U0458631

专业　让保险更保险

中国再保险行业发展报告

（2024）

中国再保险（集团）股份有限公司等 ◎ 编著

责任编辑：王雪珂
责任校对：李俊英
责任印制：陈晓川

图书在版编目(CIP)数据

中国再保险行业发展报告. 2024 / 中国再保险（集团）股份有限公司等编著. -- 北京 : 中国金融出版社, 2024. 12. -- ISBN 978-7-5220-2633-6

Ⅰ. F842.69

中国国家版本馆CIP数据核字第2024Q5V901号

中国再保险行业发展报告（2024）
ZHONGGUO ZAIBAOXIAN HANGYE FAZHAN BAOGAO (2024)

出版发行 中国金融出版社
社址 北京市丰台区益泽路2号
市场开发部 (010) 66024766，63805472，63439533 (传真)
网上书店 www.cfph.cn
(010) 66024766，63372837 (传真)
读者服务部 (010) 66070833，62568380
邮编 100071
经销 新华书店
印刷 北京侨友印刷有限公司
尺寸 169毫米×239毫米
印张 22.5
字数 270千
版次 2024年12月第1版
印次 2024年12月第1次印刷
定价 168.00元
ISBN 978-7-5220-2633-6

编委会名单

序　言

党的二十届三中全会通过的《中共中央关于进一步全面深化改革、推进中国式现代化的决定》，对进一步深化金融体制改革作出重大部署，为加快建设金融强国、推进中国式现代化注入了强劲动力。中央金融工作会议强调要做好金融“五篇大文章”，发挥保险业经济减震器和社会稳定器功能，部署了“建设再保险市场”“建立健全国家巨灾保险保障体系”重大战略任务，为保险再保险业坚定不移走好中国特色金融发展之路提供了根本遵循。国务院颁布《关于加强监管防范风险推动保险业高质量发展的若干意见》（以下简称新“国十条”），对未来5～10年保险业改革发展重点任务作出系统谋划，对再保险高质量发展提出具体要求，为保险再保险业进一步全面深化改革、更好服务经济社会发展全局指明了前进方向。

今年以来，中国经济增速在世界主要经济体中继续保持领先，持续展现出“稳”的底气、“新”的活力、“大”的潜力、“强”的韧性。中国经济长期向好的基本趋势没有改变，支撑高质量发展的要素条件没有改变。作为现代市场经济的重要组成部分，保险业必须牢牢把握高质量发展的历史性机遇，以时不我待的使命感和责任感，自觉融入中国式现代化建设全局，围绕应对气候变化、推进绿色转型、服务乡村振兴、培育新质生产力、发展低空经济和养老金融等关乎国家战略、实体经济和国计民生的重点领域，深入推进供给侧结构性改革，以改革增活力、以发展解难题，积极应对全球经济复苏缓慢、地缘政治局势紧张、极端天气频率强度加大、老龄化社会加速演进等诸多风险挑战。

再保险作为“保险的保险”，是世界各国分散和应对重大自然风险、复杂风险和特殊风险的有效方式。任何一个发达的保险市场，都离不开强大和完善的再保险体系的支撑。

再保险具有平台型公司的独特价值。当前，应对气候变化已经成为全人类的共同事业。再保险能够有效推动直再融合、产业融合和政企融合，有力支持国家巨灾保险保障体系建设，在完善巨灾保险制度建设、提高巨灾保险保障水平、提升巨灾风险管理技术、创新巨灾风险分散方式等方面发挥重要作用，助力推进国家治理体系和治理能力现代化。

再保险具有链接基因的数据优势。数字化正在深刻改变着保险业的经营逻辑和商业模式，成为行业转型升级的关键驱动力。再保险能够充分聚合保险业数据资源、促进跨行业数据融通，持续打造“再保+科技+服务”新模式，着力加强创新型产品服务供给，推动风险减量与保险增量的良性互动和循环促进，助力中国保险市场发展行稳致远。

再保险具有国际化的天然属性。对外开放是中国金融业改革发展的重要动力。作为中国加入世贸组织后最早开放的金融领域，再保险能够有效利用国内国际两个市场、两种资源，高质量服务国内国际双循环，助力共建“一带一路”。上海国际再保险中心建设的加速推进，将进一步扩大再保险高水平制度型开放，切实提升中国保险业的国际话语权和全球影响力。

中国再保险（集团）股份有限公司（以下简称中国再保）作为再保险国家队和主力军，始终坚持以习近平新时代中国特色社会主义思想为指导，全面践行金融工作的政治性和人民性，坚决贯彻落实党的二十大、二十届三中全会和中央金融工作会议精神，深入贯彻落实新“国十条”对保险业高质量发展提出的具体要求，始终聚焦再保险主责主业，不断强化再保险功能作用，持续打造再保险生态圈，加快数字化转型，推进国际化发展，全力服务国家战略、分散经济风险、护航美好生活，坚定不移向世界一流综合性再保险集团迈进。

2022年以来，中国再保在国家金融监督管理总局和中国保险行业协会的悉心指导下，在国内保险再保险业同仁的大力支持下，每年牵头组织编写中国再保险行业年度发展报告。今年，中国再保进一步汇聚再保险行业和知名高校专业力量，共同编写《中国再保险行业发展报告（2024）》，全面总结和展示了行业发展的新趋势、新特点、新成效，希望能为广大读者深入了解中国再保险行业发展状况提供有益参考，对扩大国内外交流、提升中国再保险行业社会影响力起到积极的促进作用。

展望未来，在中国式现代化新征程上，再保险行业正处于重要的战略机遇期，同时也面临很多改革发展的困难与挑战，需要汇聚多方智慧与力量认真研究解决。中国再保将主动担当、积极作为，与社会各界一道，共享机遇、共商合作、共促发展，为我国再保险行业高质量发展，为加快建设金融强国、服务中国式现代化作出新的更大的贡献！

中国再保董事长　和春雷

2024年11月

前　言[①]

2023年，是全面贯彻党的二十大精神的开局之年。我国积极应对外部风险挑战，加快构建新发展格局，着力推动高质量发展，经济社会发展取得明显成效，全年国内生产总值超过126万亿元，同比增长5.2%，增速居世界主要经济体前列，经济长期向好的趋势更为稳固，为再保险行业营造了有利的宏观环境。党的二十届三中全会、中央金融工作会议作出了深化金融体制改革、建设再保险市场的战略部署，为再保险业高质量发展提供了根本遵循和行动指南。国务院颁布的《关于加强监管防范风险推动保险业高质量发展的若干意见》赋予了再保险行业更大责任使命和发展机遇，推动再保险行业更好发挥功能作用，为经济社会发展提供强大支撑。

中国再保险行业坚持以习近平新时代中国特色社会主义思想为指导，深入贯彻党的二十大和二十届三中全会、中央金融工作会议精神，认真落实党中央、国务院决策部署以及监管机构工作要求，深刻把握金融工作的政治性、人民性，紧紧围绕科技金融、绿色金融、普惠金融、养老金融、数字金融“五篇大文章”，切实转变发展模式，

① 本报告中“中国再保险行业”或“中国保险业”是指中国大陆保险再保险行业及市场，不含港澳台地区。本报告中主要数据来自历年《中国保险年鉴》、国家金融监督管理总局官方、再保险公司年报等公开披露数据信息，以及撰写期间再保险行业调研数据信息。

不断优化再保险供给，持续推进数字化转型，全面加强风险防控，高质量发展迈出坚实的步伐。2023年，中国保险市场分出保费2 694.2亿元，再保险行业分保费收入2 296.1亿元，再保险行业总资产规模7 471.5亿元。中国再保险行业主动融入经济社会发展大局，为科技创新、绿色发展、乡村振兴、灾害管理等领域提供坚实风险保障，服务国家战略取得积极成效。中国再保险市场持续扩大对外开放，上海国际再保险中心建设取得显著进展，中国与全球再保险市场融合日益加深，再保险参与全球风险治理能力不断提升。

中国再保在2022年、2023年成功编写年度中国再保险行业发展报告的基础上，继续牵头组织《中国再保险行业发展报告（2024）》（以下简称《报告》）的编写工作。《报告》延续"主报告+专题报告"架构，分析国际国内宏观经济、政策环境、市场变化、科技创新等影响行业发展的关键因素，重点介绍市场规模、业务结构、竞争格局、创新实践、行业监管等最新情况，总结再保险行业发展成效与实践经验，研判行业发展趋势，并围绕健康养老、气候变化、巨灾保险及网络安全保险等热点领域开展了专题研究。

在《报告》编写过程中，始终得到国家金融监督管理总局财产保险监管司（再保险监管司）尹江鳌司长、中国保险行业协会于华会长等领导的悉心指导，在此致以诚挚的谢意！《报告》的出版发行，离不开中国保险再保险行业相关单位领导和专家同仁的大力支持，感谢国家金融监督管理总局财产保险监管司（再保险监管司）再保险监管处王君、金学群、郑琬冬对报告编写工作的帮助与指导！感谢中国保险行业协会统计研究部尹博、付盛麟提供的支持与协助！

《报告》由中国再保牵头，以下单位参与编写：

中国再保险（集团）股份有限公司

中国财产再保险有限责任公司

中国人寿再保险有限责任公司

人保再保险股份有限公司

前海再保险股份有限公司

瑞士再保险股份有限公司北京分公司

北京大学

中国人民大学

《报告》由中国再保秦跃光、张健统筹，官兵、马晓静统稿。各章撰写分工如下：主报告部分由中国再保负责，第一章窦健，第二章孙涛、赵心雨，第三章金笑权、于洋，第四章王洪鹏、刘爽，第五章郑利娜、范令箭。专题报告撰稿人包括：专题一张楚、王明彦、孙啸辰、郭炜钦（中国再保），专题二金笑权、邹春燕（中国再保），专题三戴鑫、陈亚新（瑞再北分），专题四蓝虹、方云龙（中国人民大学环境学院、中国再保），专题五陈思（前海再），专题六刘新立（北京大学经济学院），专题七焦健、李忠益（人保再）。

《报告》的出版发行是再保险同业和关注支持再保险发展的专家学者共同努力的结果。在此，向所有参与编写工作的机构与同仁表达诚挚的谢意，向所有为《报告》提供专业意见建议的专家学者表示衷心感谢！

当前，我国正处在以中国式现代化全面推进强国建设、民族复兴伟业的关键时期，迫切需要发挥再保险独特功能作用，为金融强国建设提供坚实有力的支撑。对此，中国再保将以更高的责任感和使命感，与同业一道，深化理论研究，加强实践探索，共同推动中国再保险行业高质量发展，走好中国特色金融发展之路，为全面建设社会主义现代化国家作出积极贡献。

中国再保险（集团）股份有限公司

2024年11月

目 录

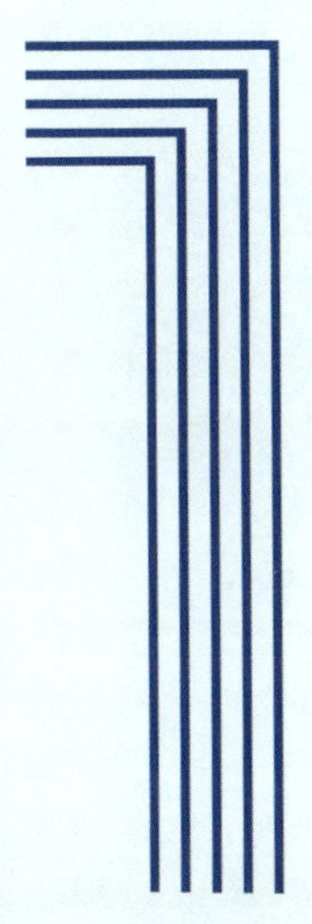

第一章 2023年中国再保险市场整体情况及发展展望

2023年，面对全球通胀压力、地缘政治紧张等复杂多变的内外部形势，中国再保险业展现出较强的韧性和适应性，市场规模持续扩大，经营效益稳健提升，国际影响力不断增强，风险防控有力有效，科技创新与数字化转型加速推进，高质量发展取得新成效。行业发展整体呈现“4D”特点：一是动态化韧性（Dynamic Resilience），再保险持续增强快速适应市场和监管变化的韧性，通过调整风险偏好、加强资本管理、创新商业模式，保持稳健的业绩增长和发展信心。二是多元化供给（Diversified Supply），再保险积极推动产品和服务多元化供给，以应对不断变化的市场需求，包括更好地满足网络安全、气候变化、生物技术等新兴风险的转移和分散需求，以及为大型基础设施项目等特殊风险提供定制化解决方案等，提供更加全面的再保险保障与风险分散。三是差异化服务（Differentiated Service），再保险积极从风险等量管理向风险减量管理服务模式转型，从重视事后经济补偿的运营模式，逐步拓展至提供事前、事中及事后全流程的服务模式，提高社会抗风险能力，降低社会风险成本。四是数字化进步（Digital Advancement），再保险着力以数字科技为支撑，发展平台生态化新模式，深挖数据要素价值，利用人工智能、大数据、区块链等新技术，加快推进经营管理和业务流程再造，以数字化驱动运营管理与服务模式转型升级。

一、再保险市场发展环境

（一）全球

2023年，全球经济从新冠疫情、能源危机、俄乌冲突等负面因素影响中艰难恢复，恢复动能不足、增长势头不稳，各国经济发展呈现明显分化态势，全球经济增长从2022年的3.4%放缓至2.6%①，经济发展和贸易增长动能持续减弱。在供给侧问题缓解和紧缩性货币政策的影响下，全球通胀水平在低增长环境中见顶，从2022年数十年最高水平的9%下降至6.8%②，主要经济体短期通胀预期有所下降，长期预期保持良好锚定。地缘政治紧张局势加剧和极端天气冲击持续形成威胁，国际贸易受到更多限制，多边合作受到更大阻碍，大宗商品价格大幅下跌，金融市场剧烈波动，全球经济下行压力增大。与此同时，全球新一轮科技革命和产业变革深入推进，有望为全球经济增长提供新机遇、创造新条件。

2023年，经通胀调整后的全球保费收入约7.2万亿美元，实际增速约2.8%，比2022年增速提高3.9个百分点，主要源于寿险市场的复苏增长。其中，寿险市场保费收入约2.9万亿美元，实际增速约1.3%，比2022年增速提高4.4个百分点；非寿险市场保费收入约4.3万亿美元，实际增速约3.9%，比2022年增速提高3.4个百分点③。

2023年，全球再保险市场机遇与挑战并存。全球宏观环境持续动荡，再保险市场面临地缘政治紧张、高利率、供给成本高昂、去全球

① 数据来源：世界银行World Economic Outlook，2024年6月。

② 数据来源：国际货币基金组织《世界经济展望》，2024年1月。

③ 数据来源：2024年第3期Sigma报告“世界保险业：焕发新生，提升全球韧性”，瑞再研究院。

化等挑战。与此同时，气候变化影响加剧，由自然巨灾导致的全球经济损失估计达3 800亿美元，保险损失连续四年超过1 000亿美元①。在多种因素综合影响下，2023年全球财产再保险市场继续走硬，费率上涨、起赔点提高，全球再保险资本供给回升，国际再保人盈利水平普遍提升。全球人身再保险市场稳步扩张，主要受益于科技进步、老龄化社会需求及新兴市场增长，但也面临着风险评估精准性与资本效率提升的挑战。

（二）中国

2023年，中国宏观经济回升向好，供给需求稳步改善，转型升级积极推进，就业物价总体稳定，民生保障有力有效，高质量发展扎实推进。国内生产总值超过126万亿元，全年经济增速约5.2%，在世界主要经济体中名列前茅②。

2023年，中国保险市场规模持续增长，保费收入约5.12万亿元，首次突破5万亿元，同比增长9.1%，全球第二的位置更为稳固③。保险密度达3 635元/人，人均保费比2022年增长304元；保险深度4.1%，同比增长0.2个百分点④。中国保险市场虽与发达保险市场存在一定差距，但也预示着中国保险市场具有较大发展潜力。

2023年，中国财产保险公司保费收入约1.59万亿元，同比增长6.7%，较2022年增速有所放缓。近年来中国财产险行业增长动能发生转化，2017年以来车险增长放缓，保费增长主要由非车险驱动。人身

① 数据来源：Aon《2024气候和自然灾害洞察报告》。

② 数据来源：《2023年国民经济和社会发展统计公报》，国家统计局，2024年2月29日。

③ 数据来源：国家金融监督管理总局披露的2023年保险行业经营情况。

④ 数据来源：国家金融监督管理总局。

保险公司保费收入约3.54万亿元，同比增长10.2%。其中，寿险保费收入增速明显高于意外险和健康险，同比增长12.8%。截至2023年末，中国保险行业资产总额达29.96万亿元，同比增长10.4%，资金运用余额达27.67万亿元，同比增长10.5%，持续保持良好发展态势[①]。

二、再保险市场发展情况

（一）市场规模

1. 原保险市场分出

（1）原保险市场分出规模

2023年，国内保险市场分出保费2 694.2亿元，同比下降3.2%。同期，国内原保险保费收入合计51 247.0亿元，同比增长9.1%（见图1、表1）。

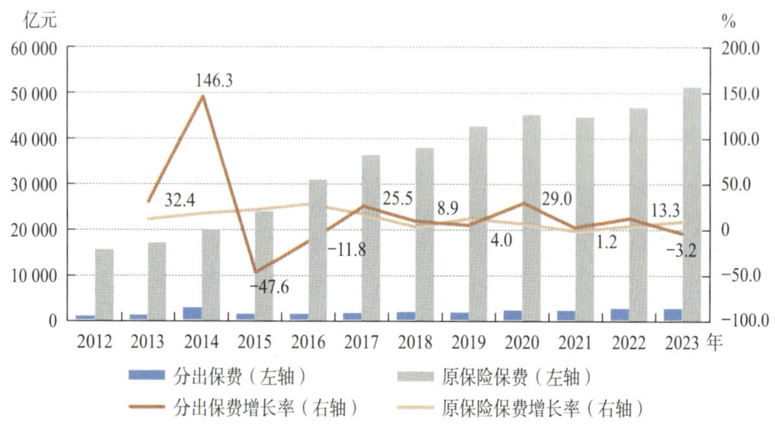

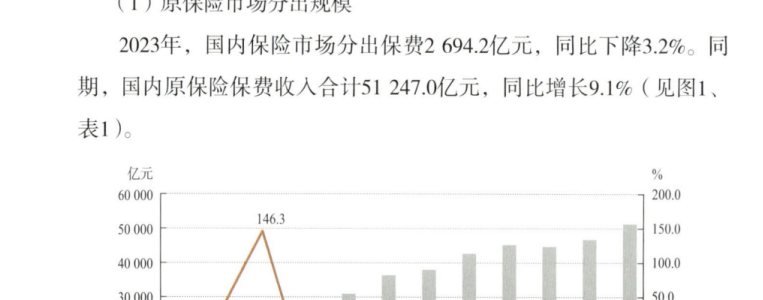

图1　2012—2023年原保险保费、分出保费及增长率情况

（数据来源：《中国保险年鉴》、国家金融监督管理总局）

① 数据来源：国家金融监督管理总局披露的2023年保险行业经营情况。

表1　　2012—2023年分出保费、原保险保费及再保险分出率情况

单位：亿元，%

年份	分出保费	增长率	原保险保费	增长率	再保险分出率
2012	879.4		15 487.8		5.7
2013	1 164.0	32.4	17 222.1	11.2	6.8
2014	2 867.2	146.3	20 234.7	17.5	14.2
2015	1 501.6	−47.6	24 282.4	20.0	6.2
2016	1 323.8	−11.8	30 959.0	27.5	4.3
2017	1 661.2	25.5	36 580.9	18.2	4.5
2018	1 808.5	8.9	38 016.6	3.9	4.8
2019	1 881.6	4.0	42 644.8	12.2	4.4
2020	2 427.1	29.0	44 257.3	6.1	5.4
2021	2 456.8	1.2	44 900.2	−0.8	5.5
2022	2 782.8	13.3	46 958.0	4.6	5.9
2023	2 694.2	−3.2	51 247.0	9.1	5.3

数据来源：《中国保险年鉴》、国家金融监督管理总局。

2023年，国内保险市场分出保费中，财产保险公司分出保费1 637.5亿元，同比增长0.5%，占总分出保费的60.8%；人身保险公司分出保费1 056.7亿元，同比下降8.4%，占总分出保费的39.2%（见图2）。

图2　2012—2023年财产险与人身险分出保费占比情况

（数据来源：《中国保险年鉴》、国家金融监督管理总局）

2012—2023年，伴随中国保险市场的不断发展，再保险需求持续提升，分出保费规模从2012年的879.4亿元增长至2023年的2 694.2亿元，年均增长率约10.7%。同期，原保险保费由15 487.8亿元增长至51 247.0亿元，年均增长率约11.5%（见图1、表1）。总体来看，分出保费与原保险保费平均增速基本一致，但各年增速差异较大，分出保费波动性明显高于原保险保费，这也是再保险经营模式的显著特征，体现再保险对原保险经营周期发挥风险分散和平滑波动作用。

（2）原保险市场分出率

2023年，国内保险市场分出率约5.3%（见图3）。其中，财产保险公司分出率约10.3%，人身保险公司分出率约3.0%。由于财产保险市场风险更为多元且巨灾风险突出，相较于人身保险，财产保险对再保险需求更大，分出率也更高。

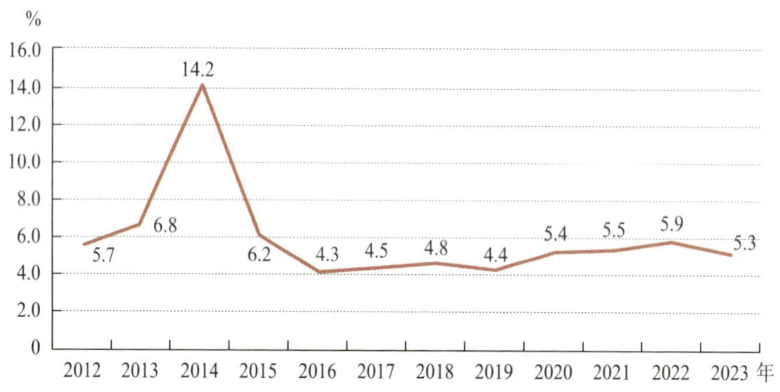

图3　2012—2023年原保险市场分出率情况

（数据来源：《中国保险年鉴》、国家金融监督管理总局）

2012—2023年，国内保险市场分出率平均约5.7%，其中2014—2016年“偿二代”监管政策过渡期间，分出率大幅波动，2014年分出需求猛增，分出率高达14.2%，随后逐步回落。不考虑2014—2016年波动影响，分出率平均约为5.2%。2016年至今，再保险分出率总体呈平稳缓升的趋势，2023年略有下降，体现出保险市场对再保险的风险分散需求正在逐步增强。

与全球市场对比，中国保险市场分出率较低，保费自留率较高。据国际保险监督官协会（IAIS）报告估算①，2022年，全球保险市场分出率约8%，北美地区分出率约12%。

2. 再保险市场分保费收入

2023年，国内再保险市场分保费收入2 296.1亿元，同比增长2.0%，与2022年相比增速有所放缓。其中，6家中资公司分保费收入1 660.1亿元，同比增长2.1%，占比约72.3%；8家外资公司分保费收入636.1亿元，同比增长1.8%，占比约22.7%。

2012—2023年，国内再保险市场分保费收入从691.2亿元增长至2 296.1亿元，年均增长率约11.5%（见图4）。总体来看，再保险分保费收入与原保险保费收入、原保险市场分出保费平均增速基本一致，但再保险分保费收入各年增速差异较大、波动性较高。特别是2014—2016年间，受"偿二代"监管政策过渡期影响，再保险公司分保费收入显著波动。自2016年"偿二代"正式实施后，分保费收入呈逐年稳步增长趋势。

① 数据来源：国际保险监督官协会（International Association of Insurance Supervisors，IAIS），Global Insurance Market Report，2023。

图4　2012—2023年再保险公司分保费收入及增长率情况

（数据来源：《中国保险年鉴》、国家金融监督管理总局）

2012—2023年，中资再保险公司分保费收入保持正增长，但2023年增速出现较大幅度下降；外资再保险公司分保费收入波动性较大（见表2、图5），体现出中资与外资公司经营策略的差异性。

表2　　2012—2023年中资与外资再保险公司分保费收入及增长率情况

单位：亿元，%

年份	分保费收入	中资公司分保费收入	增长率	占比	外资公司分保费收入	增长率	占比
2012	691.2	400.3		57.9	290.9		42.1
2013	948.6	466.8	16.6	49.2	481.8	65.6	50.8
2014	1 486.0	502.5	7.6	33.8	983.5	104.1	66.2
2015	1 066.3	543.4	8.1	51.0	522.9	−46.8	49.0
2016	958.6	552.0	1.6	57.6	406.6	−22.2	42.4
2017	1 099.6	778.7	41.1	70.8	320.9	−21.1	29.2
2018	1 370.1	949.8	22.0	69.3	420.2	31.0	30.7
2019	1 576.1	1 044.9	10.0	66.2	533.0	26.8	33.8
2020	1 809.2	1 180.1	13.1	65.2	629.1	18.0	34.8
2021	2 090.2	1 422.9	20.6	68.1	667.3	6.1	31.9
2022	2 250.2	1 625.5	14.2	72.2	624.6	−6.4	27.8
2023	2 296.1	1 660.1	2.1	72.3	636.1	1.8	27.7

数据来源：《中国保险年鉴》、国家金融监督管理总局。

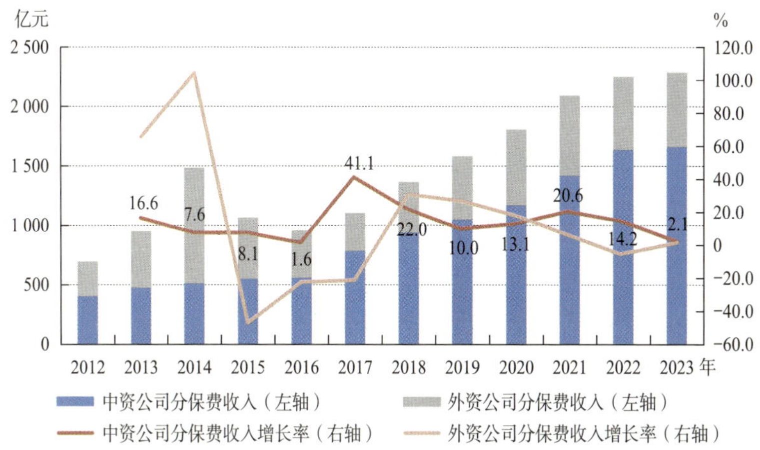

图5　2012—2023年中资与外资再保险公司分保费收入及增长率情况

（数据来源：《中国保险年鉴》、国家金融监督管理总局）

3. 再保险赔付支出

2023年，国内再保险行业赔付支出约1 247.6亿元，同比增长8.1%，占当年分保费收入约54.2%（见图6）。其中，6家中资公司赔付支出约906.8亿元，同比增长9.0%；8家外资公司赔付支出约340.7亿元，同比增长5.6%（见表3、图7）。

图6　2012—2023年再保险业赔付支出情况

（数据来源：《中国保险年鉴》、国家金融监督管理总局）

表3　2012—2023年再保险业赔付支出情况

单位：亿元，%

年份	赔付支出	中资再保险公司赔付支出	中资再保险公司赔付支出增长率	占比	外资再保险公司赔付支出	外资再保险公司赔付支出增长率	占比
2012	303.8	151.8		50.0	151.9		50.0
2013	383.7	180.6	18.9	47.1	203.1	33.7	52.9
2014	433.2	210.5	16.6	48.6	222.6	9.6	51.4
2015	668.5	263.3	25.1	39.4	405.2	82.0	60.6
2016	1 119.4	301.2	14.4	26.9	818.1	101.9	73.1
2017	489.0	254.4	−15.6	52.0	234.6	−71.3	48.0
2018	541.2	278.3	9.4	51.4	262.9	12.1	48.6
2019	670.3	350.4	25.9	52.3	320.0	21.7	47.7
2020	746.5	432.7	23.5	58.0	313.8	−1.9	42.0
2021	852.6	491.0	13.5	57.6	361.6	15.2	42.4
2022	1 154.6	831.9	69.4	72.1	322.7	−10.8	27.9
2023	1 247.6	906.84	9.0	72.7	340.7	5.6	27.3

数据来源：《中国保险年鉴》、国家金融监督管理总局。

图7　2012—2023年中资与外资再保险公司赔付支出和增长率情况

（数据来源：《中国保险年鉴》、国家金融监督管理总局）

2012—2023年，国内再保险行业赔付支出从303.8亿元增长至1 247.6亿元，年均增长率为13.7%（见图6）。总体来看，再保险赔付支出在2016年“偿二代”实施初期大幅增长，其中人身再保险赔付支出大幅增加，2017年后明显回落，政策变化期的波动性较大。

4. 再保险总资产

2023年末，国内再保险行业总资产规模约7 471.5亿元，较年初增长11.2%，高于分保费收入增速9.2个百分点。2012—2023年，国内再保险行业总资产规模从1 437.2亿元增长至7 471.5亿元，年均增长率约16.2%，高于再保险分保费收入年均增长率。总资产规模同样受到“偿二代”影响，2014—2016年呈现较大波动。自2016年开始，再保险行业总资产规模均呈稳步增长趋势，与分保费收入变化趋势保持一致。

图8　2012—2023年再保险业总资产及增长率情况

（数据来源：《中国保险年鉴》、国家金融监督管理总局）

2012—2023年，再保险行业总资产占保险业总资产规模比重相对稳定，2023年底占保险业总资产规模约2.5%，体现了再保险行业伴随保险市场发展而逐步发展壮大，在监管政策与市场环境变化下保持整体稳步增长。同时，保险业总资产占金融业总资产规模比重稳步上升，从2018年的5.6%上升至2023年的6.5%，保险业在金融行业中的作用和地位持续巩固。

表4　2012—2023年再保险业、保险业、金融业总资产规模及占比情况

单位：亿元，%

年份	再保险总资产	保险业总资产	再保险业总资产占保险业比重	金融业总资产	保险业总资产占金融业比重
2012	1 437.2	68 425.6	2.1		
2013	1 765.4	77 576.7	2.3		
2014	3 183.2	96 177.8	3.3		
2015	4 722.0	119 295.7	4.0		
2016	2 343.9	142 659.0	1.6		
2017	2 699.3	146 816.7	1.8		
2018	3 358.3	163 641.0	2.1	2 940 000	5.6
2019	4 261.3	187 495.6	2.3	3 186 900	5.9
2020	4 956.3	216 156.5	2.3	3 531 900	6.1
2021	6 057.5	248 874.0	2.4	3 819 500	6.5
2022	6 719.5	271 500.0	2.5	4 196 400	6.5
2023	7 471.5	299 573.0	2.5	4 610 900	6.5

数据来源：《中国保险年鉴》、国家金融监督管理总局、中国人民银行网站。

（二）市场格局

1. 市场主体不断丰富

经过多年的发展，我国再保险市场逐渐形成境内专业再保险人、境外离岸再保险人和直保公司共同参与的多元发展格局。

在专业市场主体方面，截至2023年底，国内再保险市场专业再保险公司共15家，其中7家中资再保险公司（含1家集团公司，即中国再保），8家外资再保险公司（见表5）。2022年西班牙曼福再保险公司（MAPFRE）获批筹建北京分公司，注册地为北京，营运资金为5亿元人民币，并于2024年7月获批开业。

在离岸市场主体方面，近年来，未在国内设立分支机构，但通过离岸交易的形式接受国内分出业务的境外离岸再保险人参与中国市场的力度不断加大。2023年，与全球超过500家离岸再保险人开展业务往来，向境外分出保费约500亿元。

此外，境内百余家财产险和人身险直保公司不同程度地参与再保险市场竞争。部分直保公司通过业务互换等方式与境外市场展开再保险业务往来。

表5　国内专业再保险公司情况概览

公司名称	成立时间	注册地	注册性质	企业性质
中国再保险（集团）股份有限公司	1996年	北京	集团公司	中资
中国财产再保险有限责任公司	2003年	北京	公司	中资
中国人寿再保险有限责任公司	2003年	北京	公司	中资
慕尼黑再保险公司北京分公司	2003年	北京	分公司	外资
瑞士再保险股份有限公司北京分公司	2003年	北京	分公司	外资
德国通用再保险股份公司上海分公司	2004年	上海	分公司	外资
法国再保险公司北京分公司	2008年	北京	分公司	外资
汉诺威再保险股份公司上海分公司	2008年	上海	分公司	外资
安盛环球再保险（上海）	2011年	上海	公司	外资
RGA美国再保险公司上海分公司	2014年	上海	分公司	外资
太平再保险（中国）有限公司	2015年	北京	公司	中资
前海再保险股份有限公司	2016年	深圳	公司	中资
人保再保险股份有限公司	2017年	北京	公司	中资
大韩再保险公司上海分公司	2020年	上海	分公司	外资
中国农业再保险股份有限公司	2020年	北京	公司	中资

注：1. 各再保险主体名称在下文中使用以下简称：中国再保或中再、中再产险或中再、中再寿险或中再、慕再或慕再北分、瑞再或瑞再北分、通用再或通用再上分、法再或法再北分、汉再或汉再上分、安盛环球、RGA美再或RGA美再上分、太平再（中国）、前海再、人保再、大韩再或大韩再上分、中国农再。

2. 信利保险（中国）有限公司于2011年成立，2020年变更为信利再保险（中国）有限公司，2024年更名为安盛环球再保险（上海）。

资料来源：《中国保险年鉴》、各再保险公司年报。

2. 双向开放格局初步形成

在“引进来”方面，自中国2001年加入WTO以来，中国再保险市场成为中国金融业开放最早、开放力度最大的领域之一，全球主要再保险公司均在国内设立分支机构、开展业务，为国内再保险市场发展带来人才、技术和资本。近年来，中国再保险行业持续深化高水平对外开放，不断完善与国际接轨的制度和标准体系，持续激活行业发展内生动力，推进高质量发展不断取得新成效。

自党的十八大以来，中国加快建设上海国际再保险中心。2023年6月，国家金融监督管理总局与上海共同发布《关于加快推进上海国际再保险中心建设的实施细则》，上海再保险“国际板”正式启动。自建设启动以来，再保险“国际板”已初步形成机构集聚形态，吸引了中外数十家保险公司和经纪公司入驻。根据规划，上海国际再保险中心建设将聚焦打造再保险“国际板”，开设面向全球的再保险分入业务交易市场，吸引全球要素在上海集聚，增强配置全球资源的能力，打造成为在岸与离岸相结合、具有国际竞争力的全球再保险交易中心，形成再保险国内大循环的中心节点、国内国际双循环的战略链接。

在“走出去”方面，中国保险市场通过离岸交易形式分入境外业务。2022年，境外分入保费规模约283亿元。与此同时，中资再保险企业走出国门，积极布局境外市场，经营管理能力显著提升，国际竞争能力不断增强。中国再保已成为全球第八大再保险集团，是国际化程度最高的中资金融保险企业之一，境外经营机构已扩展到11个国家和地区，国际业务已覆盖全球200多个国家和地区。

（三）业务结构

1. 分业务类型分保费收入

2023年，国内再保险市场分保费收入约2 296.1亿元①，其中合约业务分保费收入约2 252.4亿元，同比增长0.5%，占比约98.1%；临分业务分保费收入约43.7亿元，同比降低9.0%，占比约1.9%（见图9）。合约业务增长速度放缓，临分业务增速和占比均下降。

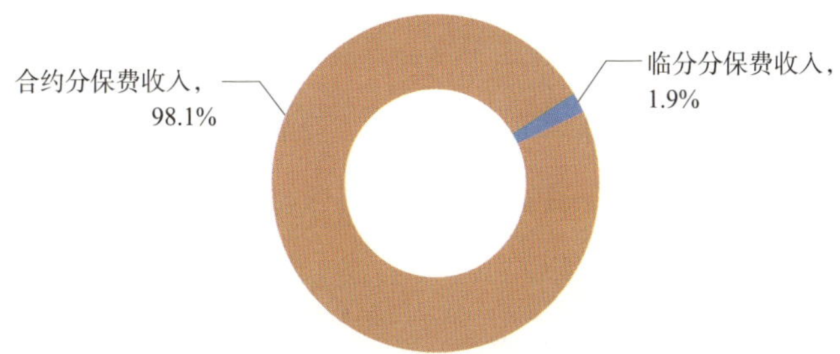

图9　2023年再保险合约与临分业务分保费收入占比情况

（数据来源：国家金融监督管理总局）

2012—2023年，合约业务分保费收入从681.9亿元增长至2 252.4亿元，年均增长率约11.5%；临分业务分保费收入从9.3亿元增长至43.7亿元，年均增长率约15.1%（见表6、图10）。总体来看，合约业务为再保险主要业务类型，占比保持在95%以上；临分业务占比较小，近两年来业务规模呈下降趋势。

表6　2012—2023年再保险合约与临分分保费收入、增长率及占比情况

单位：亿元，%

年份	合约业务分保费收入	增长率	占比	临分业务分保费收入	增长率	占比
2012	681.9		98.7	9.3		1.3
2013	940.3	37.9	99.1	8.3	-10.7	0.9

① 分保费收入已考虑公司间关联交易影响，分业务类型分保费收入未考虑关联交易影响。

续表

年份	合约业务分保费收入	增长率	占比	临分业务分保费收入	增长率	占比
2014	1 476.7	57.1	99.4	9.23	11.6	0.6
2015	1 055.2	-28.5	99.0	11.0	19.2	1.0
2016	917.9	-13.0	95.8	37.9	243.7	4.0
2017	1 080.2	17.7	98.2	19.4	-48.9	1.8
2018	1 339.4	24.0	97.8	30.7	58.5	2.2
2019	1 539.8	15.0	97.7	36.3	18.1	2.3
2020	1 774.3	15.2	97.5	45.8	26.2	2.5
2021	2 070.7	16.7	97.7	49.5	8.1	2.3
2022	2 240.6	8.2	97.9	48.0	-3.1	2.1
2023	2 252.4	0.5	98.1	43.7	-9.0	1.9

数据来源：中国保险年鉴、国家金融监督管理总局。

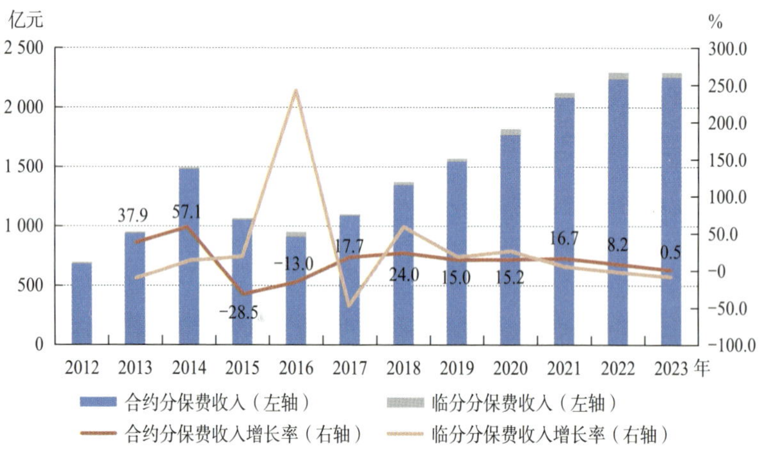

图10　2012—2023年合约、临分分保费收入及增长率情况

（数据来源：《中国保险年鉴》、国家金融监督管理总局）

2. 分险种分保费收入

2023年，国内再保险市场财产险分保费收入约1 363.0亿元，同比增长11.7%，占比约62.7%；寿险分保费收入约318.0亿元，同比降低26.6%，占比约14.6%；健康险分保费收入约445.0亿元，同比降低16.4%，占比约20.5%；意外险分保费收入约47.0亿元，同比降低26.7%，占比约2.2%（见图11）。

总体来看，一是各险种分保费收入增长趋势有所分化，财产险增长较快，寿险、健康险和意外险业务规模与2022年相比均有下降；二是与2022年相比，财产险分保费收入占比明显上升，寿险、健康险和意外险分保费收入占比均有所下降；三是人身险市场在需求端、销售端和资产端均面临压力，影响直保公司分出需求，寿险、健康险和意外险分保费收入均下降。

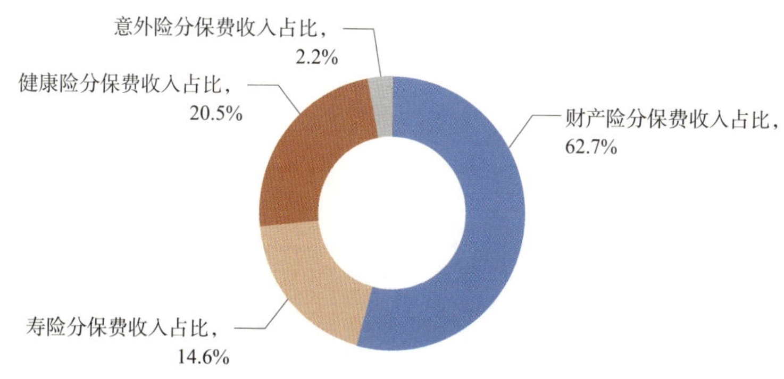

图11　2023年各险种分保费收入占比

（数据来源：国家金融监督管理总局）

2012—2023年，国内再保险市场财产险分保费收入由462.6亿元增长至1 363.0亿元，年均增长率约10.3%；寿险业务由153.0亿元增长至318.0亿元，年均增长率约6.9%；健康险业务由50.6亿元增长至445.0亿元，年均增长率约21.9%；意外险业务由25.0亿元增长至47.0亿元，年均增长率约5.9%（见表7、图12）。其中，健康险是增长最快的险种，但近年来健康险增长速度明显放缓，业务占比也有所下降（见图13）。

表7　　2012—2023年各险种分保费收入及增长率

单位：亿元，%

年份	财产险	增长率	寿险	增长率	健康险	增长率	意外险	增长率
2012	462.6		153.0		50.6		25.0	
2013	562.8	21.7	297.3	94.3	63.5	25.6	24.8	-0.6
2014	588.0	4.5	799.6	168.9	65.7	3.4	32.7	31.7
2015	598.1	1.7	320.9	-59.9	112.1	70.7	35.1	7.4
2016	480.7	-19.6	285.9	-10.9	100.1	-10.8	43.5	23.9
2017	484.9	0.9	430.2	50.5	136.1	36.0	48.4	11.3
2018	600.4	23.8	484.4	12.6	218.2	60.4	67.1	38.5
2019	729.9	21.6	421.3	-13.0	353.1	61.8	73.6	9.7
2020	840.1	15.1	441.6	4.8	454.5	28.7	73.1	-0.7
2021	1 075.6	28.0	445.0	0.8	496.5	9.2	73.1	0.0
2022	1 220.5	13.5	433.4	-2.6	532.2	7.2	64.1	12.3
2023	1 363.0	11.7	318.0	-26.6	445.0	-16.4	47.0	-26.7

数据来源：《中国保险年鉴》、国家金融监督管理总局。

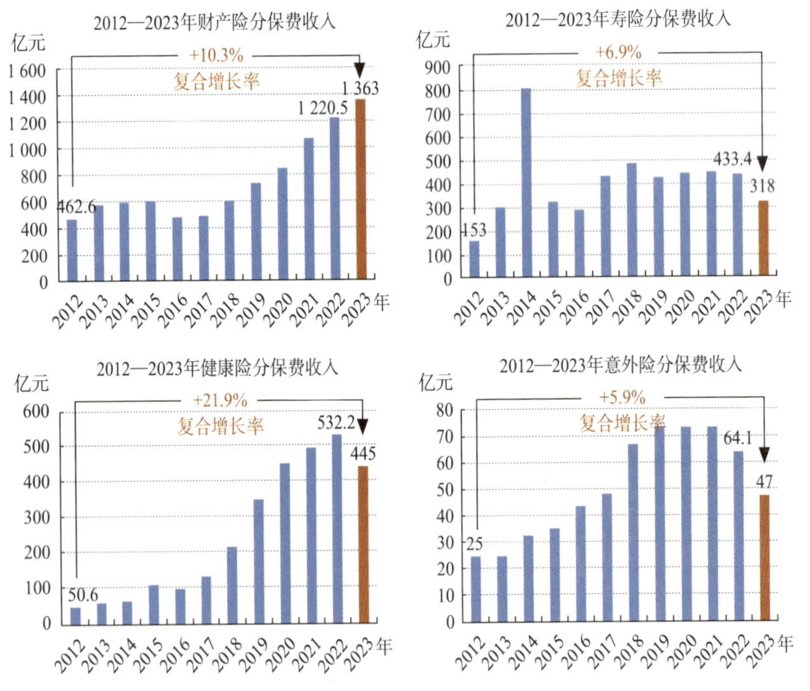

图12　2012—2023年各险种分保费收入

（数据来源：《中国保险年鉴》、国家金融监督管理总局）

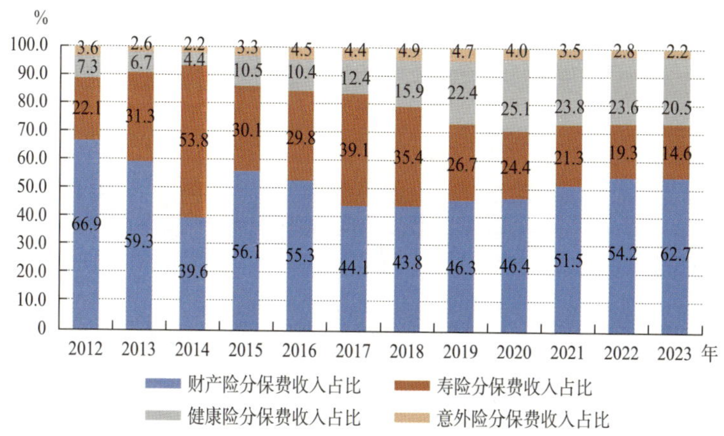

图13　2012—2023年分险种分保费收入占比情况

（数据来源：《中国保险年鉴》、国家金融监督管理总局）

（四）风险管理

1. 偿付能力情况[①]

核心偿付能力充足率是保险公司核心资本与最低资本的比值，衡量公司高质量资本的充足状况，监管达标值为50%；综合偿付能力充足率是实际资本与最低资本的比值，衡量公司资本的总体充足状况，监管达标值为100%。

2023年第一至第四季度，再保险公司的平均核心偿付能力充足率分别为240.9%、239.3%、242.3%、245.6%，均高于监管达标值50%和当季财产险公司、人身险公司的充足率水平。

2023年第一至第四季度，再保险公司的平均综合偿付能力充足率分别为277.7%、275.2%、278.3%、285.3%，均高于监管达标值100%和当季财产险公司、人身险公司的充足率水平（见图14）。

① 下文中偿付能力相关数据均为“偿二代”二期规则下的统计数据。

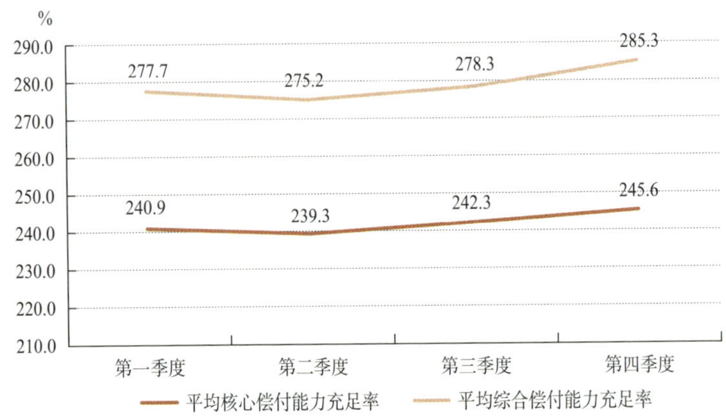

图14　2023年再保险公司偿付能力情况

（数据来源：国家金融监督管理总局）

2023年，再保险公司平均核心偿付能力充足率和平均综合偿付能力充足率较2022年均有所下降。2023年9月，国家金融监督管理总局发布《关于优化保险公司偿付能力监管标准的通知》，优化调整了《保险公司偿付能力监管规则（Ⅱ）》规定的偿付能力监管标准。自2023年第三季度以来，再保险公司偿付能力充足率有所回升。

2. 风险综合评级（IRR）情况

风险综合评级是对保险公司偿付能力综合风险的评价，衡量保险公司总体偿付能力风险的大小，分为A、B、C、D四类，监管达标值为B类。

2023年，共有14家再保险公司获得并披露了季度风险综合评级情况，评级结果均在B类及以上。

3. 风险管理能力（SARMRA）情况

偿付能力风险管理要求与评估（SARMRA）是保险业功能监管的重要内容，是通过制度健全性和遵循有效性的评估反映保险公司的风险管理水平，对于提升保险公司风险管理水平、增强行业防范化解风险能力具有重要意义。SARMRA评估分值高于80分可提高偿付能力充足率。

2023年，监管部门对36家保险公司开展了SARMRA评估，其中再保险公司3家，中国农业再保险股份有限公司首次参与评估，再保险公司评估平均分为78.81分①，比2022年降低0.92分。2023年SARMRA评估结果显示，保险公司普遍增强了风险管理意识，强化了风险管理主体责任，在风险管理方面取得了进步，搭建了较为完整的风险管理架构，制定了较为全面的风险管理制度，构建了较为合理的风险管理工作机制，建立了符合自身情况的风险偏好体系。

（五）再保险经纪市场发展情况

再保险经纪人是代表保险公司或再保险分出公司利益，向分入公司（通常是再保险公司）购买再保险保障或服务解决方案的保险经纪机构。近年来，伴随经营环境的变化和风险管理需求的多样化，再保险经纪人的商业模式已从早期安排再保险方案，逐步发展成为风险咨询、风险管理技术等综合服务提供商。

中国再保险经纪市场主体主要由国际再保险经纪人、国内再保险经纪人、国内直保经纪人兼营再保险业务等组成。中国再保险登记系统信息显示，截至2023年末，再保险经纪人共232家，其中境外机构120家，占比51.7%；境内机构112家，占比48.3%。

目前，我国境内再保险经纪市场由佳达、怡安、安睿嘉尔等三大外资巨头主导，同时中资再保险经纪人正在快速成长。外资专业再保经纪人服务全面、团队专业、资源充足，能在全球范围内进行复杂的

① 数据来源：国家金融监督管理总局发布2023年度保险公司偿付能力风险管理评估工作信息，国家金融监督管理总局网站。

再保安排。中资再保险经纪人及直保经纪人的市场份额较外资低，但具有市场化程度高、了解客户需求等特点，拥有细分险种的专业团队，服务较为全面（见表8）。

表8　　主要中资与外资再保险经纪公司情况

单位：亿元

公司名称	注册时间	注册地	资本金	2023年国内再保经纪营业收入
外资				
佳达	2003年11月	上海	0.5	2
怡安	1993年10月	北京	0.5	1.3
安睿嘉尔	2004年8月	上海	0.5	0.5
中资				
太平再保险顾问	1996年7月	香港	—	1.1
五洲经纪	2003年8月	北京	0.5	0.7
江泰再保险经纪	2015年7月	上海	0.5	0.4
中天经纪	2004年11月	北京	0.1	0.2
明睿经纪	2009年5月	上海	—	0.1
华泰经纪	1993年3月	北京	0.5	0.1

注：“2023年国内再保经纪营业收入”数据来源于中国大陆地区客户的再保经纪费收入，不包含同一经纪公司直保业务经纪费收入，数据无公开信息披露，均为根据市场信息估计。

资料来源：各公司公开披露信息。

三、再保险行业服务经济社会发展情况

2023年，中国再保险行业聚焦国家重大战略、经济社会发展和民生保障需求，着力做好科技金融、绿色金融、普惠金融、养老金融、数字金融五篇大文章，为金融强国建设贡献专业价值。

（一）大力发展科技保险，助力科技自立自强

再保险聚焦科技创新的前沿领域和重点环节，加强对科技型企业和战略性产业的保障支持，助力建设由科技创新引领的现代化产业体系。2023年，中再助力科技创新领域保额超过4 300亿元，同比增长16.4%。为国产大飞机C919首飞、国家重点卫星发射、我国自主研发的全球首台兆瓦级漂浮式波浪能发电装置等重大装备提供再保险风险保障；为重大技术装备首台套、新材料首批次、软件首版次研发提供风险保障；推出国内首个“专精特新中小企业综合保险专项合约”，研发汽车芯片保险产品，落地自动驾驶汽车保险；推动“保险+风险管理+服务”的新型网络安全保险模式在北京、上海复制推广。人保再开发中小企业网安核保定价平台“网安e保”，全面扫描评估中小企业网络安全，并提供详细的评估报告和安全建议，赋能网安产品研发、风险核保和方案落地。前海再参与国内头部产险公司的首台套、新材料合约，全力助推“中国制造2025”，助力我国重大技术装备制造业转型和升级。

（二）大力发展绿色保险，助力达成“双碳”目标

再保险聚焦低碳转型和生态保护，不断拓展绿色保险覆盖面，创新绿色保险产品供给，推动现代产业绿色升级。2023年，中再服务绿色发展领域保额超过3万亿元，同比增长26.8%。中再积极发挥中国核保险共同体主席单位作用，支持全球首座第四代核电站商业运行，落地核燃料循环前端设施保险、核技术利用责任保险，支持国家核能事业发展；为8900多个风电、光伏等绿色能源项目提供全生命周期综合保险。中再、瑞再深度参与中国保险行业协会绿色保险分类指引编制

工作，为《绿色保险分类指引（2023版）》的成功发布贡献专业力量；瑞再针对海洋经济绿色转型的新兴领域，瑞再研究院发布《保险助力蓝色经济发展》，首次探究蓝色保险的内涵与业务范畴，推动新兴业务领域发展。人保再自去年以来，在海上风电投放的承保能力同比提升100%，服务国家战略能力全面提升。前海再参与财产险直保公司的责任险超赔合约，支持前端环境污染责任险的开展；支持光伏电站、风力发电等清洁能源的财产保险业务，如支持电力系保险公司的财产工程险合约。

（三）大力发展普惠保险，助力实现美好生活

一是防范化解小微企业经营风险，护航民营经济发展。2023年，中再服务中小微企业372万家，同比增长150.8%。持续聚焦增强企业抗风险能力，促进扩大内需和稳定就业。在山西助力全国首个省域“惠商保”落地，倾力纾困解难；满足餐饮民宿、文化旅游、社区托育等特定需求，创新定制行业与地方特色产品540余款，提振企业经营信心。

二是支持多层次社会保障体系建设，聚焦重点人群，以普惠性保障增进民生福祉。2023年，中再助力健康中国服务人群2.1亿人次，同比增长78.5%。支持政府惠民，为北京、江苏苏州等地“惠民保”增加特药、一站式理赔结算等优质服务；创新研发青少年系列保险产品，助力青少年健康成长。前海再开展覆盖北京市、深圳市、海南省、贵州省、安徽省、广西南宁市、厦门市、苏州市、湖北云梦县等地区9个惠民保项目，惠及人员超过800万人。持续推广非标体系统及创新产品，服务弱势人群，截至2023年末，与国内10多家寿险公司合作多款非标体产品，在5个互联网保险平台上线，为100多种疾病人群提供了

健康保障。同时，在非标体项目基础上，与多家保险公司合作开发了多款针对肺结节、乳腺结节、甲状腺结节、甲癌术后、乳癌术后、“三高”、肾病、肝病等常见慢病的专属健康险产品。瑞再专注于老年人群的产品创新，加快核保核赔技术电子化步伐，深度参与《中国人身保险业第四套经验生命表》的编制工作，积极助力中国寿险市场高质量发展。

三是推进农业强国建设，以农业保险保障粮食安全。中再深入推进高标准农田保险工作，探索开发林业草原碳汇指数保险，2023年服务乡村振兴领域保额7051.5亿元，同比增长12.9%。瑞再联合相关企业推出《高标准农田基础设施工程质量缺陷保险（IDI）风险管理服务（TIS）作业指南》，依托国内外IDI保险实施中的TIS实践经验，帮助保险行业加深对新型风险的了解、掌握管理风险的方法、建立风险评价体系、制定理性健康的核保和业务发展策略，同时通过系统性、全生命周期的风险管理，提升农田基础设施的建设质量。发布《农产品质量安全保险创新研究》报告，着眼于农产品全产业链的各类质量安全风险，指出风险管理已成为增强农产品质量安全的核心，保险作为有效的风险转移工具，可以实现从损失预防、风险管理到经济补偿全方面的保障作用，助力新时期农产品质量安全的进一步提升。前海再积极参与全国首个乡村振兴专项再保险合约，重点围绕高标准农田建设、农业机械化率提升和美丽乡村建设等方面开拓“三农”市场新业务，为农业农村领域提供多元化、定制化、一体化的风险保障，推动服务乡村振兴战略的新生态建设；支持新设立的中国渔业互助保险社的再保险合约，进一步提升我国渔业风险保障水平，推动渔业高质量发展。

四是助力巨灾保险保障体系建设，服务社会治理体系现代化。中再服务防灾减灾救灾，承担国内地震、洪水和台风风险责任25.8万亿元，同比增长11%；参与全部19个省市巨灾保险试点项目，在80%的项目中担任首席再保人，为京津冀暴雨洪涝等灾害赔付6.5亿元；迭代升级具有自主知识产权的地震、台风、洪涝等系列巨灾模型。积极应对气候变化，配合人民银行研发气候变化物理风险压力测试模型，牵头科技部“重大自然灾害防控与公共安全”国家重点研发计划，就巨灾保险体系建设等重大问题向国家建言献策，提升国家灾害防治能力。人保再开发的巨灾风险可视化管理平台“巨灾经纬”，运用区域巨灾风险理论和地理信息系统（GIS）技术，保障保险公司实现多维度、多场景、多因素的巨灾风险综合管控以及行业风险减量和精细化管理，平台注册公司已达40家。

（四）大力发展养老保险，助力应对老龄化趋势

再保险助力提升老年人群风险保障和服务水平，推动完善多层次养老保障体系。中再积极推动老人保险产品服务创新。提供“慢病+重疾+护理”保障，与慢病管理服务、康护服务相结合，创新提出重疾型护理险概念，并推动产品落地；创新推出市场首款失能险，将失能护理给付前移，提升百姓获得感；创新老年医疗保险，为银发一族提供医疗费用保障；推广“保险+诊疗+康复服务”模式，打造行业长护险样板，2023年长护失能产品新单销量超过50万单。瑞再与中国保险行业协会深化合作，共同完成《中国中老年人风险保障研究》，首次对中国中老年群体的保险保障状况及消费者保险需求偏好进行了系统性梳理和分析，为行业创新开发中老年保险产品奠定基础。前海再高度关注老年人群保障需求，截至2023年末，与10余家保险公司合作开发了一系列针对慢病群体和银发群体的专属健康险产品，如针对慢病人群的百万医疗产品、线上复诊与慢病药品报销的医疗险、针对中老年有

认知症风险人群的认知症防护险等多款老年专属医疗险产品。

（五）大力发展数字保险，提升风险减量服务能力

再保险通过数字技术赋能，推动保险服务提质增效。中再迭代升级“数字中再”战略，成立中再保数字科技有限责任公司（以下简称中再数科），发布数字化转型拓扑图和路线图，构筑起以中再巨灾和中再数科为科技两翼、赋能再保险主业创新发展的战略新架构。研发推出“再·耘”农险科技平台，是行业首个具备遥感指数保险产品方案自动设计的服务平台。瑞再发布“信瑞智农”农业风险管理平台，利用实时灾害分析功能，对“杜苏芮”台风影响的省份进行强降水灾害全程跟踪监测及风险评估，基于大数据、人工智能和农业风险管理模型推动农业风险减量服务，助力政府部门、保险行业和农业企业更主动地、更有针对性地开展防灾减损和灾后救援工作。前海再选择神经网络模型作为重货车险智能定价引擎的核心算法并开发了API接口，帮助保险公司有效解决了重型货车长期以来存在的“投保难”问题；在寿险方面，前海再获得“非标体自动核保系统”和“寿险预估系统”两项软件著作权，联合合作伙伴开发出全人群医疗险、慢病人群医疗险等行业创新产品。

四、再保险发展趋势展望

（一）机遇与挑战

1. 机遇

一是中国经济增长为再保险行业发展提供坚实基础。2023年10月召开的中央金融工作会议指出要着力营造良好的货币金融环境，12月

召开的中央经济工作会议强调2024年继续实施积极的财政政策和稳健的货币政策。尽管全球经济环境面临不确定性，伴随着宏观政策效力持续显现，中国经济仍将保持相对稳健的增长态势，经济增长仍具有巨大的发展韧性和潜力，持续推动产业升级、消费升级和绿色低碳转型，促进企业扩大规模和投资，带动财产再保险市场需求，以及健康险、养老保险等个人保险产品的快速发展，拓宽人身再保险市场发展空间。

二是中国保险业发展空间依然广阔。自改革开放以来，中国保险业快速发展，已成为现代经济的重要产业和风险管理的基本手段，但仍处于发展初级阶段，保险深度和保险密度相比发达国家仍有较大提升空间。党的二十大擘画了以中国式现代化全面推进中华民族伟大复兴的宏伟蓝图，保险作为现代市场经济的基础性制度安排，正迎来高质量发展的重要机遇，将在医疗保障、养老保障、环境治理、社会管理、生产安全、公共安全、灾害预防与救助等方面，发挥增强社会韧性、保障发展安全的重要作用。

三是国际市场面临发展机遇。在中国经济融入全球步伐不断加深的背景下，国际市场持续展现多元发展潜力，为中国再保险行业加快“走出去”步伐、全面融入国际保险市场、提升全球竞争力与影响力、加快反哺国内保险产业转型升级提供了重要战略机遇。新冠疫情冲击后，欧美市场周期性复苏，有力支撑发达保险市场的增长前景；新兴保险市场特别是亚洲、非洲等地区的发展，为再保险市场带来新的增长点。与此同时，中国共建“一带一路”深入实施，海外能源、基础设施建设、制造业和高科技产业等行业的特殊风险应保未保的问题突出，保险保障需求日趋旺盛，为中国再保险公司提供了海外市场空间。此外，面对全球气候变化等挑战，国际合作与风险共担的需求日益增加，为中国再保险企业带来海外业务布局、提升国际影响力的机会。

2. 挑战

一是宏观环境复杂多变，面临全球经济波动与国内转型双重考验。国际上，贸易保护主义抬头、地缘政治局势紧张、全球供应链重构以及多国货币政策的收紧，直接影响保险需求稳定性、资产配置收益率以及赔付风险评估。当前，中国处在转变发展方式、优化经济结构、转变增长动力的攻坚期，国内有效需求不足、部分行业产能过剩、社会预期偏弱、风险隐患依然较多，可能影响企业和个人的保险购买力，进而间接对再保险市场产生压力。自然灾害频发和全球公共卫生事件的潜在威胁，不仅考验保险业的赔付能力，也对再保险公司的精算模型和风险评估机制提出了新的挑战。国内低利率环境仍将持续，境内外的利差空间将趋势性缩窄，保险再保险企业的资产负债管理难度进一步加大。

二是市场竞争越发激烈，业务创新与差异化竞争压力增大。在财产险领域，由于受到自然灾害频发影响，赔付成本上升，市场竞争加剧，尤其是在巨灾风险转移方面，保险公司寻求更高效率的风险分散解决方案，促使再保险公司不断创新产品和服务。人身险领域，市场份额争夺激烈，对满足个性化需求、提供差异化的创新产品提出更高要求，如在长寿风险、重大疾病保障等领域，要求寿险公司具有更高的定制化能力和市场敏感性。健康险领域，伴随中国人口老龄化和医疗费用上涨趋势，健康险需求不断扩大，吸引科技公司和专业健康险再保险公司纷纷涌入，健康管理、远程医疗、大数据分析等技术应用成为新的竞争优势，要求再保险公司具备处理大规模个人健康数据的能力，并确保隐私与安全，显著增加了运营复杂度。

（二）趋势展望

一是再保险将着力服务实体经济发展。随着中国经济结构调整和产业升级，中国再保险行业将积极适应新变化，不断创新风险保障服务模式，高质量服务国家重大战略和实体经济新需求。在基础设施建设、高新技术产业、现代农业、绿色能源等领域，再保险将发挥更加重要的风险保障作用。例如，通过提供长期稳定的再保险支持，促进基础设施项目融资和建设，降低因自然灾害、技术风险等因素导致的潜在损失，保障项目顺利实施。将聚焦绿色保险、健康保险、小微企业保险等重要领域，为满足多元化需求提供一揽子定制化再保险解决方案。

二是再保险经营模式将持续创新迭代。近年来，保险科技发展迅猛，特别是生成式人工智能逐步推广应用，正在重塑保险行业的业务模式和服务方式。中国再保险行业将以数字化转型为驱动力，深入推动再保险模式升级，加快高质量发展步伐。将持续深化直再融合、产业融合与政企融合，延伸服务链条，向社会输出风险管理专业技术和能力。将整合上下游资源，引领产品服务创新，完善基础设施建设，丰富公共产品供给。将打造“再保+科技+服务”新商业模式，建设服务国家战略、社会治理与民生保障的平台生态圈，拓展服务广度。将加快经营管理和业务流程的数字化、智能化再造，利用数字技术提升量化、识别和管理风险的能力，推进运营管理智能升级。

三是再保险市场将加快双向开放。中国再保险市场将进一步提升开放程度，形成内外并重、双向开放的新格局，不断提升行业竞争力和国际化水平。一方面，国际大型再保险公司继续加大在中国市场的布局，引入先进的管理经验和技术，促进中国再保险市场发展，提升市场整体服务水平和创新能力。另一方面，伴随上海国际再保险中心建设不断提档加速，国内再保险公司也在加快“走出去”步伐，通过设立海外分支机构、参与国际再保险业务、建立国际合作网络等方式，积极参与国际市场竞争，提升全球服务能力。

四是再保险政策体系将持续优化完善。2023年10月，中央金融工作会议要求做好金融“五篇大文章”，后续出台了一系列政策指导意见，明确发展导向、系统谋划部署，指导保险再保险行业进一步提升服务实体经济和社会民生的质效。2024年9月《国务院关于加强监管防范风险　推动保险业高质量发展的若干意见》（国发〔2024〕21号）发布，要求充分发挥保险业经济减震器和社会稳定器功能，大力提升保险保障能力和服务水平。明确的政策导向将推动保险业不断强化系统整治，推进合规经营，加强风险处置，创造更规范的竞争环境和市场秩序，也将推动再保险公司提升风险管理、产品服务创新、风险减量等专业能力，走好高质量、可持续发展之路。

第二章 2023年中国财产再保险市场回顾及展望

一、财产再保险市场规模

（一）分出保费规模

2023年，国内财产保险公司分出保费1 637.5亿元，同比增长0.5%；同期，财产保险公司原保险保费收入15 867.8亿元，同比增长5.6%；分出保费增速低于同期原保险保费收入增速约5.1个百分点（见图1、表1）。

2013—2023年，国内财产保险公司分出保费从865.2亿元增长至1 637.5亿元，年均增长率约6.6%；同期，财产保险公司原保险保费收入由6 480.9亿元增长至15 867.8亿元，年均增长率约9.4%；分出保费年均增速低于同期原保险保费收入增速约2.8个百分点（见图1、表1）。

图1　2013—2023年财产保险公司原保险保费、分出保费及增长率情况

（数据来源：《中国保险年鉴》、国家金融监督管理总局）

表1　2013—2023年财产保险公司分出保费、原保险保费及分出率情况

单位：亿元，%

年份	分出保费	增长率	原保险保费	增长率	分出率
2013	865.2	17.1	6 481.2	17.2	13.3
2014	929.8	7.5	7 544.4	16.4	12.3
2015	946.0	1.7	8 423.3	11.6	11.2
2016	887.9	-6.1	9 266.2	10.0	9.6
2017	938.8	5.7	10 541.4	13.8	8.9
2018	1 072.3	14.2	11 755.7	11.5	9.1
2019	1 207.7	12.6	13 016.3	10.7	9.3
2020	1 383.4	14.5	13 583.7	4.4	10.2
2021	1 460.5	5.6	13 816.2	1.7	10.6
2022	1 629.5	11.6	15 019.4	8.7	10.8
2023	1 637.5	0.5	15 867.8	5.6	10.3

数据来源：《中国保险年鉴》、国家金融监督管理总局。

（二）分出率

2023年，国内财产保险公司的分出率约10.3%，较上年下降0.5个百分点（见图2），连续四年超过10%。

2013—2015年，财产保险分出率逐年下降，但均高于10%；2016—2022年，分出率呈现先降后升的变化趋势；2023年，分出率回落0.5个百分点至10.3%。2016年主要受“偿二代”实施的影响，分出率大幅下降至不足10%；2017年“偿二代”影响延续，分出率降至不足9%；2018年以来，在非车险业务增长的拉动下，分出率逐年提升；2020—2023年，分出率保持在10%以上。

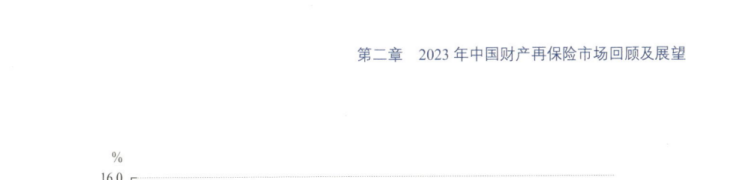

图2 2013—2023年财产保险公司再保险分出率情况

（数据来源：《中国保险年鉴》、国家金融监督管理总局）

二、财产再保险需求侧分析

（一）财产保险公司分出保费分布情况

2023年，分出保费规模超过100亿元的财产保险公司共4家，合计分出保费1 014.9亿元，占行业分出保费规模的61.8%；分出保费规模在10亿~100亿元的财产保险公司共18家，合计分出保费429.6亿元，占行业分出保费规模的26.2%；分出保费规模在1亿~10亿元的财产保险公司共49家，合计分出保费192.7亿元，占行业分出保费规模的11.7%；分出保费规模不足1亿元的财产保险公司共18家，合计分出保费5.6亿元，占行业分出保费规模的0.3%（见表2）。

表2 2023年财产保险公司分出保费的规模分布情况

单位：家，亿元，%

规模	数量	合计分出保费	占全行业分出保费的比例
分出保费规模超过100亿元	4	1 014.9	61.8
分出保费规模在10亿~100亿元	18	429.6	26.2

续表

规模	数量	合计分出保费	占全行业分出保费的比例
分出保费规模在1亿~10亿元	49	192.7	11.7
分出保费规模不足1亿元	18	5.6	0.3

数据来源：国家金融监督管理总局。

（二）财产保险公司分出保费变化情况

2023年，分出保费较上年增长的财产保险公司数量55家，占比61.8%。其中，较上年增长10%以内的公司数量14家，占比15.7%；较上年增长10%~20%的公司数量13家，占比14.6%；较上年增长超过20%的公司数量28家，占比31.5%（见表3）。

表3　　2023年财产保险公司分出保费的增速分布情况

单位：家，%

	数量	占比
分出保费较上年增长的财产保险公司	55	61.8
其中：较上年增长10%以内的公司	14	15.7
较上年增长10%~20%的公司	13	14.6
较上年增长超过20%的公司	28	31.5

数据来源：国家金融监督管理总局，不包含劳合社中国的业务。

（三）财产保险公司分出率分布情况

2023年，分出率超过20%的财产保险公司数量40家，较上年减少1家，占比44.9%；分出率15%~20%的公司数量7家，较上年增加1家，占比7.9%；分出率10%~15%的公司数量9家，较上年减少1家，占比10.1%；分出率5%~10%的公司数量15家，较上年减少1家，占比16.9%；分出率低于5%的公司数量18家，较上年增加4家，占比20.2%（见表4）。

表4　　2016—2023年各财产保险公司分出率分布情况

单位：家

分出率区间＼年份	2016	2017	2018	2019	2020	2021	2022	2023
>20%	26	26	28	34	32	38	41	40
15%~20%	4	5	8	2	10	5	6	7
10%~15%	12	12	11	15	7	8	10	9
5%~10%	14	17	15	11	12	18	16	15
<5%	24	24	25	25	26	17	14	18
合计	80	84	87	87	87	86	87	89

数据来源：国家金融监督管理总局。

三、财产再保险供给侧分析

2023年，在境内注册、经营财产再保险业务的专业再保险公司共12家，中资再保险公司5家，外资再保险公司7家。其中，中再产险发挥国内再保险市场主渠道作用，市场份额排名第1位。

（一）车险业务

2022年，在财产再保险市场中，专业再保险公司的车险分保费收入199.4亿元，同比下降2.5%；2012—2022年，年均增长率约-3.3%，业务规模整体呈下降态势。从车险业务逐年分保费收入来看，2013年增幅较大，增速达27.7%；2016年降幅最大，降低约42.6%；从2016年开始，业务规模由超过300亿元降至200亿元左右，2022年业务规模首次降至200亿元以下（见表5）。

表5　　2012—2022年专业再保险公司车险业务分保费收入情况

单位：亿元

公司名称＼年份	2012	2013	2014	2015	2016	2017	2018	2019	2020	2021	2022
中再产险	147.0	170.0	174.9	181.5	94.3	91.2	88.4	83.5	98.1	81.0	84.6
慕再北分	39.3	65.6	46.6	45.5	43.3	30.3	41.6	28.3	28.7	25.7	22.6
瑞再北分	78.2	103.1	106.3	83.1	38.3	38.5	33.8	42.9	44.7	42.9	32.7
法再北分	3.7	9.1	14.1	16.4	14.6	12.5	12.1	10.6	4.5	4.3	4.5
通用再上分		0.1	0.1	0.2	0.2	0.2	0.2	0.2	0.2	0.2	0.1
汉再上分	10.3	3.7	3.4	20.7	6.2	4.6	8.2	12.0	14.4	14.6	13.5
太平再（中国）		4.0	4.6	6.4	6.3	7.6	11.5	11.8	11.9	11.6	15.7
前海再						1.4	2.5	5.2	3.9	3.8	3.3
人保再						15.6	10.1	10.6	21.6	20.4	22.2
大韩再										0.1	0.2
合计	278.4	355.5	350.0	353.8	203.2	201.8	208.4	205.1	228.1	204.5	199.4

数据来源：《中国保险年鉴》。

从各市场主体车险分保费收入情况来看，中再产险居于行业第1位，2022年分保费收入84.6亿元，其他公司的车险分保费收入均在40亿元以下。

（二）非车险业务

2022年，在财产再保险市场中，专业再保险公司的非车险分保费收入956.5亿元，同比增长16.2%；2012—2022年，年均增长率约17.9%，业务规模整体呈较快增长态势。从非车险业务逐年分保费收入来看，除2015年和2017年出现下降外，其余年度均实现增长；非车险业务的增长率较高，分保费收入在2018年和2019年先后突破400亿元和500亿元，2022年突破900亿元（见表6）。

表6　　2012—2022年专业再保险公司非车险业务分保费收入情况

单位：亿元

年份 公司名称	2012	2013	2014	2015	2016	2017	2018	2019	2020	2021	2022
中再产险	93.5	114.2	118.1	114.8	123.6	128.9	162.9	203.7	235.4	269.3	336.4
慕再北分	25.4	23.1	26.3	27.6	41.2	16.5	41.5	46.6	38.9	50.3	53.7
瑞再北分	46.2	53.2	52.6	60.3	59.3	37.0	58.8	76.7	81.0	95.9	89.9
法再北分	12.6	15.2	18.3	19.2	23.1	22.8	21.3	22.1	23.0	29.7	28.7
通用再上分	0.2	0.3	0.5	0.4	0.3	0.7	1.5	1.9	3.2	2.2	2.9
汉再上分	6.3	5.5	30.7	10.5	16.2	20.7	33.4	54.5	81.4	68.4	77.3
安盛环球										4.8	3.1
太平再（中国）		9.4	11.0	12.0	14.2	22.8	32.5	38.9	39.0	39.8	47.5
前海再						4.7	19.1	18.2	21.3	25.5	25.5
人保再						19.1	38.8	47.0	29.9	40.6	45.0
大韩再									0.7	5.0	5.7
中国农再										191.7	240.8
合计	184.2	220.8	257.4	244.8	278.1	273.2	409.8	509.6	553.8	823.1	956.5

数据来源：《中国保险年鉴》。

从各市场主体非车险分保费收入情况来看，中再产险居于行业第1位，2022年分保费收入336.4亿元，其余公司的非车险分保费收入均在250亿元以下。

四、财产再保险市场机遇与挑战

（一）财产险市场发展机遇

1. 聚焦做好金融“五篇大文章”，财产保险业将在培育壮大战略性新兴产业、助力绿色低碳发展、加大民生保障力度等领域具有较大发展空间

2023年10月，中央金融工作会议提出要“做好科技金融、绿色金

融、普惠金融、养老金融、数字金融五篇大文章”。财产保险业将围绕金融“五篇大文章”，积极发展科技保险、绿色保险、普惠保险、养老保险和数字保险，以下险种将具有较大发展潜力。

一是城市定制型家庭财产险，家财险版“惠民保”提供“保险+服务”综合保障，目前已在多个省市开售。二是无人机责任保险，根据《无人驾驶航空器飞行管理暂行条例》，2024年起将实施强制责任保险，要求经营性飞行和除微型、轻型飞行器以外的非经营性飞行均应投保。三是民营商业航天保险，目前，民营商业航天企业已研发多型号多类型火箭，保险业探索出“阶梯式参保”模式。四是渔业保险，2023年中央一号文件提出“鼓励发展渔业保险”，中国渔业互助保险社获批开业，丰富了商业保险市场的细分险种。五是巨灾保险，河南郑州暴雨洪涝灾害后，河南巨灾保险试点落地。2023年京津冀特大暴雨灾害再次启示，目前自然灾害风险保障不足，巨灾保险有进一步发展空间。六是网络安全保险，工信部与国家金融监督管理总局联合发文，促进网络安全保险规范健康发展。国际市场网络安全保险的保费规模已达百亿美元，相比之下，国内企业的网络安全风险保障不足，市场发展空间较大。

2. 政策引导财产保险业中长期向风险减量服务积极转型

2023年1月，原中国银保监会发布《关于财产保险业积极开展风险减量服务的意见》，要求加快发展财险业风险减量服务。行业主体开展了多样化的实践探索，如营运货车保险，为货车加装监控设备，降低驾驶员因视觉盲区和疲劳驾驶的风险；安全生产责任保险，开展风险教育培训，排查事故隐患；建筑工程潜在缺陷保险，聘请第三方机构，开展全流程的建筑质量风险检验；工程项目保险，工程师现场查勘，出具防灾防损建议；电梯设备保险，通过整合维保维修服务，确保设备“按时保养、保养到位”。

同时，财产险公司创新服务内容，深耕细分市场，构建服务新模式，提升服务便利性，加快科技创新与风险减量服务融合。例如，通过集成承保理赔数据、地质地理数据、天气气象数据等跨行业信息，聚焦风险场景、绘制风险地图，让大数据技术在更多场景下为风险减量服务决策提供基础信息；应用卫星遥感技术对工程项目的周边环境进行风险查勘，对森林火点进行预警和风险检测，对农业气象灾害进行预警；应用无人机开展电网线路巡检、项目风险查勘、农药喷洒防治农业病害；应用物联网技术，建设智慧消防平台、开展电气火灾监控、实施水浸智能监测等。

（二）财产再保险市场发展机遇

一是聚焦金融“五篇大文章”，再保险助力服务国家战略。财产保险公司聚焦金融“五篇大文章”，在科技保险、绿色保险、普惠保险、养老保险、数字保险等领域拓展保险保障，创新保险险种。再保险助力服务国家战略，为农业保险、巨灾保险等领域提供再保险保障支持，同时与直保公司合作，围绕金融“五篇大文章”开展风险研究与产品创新。

二是聚焦新质生产力发展，再保险助力产品与服务创新。加快发展新质生产力成为推动高质量发展的新要求，在低空经济、新能源等新兴领域，新的风险需求要求财产保险加快产品与服务创新。再保险天然具有平台化基因，基于数据积累、技术能力和合作网络优势，可以为直保公司产品设计、产品定价、条款设计、风险管理等提供支持。

三是聚焦风险减量，再保险助力开展风险减量服务。再保险在助力财产保险业开展风险减量服务方面具有独特作用和价值，可以在自然灾害风险、农业风险、建筑质量风险、新兴风险等领域，与财产保险公司共同开展风险减量服务。

（三）财产险及再保险市场面临的风险挑战

一是中长期气候风险加剧，自然灾害损失预期将增加。亚洲是全球自然灾害高发地区，当前气候变化影响正在加剧①。中国气象局气候变化中心《中国气候变化蓝皮书（2023）》中指出中国升温速率高于同期全球平均水平，中国气候风险指数呈升高趋势，具体表现为极端高温事件频发趋强，极端强降水量事件增多，台风平均强度波动增强等。同时，世界气象组织宣布厄尔尼诺条件形成，厄尔尼诺年将使气候更加复杂。气象部门预计，将出现有的年份全国大部分地区降水偏多，有的年份淮河流域洪涝，有的年份长江流域洪涝，有的年份长江以南地区降水明显偏多等多种情景的可能。

2023年，中国自然灾害频发，损失加重。5月底，豫南麦收时节的“烂场雨”导致河南夏粮减产50余亿斤，保险赔付超过20亿元；7月底、8月初，台风“杜苏芮”及京津冀暴特大暴雨影响十余个省市，保险估损超过百亿元。极端天气灾害损失加重的趋势下，财产保险业的自然灾害责任累积增长较快，台风、洪水风险暴露的复合增长率超过10%，超过同期相关险种的保费增速，应对灾害风险的保费充足率持续承压。

① 世界气象组织《State of the Climate in Asia 2022》。

专栏：中国2023年自然灾害[①]和保险赔付[②]情况

2023年，中国自然灾害以洪涝、台风、地震和地质灾害为主，干旱、风雹、低温冷冻和雪灾、沙尘暴和森林草原火灾等也不同程度地发生。初夏，河南等地出现连阴雨天气，给夏收造成不利影响。进入主汛期，超强台风“杜苏芮”、海河流域性特大洪水、松辽流域严重暴雨洪涝等重大灾害相继发生。12月中旬山西等地发生低温雨雪冰冻灾害，对群众生产生活造成较大影响，12月18日，甘肃积石山6.2级地震造成甘肃、青海两省重大人员伤亡。

全年各种自然灾害共造成9 544.4万人次不同程度受灾，因灾死亡失踪691人，紧急转移安置334.4万人次；倒塌房屋20.9万间，严重损坏62.3万间，一般损坏144.1万间；农作物受灾面积10 539.3千公顷；直接经济损失3 454.5亿元。与近5年均值相比，受灾人次、因灾死亡失踪人数和农作物受灾面积分别下降24.4%、2.8%和37.2%，倒塌房屋数量、直接经济损失分别上升96.9%、12.6%。

在保险赔付方面，2023年保险业涉及重大自然灾害的赔付约252.59亿元，投入防灾、减灾资金约6.61亿元，投入防灾、减灾人力约11.31万人次，发送预警信息约1.30亿人次，排查企业客户风险约17.14万次，预计减少灾害损失约37.09亿元。

二是安全生产风险形势值得关注。应急管理部门信息披露，过去5年全国安全生产事故总量和死亡人数比此前5年分别下降80%和50%。但自2023年以来，重特大事故数量有所回升，特别是矿山、消防、危险化学品等领域的安全风险值得关注。

三是新型保险标的增多，承保面临新挑战。近年来，海洋牧场、

① 数据来源：应急管理部发布的2023年全国自然灾害基本情况，应急管理部网站。

② 数据来源：“中国保险行业协会组织行业开展2024年全国防灾减灾日有关工作”，中国保险行业协会网站。

国产大型邮轮、海上光伏、电动船舶、漂浮式海上风电等新型保险标的涌现，其中部分已经开始规模化推广，但保险经营数据有限，相关风险尚未暴露，承保新型保险标的面临新挑战。

四是新能源汽车运输风险涌现。中国新能源汽车出口大幅增长带来新的风险变量，2022年共发生十余次新能源汽车运输船火灾。汽车运输船一旦发生火灾，救援难度较大，航运保险的风险敞口较高。包括新能源汽车在内的汽车海上运输安全成为航运业关注焦点，为航运保险带来新挑战。

五是建筑安全领域风险隐患导致较大风险敞口。建筑材料风险方面，无机砂浆外保温层空鼓、脱落等导致的安全事故，将导致建筑质量潜在缺陷保险承担大额赔付，风险敞口达10亿元。2023年5月，天津某居民社区地面突发沉降，导致居民财产损失；7月，黑龙江省某中学体育馆发生坍塌事故，导致人身和财产损失。建筑安全隐患引发公众担忧，保险业风险减量服务在建筑安全领域应发挥更大作用。

六是关注境外分入业务的风险。一方面，境外分入业务自然巨灾风险暴露高、营业中断赔付重。以汽车、化工行业的全球保单为例，超过1亿美元的赔付案例较多，远远高于国内市场同类标的可预期的损失水平。另一方面，直保端及再保险各环节的价格信息不透明，境内与境外市场价格差异较大，相关业务风险值得关注。

五、财产再保险市场发展展望

（一）对再保险分出需求变化的展望

一是在传统风险领域，财产保险公司向再保险市场转移风险的需求不断提升。传统风险因素影响延续，气候变化带来的极端天气加重灾害损失，保险公司的地震、洪水、台风等巨灾风险快速累积，成为影响行业稳健经营的重大风险，财产保险公司向再保险市场转移风险的需求预期将提升。

二是在新型风险领域，财产保险公司的再保险需求保持强劲。网络风险、新能源汽车风险、新型责任风险、境外风险等新型风险凸显，保险业务的风险构成日趋复杂，再保险需求持续增长。再保险公司将与直保公司合作，为新兴风险开发更有针对性的保险产品，提供更加全面的风险保障。同时，再保险将发挥平台和专业优势，通过整合行业与第三方资源，积极推动行业平台建设，加快风险管理模型工具开发，不断提高行业风险减量综合服务能力。

三是财产保险公司将更加注重与财务实力稳健的专业再保险公司合作。财产保险公司对再保险人的选择及份额进行调整，将进一步向境内财务实力稳健的专业再保险公司倾斜。

（二）对专业再保险公司业务承保策略变化的展望

市场整体角度，在国际再保险“硬市场”环境下，受外部市场关注和内部定价底线的共同约束下，再保险人首席报价将更加谨慎。

价格与风险角度，在国际再保险“硬市场”环境下，再保险人自身的业务经营承压，转分成本刚性上涨。在极端天气影响下，历史年度再保险合同赔付恶化，暴雨、内涝等非模型损失加重，但目前国内再保险市场对极端天气风险的附加定价存在不足，再保险人开展业务的压力不断上升。

市场格局角度，一方面，影响保险经营的新风险、新挑战增多，行业需要一定时间提升应对和管理能力；另一方面，影响再保险供给的外部环境更加复杂严峻。再保险供给呈现本地再保险支持加强、外部再保险供给降低的趋势。

整体而言，极端天气将加重灾害损失，再保险经营管理难度增加，实现定价利润面对较大困难，同时气候变化影响使再保险公司风险偏好更加谨慎。再保险公司需要遵循的内部“硬约束”增多，再保险市场供需关系处于“紧平衡”状态，预期再保险市场将进一步提升价格水平以反映风险趋势变化。

第三章 2023年中国人身再保险市场回顾及展望

一、人身再保险市场规模

二、人身再保险需求侧分析

三、人身再保险供给侧分析

四、人身再保险市场机遇与挑战

五、人身再保险市场发展展望

一、人身再保险市场规模

（一）人身险市场情况

2023年，中国人身险市场继续在转型中前行，长期储蓄类业务增长较快，保障类业务短期下降，人身保险公司经营压力和资本需求较大，对人身再保险市场发展既带来机遇，也带来挑战。

业务规模方面，2023年，国内人身保险公司保费收入35 379.0亿元，按可比口径，同比增长10.2%。

业务结构方面，寿险保费收入27 646.0亿元，同比增长12.8%；健康险保费收入7 283.0亿元，同比增长3.0%，增速较2022年稍有回升，但仍维持低速增长水平；意外险保费收入450.0亿元，同比下降9.8%，放缓速度较2022年有所收窄。

（二）分出保费规模

2023年，国内人身保险公司分出保费1 056.7亿元，同比下降8.4%。同期，人身保险公司原保险保费收入35 379.0亿元，按可比口径同比增长10.2%（见图1、表1）。总体来说，人身险分出保费规模不同年份之间呈波动趋势。当前，中国宏观经济发展具有较强韧性，长期向好的基本趋势没有改变，但仍需要克服有效需求不足、社会预期偏弱、风险隐患较多等困难。受美国加息等影响，资本市场波动性增强，人身险直保市场面临发展转型压力，给人身再保险市场增长带来一定冲击和挑战。

2013—2023年，国内人身保险公司分出保费由298.8亿元增长至1 056.7亿元，年均增长率约13.5%，整体稳中有升。其中，2013—2014

年，分出保费快速增长；2015—2016年大幅回落；2017—2020年波动上涨；2020年后，人身再保险市场整体规模保持千亿元水平。

图1　2013—2023年人身保险公司原保险保费、分出保费及增长率情况

（数据来源：《中国保险年鉴》、国家金融监督管理总局）

表1　2013—2023年人身保险公司分出保费、原保险保费及再保险分出率情况

单位：亿元，%

年份	分出保费	增长率	原保险保费	增长率	分出率
2013	298.8		11 010.0		2.7
2014	1 937.4	548.4	12 592.3	14.4	15.4
2015	555.6	-71.3	15 724.0	24.9	3.5
2016	435.9	-21.5	21 662.8	37.8	2.0
2017	722.4	65.7	25 972.7	19.9	2.8
2018	736.2	1.9	26 232.5	1.0	2.8
2019	673.9	-8.5	27 792.6	5.9	2.4
2020	1 043.7	54.9	29 500.7	6.1	3.5
2021	996.3	-4.5	31 224.0	14.0	3.0
2022	1 153.3	15.8	32 091.0	2.8	3.6
2023	1 056.7	-8.4	35 379.0	10.2	3.0

数据来源：《中国保险年鉴》、国家金融监督管理总局。

（三）分出率

2023年，国内人身保险公司分出率约3.0%，较去年下降0.6个百分点（见图2）。当前，国内人身险分出率低于全球平均水平。从业务结构看，以风险保障为目的的传统再保险业务分出比例较高，以储蓄型为主的人身险分出比例较低。境外存量市场业务变动主要受国际并购、年金业务等大宗交易业务影响，增长有限，整体格局稳定。

2013—2023年，人身保险公司分出率整体呈现稳中有升趋势（见图2）。其中，2013—2014年，分出率提升并达到高峰；2015年大幅回落；2016—2020年，分出率出现波动并呈上升趋势；2020年后，分出率基本维持在3%左右。

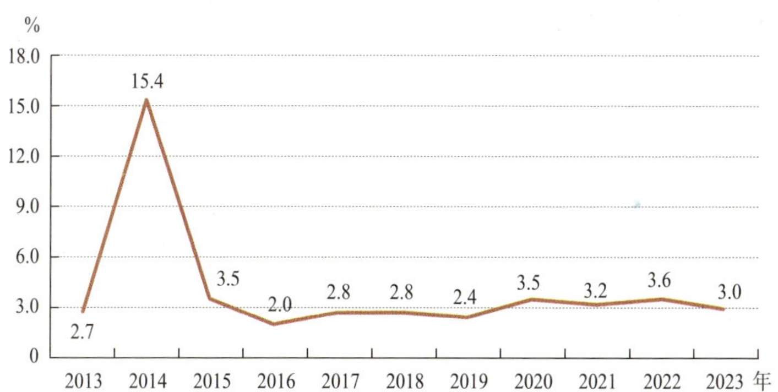

图2　2013—2023年人身保险公司再保险分出率情况

（数据来源：《中国保险年鉴》、国家金融监督管理总局）

二、人身再保险需求侧分析

（一）人身保险公司分出保费分布情况[①]

2023年，分出保费规模超过50亿元的人身保险公司共11家，合计分出保费710.8亿元，占行业分出保费规模的66.4%；分出保费规模在10亿~50亿元的人身保险公司共15家，合计分出保费271.6亿元，占行业分出保费规模的25.4%；分出保费规模不足10亿元的人身保险公司共61家，合计分出保费87.3亿元，占行业分出保费规模的8.2%（见表2）。

表2　　2023年人身保险公司分出保费的规模分布情况

单位：家，亿元，%

规模	数量	合计分出保费	占全行业分出保费的比例
分出保费规模超过50亿元	11	710.8	66.4
分出保费规模在10亿~50亿元	15	271.6	25.4
分出保费规模不足10亿元	61	87.3	8.2

数据来源：国家金融监督管理总局。

（二）人身保险公司分出保费变化情况

2023年，分出保费较上年增长的人身保险公司数量42家，占比48.8%。其中，较上年增长超过50%的公司数量16家，占比18.6%；较上年增长20%~50%的公司数量3家，占比3.5%；较上年增长20%以内的公司数量23家，占比26.7%（见表3）。

① 部分人身保险公司2023年分出保费规模数据为负数。

表3　　2023年人身保险公司分出保费的增速分布情况

单位：家，%

规模	数量	占比
分出保费较上年增长的人身保险公司	42	48.8
其中：较上年增长超过50%的公司	16	18.6
较上年增长20%~50%的公司	3	3.5
较上年增长20%以内的公司	23	26.7

数据来源：国家金融监督管理总局。

三、人身再保险供给侧分析

2023年，在境内注册、经营人身再保险业务的专业再保险公司共10家。其中，市场份额超过50%的公司1家，市场份额10%~15%的公司1家，市场份额5%~10%的公司3家，市场份额低于5%的公司5家。中再寿险发挥国内再保险主渠道作用，市场份额排名第1位。其他主要参与者包括国际大型再保险公司，以及前海再、太平再（中国）、人保再等本土再保险公司。

（一）寿险业务

2022年，人身再保险市场中，专业再保险公司的寿险分保费收入519.7亿元，同比下降11.5%；2012—2022年，年均增长率约13.0%，整体呈波动增长态势（见表4）。从寿险业务逐年分保费收入来看，2013—2014年大幅增长，2015—2016年显著下降，2017年开始稳步回升，除2019年和2022年外，2017—2022年多数年份保持正增长。

表4　　2012—2022年专业再保险公司寿险业务分保费收入情况

单位：亿元

公司名称＼年份	2012	2013	2014	2015	2016	2017	2018	2019	2020	2021	2022
中再寿险	125.7	142.2	166.0	178.1	252.9	368.5	404.6	390.0	464.8	443.7	379.4
慕再北分	4.0	20.4	23.1	30.3	9.3	6.2	4.2	5.0	7.9	6.1	6.6
瑞再北分	1.0	0.8	1.3	1.6	0.8	1.9	2.4	1.1	3.4	3.4	4.5
法再北分	0.3	10.6	19.0	10.8	2.1	3.8	10.1	7.3	8.0	40.0	27.3
通用再上分	2.3	2.6	3.1	3.8	4.0	5.1	5.6	7.1	8.0	9.8	12.1
汉再上分	19.7	120.7	586.9	96.3	16.7	9.3	12.5	17.6	18.8	16.4	10.2
RGA美再上分				0.1		2.1	2.9	2.0	2.4	2.5	2.7
太平再（中国）										0.1	0.2
前海再						33.3	42.2	29.0	49.1	62.5	71.1
人保再										2.4	5.5
合计	153.0	297.3	799.6	320.9	285.8	430.2	484.4	459.0	562.5	587.1	519.7

数据来源：《中国保险年鉴》。

从各市场主体寿险分保费收入情况来看，中再寿险居于行业第1位，2022年分保费收入379.4亿元，市场份额约为73.0%；其次是前海再、法再，2022年市场份额分别约为13.7%、5.3%；其余公司的寿险分保费收入均在20亿元以下。

（二）健康险业务

2022年，人身再保险市场中，专业再保险公司的健康险分保费收入477.4亿元，同比下降0.6%；2012—2022年，年均增长率约25.2%（见表5）。近年来，健康险分保费收入增长较快，2022年健康险分保费收入为2012年的9.4倍，但2022年健康险分保费收入普遍下降，行业整体增长趋势明显放缓。

表5 2012—2022年专业再保险公司健康险业务分保费收入情况

单位：亿元

年份 公司名称	2012	2013	2014	2015	2016	2017	2018	2019	2020	2021	2022
中再寿险	16.2	26.8	25.1	32.5	37.3	50.6	97.6	139.3	175.6	212.3	261.3
慕再北分	10.6	10.8	10.8	17.3	24.5	28.5	26.3	36.4	44.3	37.5	23.8
瑞再北分	18.9	18.7	21.1	20.3	21.5	20.1	17.3	38.1	46.6	48.6	48.5
法再北分	1.5	2.0	2.5	1.4	1.2	5.0	13.7	21.8	30.7	26.3	23.8
通用再上分	0.5	0.4	1.2	2.1	2.9	7.8	23.4	37.0	40.9	41.7	26.0
汉再上分	2.9	4.8	4.7	38.2	12.7	19.7	28.8	41.6	51.9	58.4	47.0
RGA美再上分				0.4		3.9	7.8	8.5	8.2	8.9	11.4
太平再(中国)								0.6	1.4	2.4	3.0
前海再						0.4	2.1	12.2	27.8	39.8	26.0
人保再									0.4	4.6	6.6
合计	50.6	63.5	65.4	112.2	100.0	135.9	216.9	335.6	427.8	480.5	477.4

数据来源：《中国保险年鉴》。

从各市场主体健康险分保费收入情况来看，中再寿险居于行业第1位，2022年分保费收入261.3亿元，市场份额约为54.7%；瑞再、汉再、通用再、前海再、慕再、法再2022年健康险分保费收入在20亿~50亿元之间。其余公司的健康险分保费收入均在15亿元以下。

（三）意外险业务

2022年，人身再保险市场中，专业再保险公司的意外险分保费收入50.1亿元人民币，同比下降23.9%；2012—2022年，年均增长率约7.6%，整体呈增长趋势，但2022年显著降低（见表6）。

表6 2012—2022年专业再保险公司意外险业务分保费收入情况

单位：亿元

年份 公司名称	2012	2013	2014	2015	2016	2017	2018	2019	2020	2021	2022
中再寿险	17.1	13.6	18.3	18.1	22.2	23.0	21.5	25.1	24.6	37.0	21.2
慕再北分	2.8	1.3	6.2	3.8	5.5	8.3	11.5	12.6	13.0	11.6	11.3

续表

公司名称 \ 年份	2012	2013	2014	2015	2016	2017	2018	2019	2020	2021	2022
瑞再北分	1.9	0.9	0.6	1.1	-0.6	0.5	0.9	1.5	1.7	1.4	1.5
法再北分	0.6	0.9	2.2	3.8	4.8	3.9	2.2	2.1	2.3	2.6	2.0
通用再上分	0.2	0.3	1.3	3.6	5.3	5.2	6.8	7.7	6.3	4.9	5.1
汉再上分	1.4	7.0	3.1	4.1	5.5	6.0	12.3	13.1	14.1	6.8	8.2
太平再（中国）								0.3	0.5	1.0	0.2
前海再						0.1	0.6	0.5	0.6	0.4	0.3
人保再										0.1	0.3
合计	24.1	24.0	31.7	34.6	42.8	46.8	55.7	62.9	63.0	65.8	50.1

数据来源：《中国保险年鉴》。

从各市场主体意外险分保费收入情况来看，中再寿险居于行业第1位，2022年分保费收入21.2亿元，市场份额约为42.3%；其次是慕再、汉再、通用再，市场份额分别约为22.6%、16.4%、10.2%；其余公司的意外险分保费收入均在5亿元以下。

（四）全球人身再保险市场格局

从全球市场格局来看，AM.Best数据显示，全球再保险集团排名中，人身再保险业务至少占总保费收入的30%，整体格局较稳定。2022年全球人身再保险公司排名中，各再保集团人身再保险业务规模普遍略有下降，排位总体保持稳定，加拿大人寿再继续居第1位；中再寿险排名第7位（见表7）。

表7　2022年全球前十大人身再保险集团

单位：亿美元

排名	公司名称	毛再保保费规模
1	加拿大人寿再	234.1
2	瑞再	159.9
3	慕再	146.0

续表

排名	公司名称	毛再保保费规模
4	RGA美再	138.2
5	法再	103.7
6	汉再	96.4
7	中再	91.8
8	伯克希尔公司	51.9
9	大西洋再	30.0
10	Assicurazioni Generali SPA	24.5

数据来源：AM. Best。

四、人身再保险市场机遇与挑战

2023年，在世界经济复苏乏力、各经济体分化加剧的复杂环境下，中国经济转方式、调结构、增动能取得新成效，增速领先全球主要经济体，GDP同比增长5.2%，居民可支配收入同比增长6.3%。中国人身保险业也在2023年实现保费规模重返两位数的增长。当前，中国人身保险业仍处于深度转型期，面临诸多挑战，需要把握高质量发展新阶段的重要历史机遇，突破发展瓶颈，实现长期价值增长。

（一）人身险市场发展机遇

一是国家层面利好政策频出。国家顶层设计中对人身险定位更加明确，重要性更加突出。中央金融工作会议要求保险业发挥经济减震器和社会稳定器功能，金融“五篇大文章”中普惠金融、养老金融均受到高度关注，中国人身保险业在服务养老、医疗等领域将大有可为，成为多层次保障体系的重要组成部分。税优、税延政策逐步完善并落地实施。自2023年以来，税优健康、税延养老政策陆续出台，配套细则扎实推进，打开了广阔增长空间，成为推动商业健康险、商业养老险长期向好发展的重要因素。

二是宏观经济回升并长期向好。人身险市场发展速度与宏观经济高度正相关。2023年中国GDP增速达到5.2%，经济持续恢复、回升向好，高质量发展不断取得新成效，为保险业高质量发展提供了有力支撑。根据成熟市场经验，在人均GDP达到约3万美元时，保险进入相对饱和期。当前，中国人均GDP约1.26万美元，保险业依然蕴含巨大增长空间。

三是老龄化趋势带来新机遇。国家统计局数据显示，2023年末中国65岁及以上人口达2.17亿人，占全国人口的15.4%，中国老龄化程度进一步加深，未来健康养老保障和服务需求巨大，将推动人身险市场向寿险、养老年金险和健康险多元发展，市场整体规模预期将逐步扩大。

四是数字技术应用驱动创新发展。新技术的加速应用正在深刻改变包括人身保险业在内的各行各业。大数据的应用大幅拓展了承保风险的边界，人工智能理赔、核保等显著提升了经营效率。保险再保险公司通过应用新技术创新商业模式，提升经营业绩，增强服务能力，将有力推动行业长期高质量发展。

（二）人身险市场面临的风险挑战

一是市场供求存在一定错配。需求端，客户对保险产品感知度尚待提升，对个人人身风险保障需求和所购买的产品及服务缺乏更深层和更细化的认知，商业保险赔付在整体医疗费用支出中的占比仍然不高。供给端，保险保障功能发挥仍有较大提升空间，医疗保障产品责任仍需完善，与医院、医生等相关方的服务融合还不够紧密，保险公司以经营寿险的理念经营商业医疗险，对老人、慢性病患者等亟须保障的群体覆盖面仍然有限。养老产品设计偏重金融属性，服务功能较为欠缺，缺乏长期保障、康养配套服务等特色，存在与其他金融理财产品同质化的问题。

二是传统流量驱动模式逐渐失效。随着社会老龄化程度逐步加深，人口红利减少，同时直播、送货等新业态模式出现，传统代理人收入已缺乏比较优势，个险渠道“人海战术”已成为过去式。自2023年以来，监管政策严格要求渠道费用“报行合一”，银保渠道更加规范。互联网平台方面，流量成本数倍提升，通过互联网渠道推出爆款产品越发困难。总体来看，通过流量驱动的粗放式增长模式缺乏竞争力，渠道面临较大转型压力。

三是传统盈利模式面临重构。境内债券市场利率中长期呈持续下行趋势，同时面临信用风险等挑战，人身险公司传统盈利模式主要依靠利差获取利润，新形势下利差已明显收窄，盈利模式面临挑战和重构。面对长期低利率环境，人身险公司需要强化资产负债匹配管理，更好地防范风险；更需加强精细化管理，推动业务提质增效，加强从费差和死差中寻找潜在收益。

（三）人身再保险市场面临的机遇与挑战

发展机遇方面：一是面对中国社会日益增长的健康保障需求以及供给侧对健康险市场的热切期待，监管机构陆续出台多项利好政策，激发市场对长期护理保险、失能保险、税优健康险、普惠健康险、短期健康险等重点领域的产品创新需求，再保险在产品创新和风险管理等方面具有专业优势，可提供有力支撑，发挥创新引领作用；二是在直保渠道转型升级、产品服务供给侧结构性改革的背景下，保险公司对再保险在数据、产品、服务、销售支持等方面的需求显著提升，再保险在风险定义、产品升级、风险定价和管理方面的专业价值将进一步凸显；三是在保险与健康产业融合创新过程中，再保险可在“保险+服务”的新模式下发挥重要桥梁纽带作用，通过统筹资源、链接各方，更好地发挥平台作用和专业价值；四是再保险在人身险行业基础设施建设中，如生命表、重疾表、意外表的制定工作中，将持续发挥数据技术方面的优势，为行业贡献力量；五是“偿二代”二期、IFRS 17等新政策实施，保险公司偿付能力普遍面临压力，对再保险存在一定需求。

发展挑战方面：一是中国宏观环境仍面临多重压力，经济恢复的基础尚不牢固，给人身保险业和再保险业发展都带来一定影响；二是人身险市场在需求端、销售端和资产端都存在较大压力，保障需求在短期内仍未有效激发，长期储蓄意愿不断上升，直保公司分出需求不强，将影响人身再保险业发展；三是重疾经验持续恶化，医疗费用支出不断提高，长期医疗险管理机制仍需完善，健康险发展面临风险暴露增多、业务管理难度持续增大的问题；四是境外再保险机构通过离岸方式加大参与中国市场力度，人身再保险市场竞争日趋激烈。

五、人身再保险市场发展展望

中央金融工作会议要求做好科技金融、绿色金融、普惠金融、养老金融、数字金融“五篇大文章”。党的二十届三中全会为保险再保险业下一步深化改革创新、加快高质量发展指明了方向。从产品和服务端来看，短期内寿险产品仍是人身险业的主力产品。人民群众对稳定收益和资产保值的需求仍然突出，与基金、储蓄、银行理财等其他金融产品相比，寿险产品具有长期、稳定等优势。与此同时，随着寿险产品预定利率调整，仅含储蓄功能的寿险产品吸引力不断下降，兼具储蓄和保障功能的人身险产品更能满足人民群众不断提升的健康保障需求。健康险预计将在长期护理保险领域迎来新突破。从业务渠道端看，监管机构持续推进“报行合一”政策，加强产品在不同渠道的精细化、科学化管理，将进一步推动行业规范销售行为，维护市场有序竞争。未来业务渠道发展将突出各家公司自身优势，把转型重点放在深入理解客户需求、优化产品组合、提升客户体验与服务质量等方面，实现更加精准、有效的市场渗透，从而推动销售增长。从资产端看，受中长期利率中枢下行等因素的影响，防范利差损风险将成为行业未来一段时期的重点任务。行业将逐步降低负债成本，同时为应对投资环境的不确定性，将注重资产配置策略的稳健与安全，保证资产流动性充足。

再保险也将积极发挥在产品创新、生态联动和数据技术等方面的专业优势，持续深化直再合作，有效助力行业转型发展。一是引领产品创新，持续推动人身险供给侧结构性改革，加快长期护理保险、失能保险等细分险种的研发推广，增强商业健康险补充保障作用。二是强化生态联动作用，持续加强与医疗服务机构、健康服务机构等的合作，进一步促进医疗与保险产业融合，在慢病管理、健康管理等领域积极探索突破，助力直保公司以产品结构优化升级带动渠道专业化发展，赋能销售渠道创新转型。三是运用人工智能等技术深度开发利用数据资源，助力直保公司降本增效，提升风险防控能力和精细化管理能力，助力行业向多元化价值创造转型升级，推动高质量发展。

第四章 2023年中国再保险行业双向开放回顾及展望

随着中国金融领域高水平制度型开放深入推进，保险业对外开放的深度和广度不断提升。中国再保险市场也已初步形成双向开放新格局。一方面，中国再保险市场开放力度不断加大，全球主要再保险公司均已在中国设立分支机构、开展业务，有力推动了中国再保险市场发展。与此同时，上海国际再保险中心建设不断提档加速，旨在逐步打造一个具有全球影响力、在岸与离岸相结合的全球再保险交易中心。另一方面，中国再保险企业稳步推进国际化发展，加强全球网络布局，提升国际化经营管理能力，积极参与全球风险治理，国际市场竞争力和影响力日益提升。

一、外资再保险企业在中国发展情况

（一）外资再保险公司在华发展概况

回顾中国金融业对外开放历程，2001年中国正式加入WTO是重要的历史节点。加入WTO后金融领域率先实现开放的便是再保险市场。从2002年至2005年底，逐步取消再保险和再保险经纪业务跨境交易限制，允许国外再保险人在国内设立机构开展经营活动；再保险法定分保比例逐年降低，2006年彻底取消法定分保，全面实现商业化分保。再保险成为中国金融业中开放程度最深、国际化程度最高的领域之一。

截至2023年底，中国境内再保险市场专业再保险公司共有15家，其中7家中资再保险公司（含1家集团公司，即中国再保），8家外资再保险公司（见表1）。国际头部再保险公司通过在华设立分支机构积极参与中国市场业务。

表1　2023年外资公司在华机构保费收入排名

单位：亿元

排名	在华外资机构	2023年分保费收入
1	瑞再北分	195.5
2	法再北分	134.9
3	汉再上分	128.7
4	慕再北分	113.6
5	通用再上分	43.9
6	RGA美再上分	13.8
7	大韩再上分	5.8
8	安盛环球	0.1

数据来源：各公司2023年信息披露报告。

外资再保险公司根据其自身经营特点，制定了差异化的在华发展策略。比如，有的外资公司在中国聚焦政府与科技领域业务，一方面注重与中国政府合作，对政府重点关注的医疗、“三农”、环境污染及食品安全等领域，重点发展相应的健康险、农险、责任险等险种；另一方面，利用新技术推动创新，与许多直保公司在车联网、物联网、数据挖掘等方面开展合作。再如，有的外资公司更注重业务质量，强调在业务端实现可持续、有利润的增长，因而特别注重技术提升、市场研判和早期投入。还有的外资公司注重经营效益，强调业务端利润，同时善于通过精细化管理降低成本以维持高于同业的盈利能力。

（二）2023年外资再保险公司在华经营情况

2023年，外资再保险公司业务发展整体保持稳健，盈利能力不断提升，竞争力进一步增强，已成为中国再保险市场的重要组成部分。

1. 业务规模情况

2018—2023年，外资再保险公司业务规模整体稳定。2023年，外资再保险公司分保费收入较2022年小幅上升。其中，瑞再北分和法再北分分保费收入较2022年有所上升，汉再上分和慕再北分分保费收入较2022年均有下降。瑞再北分业务规模仍居外资再保险公司首位，2023年分保费收入195.5亿元。法再北分2023年分保费收入达134.9亿元，超越汉再上分和慕再北分，排名第2位（见图1）。

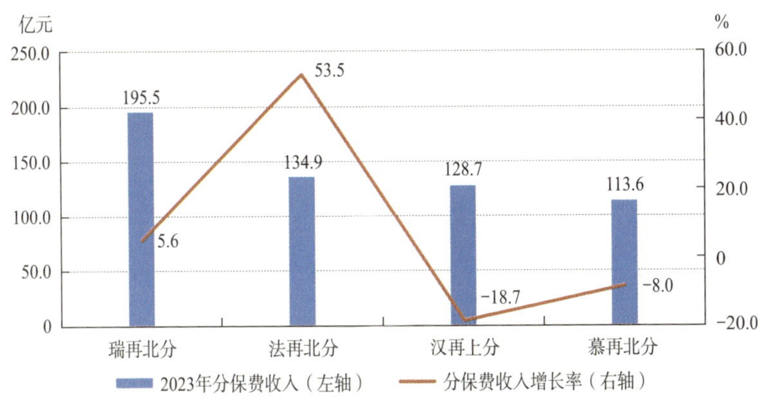

图1　2023年外资再保险公司分保费收入及增长率情况

（数据来源：各公司 2023 年信息披露报告）

（1）瑞再北分

从分保费收入看，瑞再北分作为外资再保险在国内的龙头公司，2023年分保费收入195.5亿元，同比上升5.6%。近年来，瑞再北分的财产险业务规模逐年增加，财产险业务贡献了瑞再北分总保费收入的七成左右，远高于寿险和健康险。

从业务结构看（见表2），2023年瑞再北分财产险分保费收入占比69.1%，其中占比较高的为财产及责任险（41.9%）与车险（19.5%）。人身险分保费收入占比30.9%。近年来，由于中国市场寿险及健康险发展前景较好，人身险分保费收入也呈现上升趋势。

表2　　瑞再北分业务结构情况

单位：亿元，%

业务条线	2023年分保费收入	2023年分保费占比
人身险	60.4	30.9
寿险	11.0	5.6
健康险	49.4	25.3
财产险	135.1	69.1
车险	38.2	19.5
财产及责任险	81.8	41.9
水险	13.2	6.7
其他	1.9	1.0
合计	195.5	100

数据来源：公司2023年信息披露报告。

（2）法再北分

从分保费收入看，2023年法再北分分保费收入134.9亿元，同比上升53.5%，超越汉再上分和慕再北分，在外资再保险公司中排名第2位。其中，寿险分保费收入106.8亿元，同比上升101.1%，非寿险分保费收入28.1亿元，同比下降19.3%。

从业务结构看（见表3），法再北分近年来寿险业务占比超过六成，2023年寿险业务规模大幅增加，占比达79.2%，非寿险业务占比降为20.8%。

表3　　法再北分业务结构情况

单位：亿元，%

业务条线	2023年分保费收入	2023年分保费占比
寿险	106.8	79.2
非寿险	28.1	20.8
合计	134.9	100

数据来源：公司2023年信息披露报告。

（3）汉再上分

从分保费收入看，汉再上分2023年分保费收入128.7亿元，同比下降18.7%。

从业务结构看（见表4），汉再上分非寿险业务占比54.5%，寿险业务占比45.5%。寿险业务中占比最高的为健康险，占比达31.2%。非寿险业务中占比较高的包括信用险，占比12.9%；责任险，占比12.7%；财产险，占比9.5%；车险，占比8.8%。

表4　汉再上分业务结构情况

单位：亿元，%

业务条线	2023年分保费收入	2023年分保费占比
寿险	58.6	45.5
健康险	40.2	31.2
人寿险	11.4	8.8
意外险	7.1	5.5
非寿险	70.1	54.5
责任险	16.3	12.7
财产险	12.2	9.5
信用险	16.7	12.9
机动车辆及第三者责任险	11.3	8.8
农业险	4.0	3.1
工程险	4.7	3.7
货物运输险	2.3	1.8
健康险	-0.2	-0.1
船舶险	1.8	1.4
意外险	0.5	0.3
其他	0.6	0.5
合计	128.7	100

数据来源：公司2023年信息披露报告。

（4）慕再北分

从分保费收入看，2023年慕再北分分保费收入113.6亿元，同比下降8.0%。其中，非寿险分保费收入84.4亿元，同比上升3.4 %；寿险分保费收入29.2亿元，同比下降30.1%。

从业务结构看（见表5），2023年慕再北分非寿险业务84.4亿元，占比74.3%，寿险业务29.2亿元，占比25.7%，寿险分保费收入呈现下降趋势。

表5 慕再北分业务结构情况

单位：亿元，%

业务条线	2023年分保费收入	2023年分保费占比
非寿险	84.4	74.3
寿险	29.2	25.7
合计	113.6	100

数据来源：公司2023年信息披露报告。

2. 盈利情况

2023年，外资再保险公司在华机构盈利整体保持稳健（见表6）。需要说明的是，由于外资再保险机构业务转分比例较高，盈利水平会受到转分安排影响，因此净利润指标并不一定能够客观、全面地反映其经营状况和业务质量。

表6 外资再保险公司在华机构净利润情况

单位：万元，%

公司	2022年净利润	2023年净利润	净利润增长率
瑞再北分	27 617	22 104	-20
法再北分	24 129	19 726	-18
汉再上分	-84 973	9 466	111
慕再北分	39 374	19 730	-50

数据来源：各公司2023年信息披露报告。

3. 偿付能力情况

偿付能力方面，上述4家外资再保险公司2023年偿付能力充足率较高，其中瑞再北分偿付能力充足率最高，达343%（见表7）。外资再保险公司整体资本实力较强，有较大能力来承保高质量业务，为其深耕中国再保险市场奠定了坚实基础。

表7　　外资再保险公司在华机构偿付能力情况

单位：%，亿元

公司	2023年底 综合偿付能力充足率	2023年底营运资金	2023年底净资产
瑞再北分	343	43.5	87.2
法再北分	247	20.6	29.5
汉再上分	241	72.5	71.5
慕再北分	266	16.5	48.1

数据来源：各公司2023年信息披露报告。

二、中资再保险企业国际化发展情况

在金融业推动双向开放过程中，以中国再保、太平再保险为代表的中资再保险企业也在积极推进国际化发展进程，主动参与全球再保险市场竞争，加快融入全球保险价值链。同时，上海国际再保险中心建设在加速推进中，也将推动中资再保险企业进一步融入全球再保险市场，提升中国再保险市场的国际竞争力和影响力。

（一）中国再保国际化发展情况

作为中国再保险业“走出去”的先行者，中国再保多年来坚定推进国际化战略，国际化发展格局初具规模。2010年首获国际评级，2011年正式进入劳合社市场，2015年在香港上市，2018年成功收购英国桥社保险公司，陆续设立中再资产香港子公司、集团新加坡分公司、中再寿险香港子公司。目前，中国再保在全球11个国家和地区设有境外机构，国际业务已覆盖全球200多个国家和地区，合作伙伴超过1 000家，是国际化程度最高的中资保险企业之一。

（二）太平再保险有限公司国际化发展情况

太平再（中国）的母公司太平再保险有限公司于1980年9月在中国香港注册成立，是中国太平保险集团旗下专业再保险子公司，承保来自全球的财产及人身再保险业务，总部设在中国香港，并在北京、英国伦敦设有全资子公司，在马来西亚纳闽岛设有分公司，在日本东京和中国澳门设有代表处。

太平再保险有限公司依托其上市母公司——中国太平保险控股有限公司，以及战略股东比利时富杰保险国际股份有限公司的支持，坚持稳健、高效、灵活的承保政策和管理手段，财务实力雄厚，经营业绩良好，连续多年获国际评级机构标准普尔、贝氏和惠誉财务实力A评级。

太平再保险有限公司是亚洲地区知名的专业再保险公司，保持香港财产险专业再保险市场排名首位，业务范围覆盖全球五大洲的100多个国家和地区，服务客户达1 000余家。2023年，太平再保险有限公司实现保险服务收入94.2亿港元，总资产481.8亿港元。

（三）中资再保险企业服务共建“一带一路”情况

中国再保积极以主责主业服务实体经济，从推动保险业供给侧结构性改革、提升海外风险保障能力等方面，高质量服务共建“一带一路”。一是助力完善“一带一路”保险机制顶层设计。2020年，在监管机构的指导支持下，中国再保牵头保险行业成立国内唯一专门从事“一带一路”风险管理的行业平台——中国“一带一路”再保险共同体，并担任共同体主席单位和管理机构；分别在新加坡、英国牵头组建“一带一路”保险再保险行业性组织，专门为“一带一路”中国海外利益提供风险保障。二是全面搭建“一带一路”风险保障服务网络。中国再保利用全球化布局，着力打造“一带一路”全方位服务保障体系。通过北京、新加坡、英国三地“一带一路”保险再保险行业平台，搭建起遍及136个国家和地区的战略合作“朋友圈”，积极服务“一带一路”沿线区域的中国海外利益项目。近三年，累计为“一带一路”项目提供综合风险保障超过9 000亿元。三是持续引领“一带一路”保险产品与服务创新。中国再保积极打通国内和国际两个市场，从海外成功引进政治暴力险、恐怖主义保险等特殊风险保障产品，首创中国视角境外国家恐怖主义风险评估体系。加强与大型企业协同，为中老铁路、瓜达尔港等具有全球影响力的重大标志性项目提供再保险保障。不断强化科技赋能，率先利用卫星遥感技术开展风险查勘和风险减量管理，支持“一带一路”重要项目获得全面风险保障。积极推动绿色转型，在“中巴经济走廊”项目卡洛特水电站的保险定价中，首次引入绿色因子，创新绿色金融解决方案。

（四）上海国际再保险中心建设情况

2023年6月，国家金融监督管理总局与上海市共同发布《关于加快推进上海国际再保险中心建设的实施细则》，上海再保险“国际板”正式启动，以构建面向全球的富有竞争力的国际再保险交易市场为核心，通过建立中国规制、标准，引导中国再保险市场由“单向开放”向“双向开放”转型升级，深度参与全球再保险产业合作，为全球风险保障和金融治理体系提供中国方案，助力维护多元稳定的国际风险保障格局和金融合作关系。

2024年8月，国家金融监督管理总局会同上海市人民政府联合印发《关于加快上海国际再保险中心建设的实施意见》，在中国（上海）自由贸易试验区临港新片区建设要素集聚、业务集中、交易活跃、规则完善的上海国际再保险登记交易中心，将上海打造成为具有国际竞争力的再保险中心。着力发展再保险增量市场，强化再保险供给能力，健全风险管理制度机制，有效发挥再保险分散保险风险的功能，建设现代再保险市场体系。

自上海再保险"国际板"建设启动以来，各项工作不断提档加速，实现了战略定位、发展路径、规则体系、交易系统等一系列重大突破。在规则制定方面，再保险"国际板"登记、交易、保费统计、差异化监管等首批4项业务规则已正式发布，入场交易的再保险业务、交易席位、信息等第二批4项业务规则也已完成制定。除了监管政策的落地之外，再保险"国际板"启动一年来也聚集了越来越多的保险机构。在业务开展方面，再保险"国际板"正式上线了具备交易确认、合同存证、账单确认、账务清算等功能的国际再保险业务平台。基于该业务平台，首单境外再保险分入合约已于上海国际再保险登记交易中心正式签署。入驻保险机构的首单业务陆续落地，再保险"国际板"业务平台的登记、交易、清结算等功能已逐渐跑通，下一步将持续改进完善并逐步扩大规模。未来中资再保险企业预期将进一步释放境外分入承保能力，稳健承保境外风险业务，不断提高风险管理能力，持续提升中国再保险市场国际竞争力和影响力。

三、中国再保险行业国际化发展展望

（一）外资再保险企业对中国市场的发展展望

市场潜力方面，中国保险市场规模巨大，具备较大发展潜力。中国经济韧性强，经济增长质量也将提升。瑞再研究院预计，2024年中国经济将增长4.5%左右。经济的稳健复苏将带动保险业的整体发展，中国市场仍将是未来全球保险业增长的重要引擎，中国在全球保险市场的份额预计将继续上升。未来十年，中国保险市场规模预期将翻一番，有望成为全球第一大保险市场、第二大再保险市场。增长驱动力主要来自经济稳定增长、中等收入阶层不断增加、社会风险意识不断增强等。

监管政策方面，中国保险市场持续推进双向开放，监管环境友好且可预期。近年来，国家金融监督管理总局先后出台了涉及保险业对外开放措施十余条。外资再保险公司纷纷加大对中国市场的战略布局。中国市场最早被瑞再定位为新兴市场，后来调整为高增长市场。法再近期也表示将抓住中国经济的长期增长机遇，增加对中国市场的投入。

（二）中国再保险企业国际化发展展望

受益于疫情后经济复苏、商业险种费率大幅提高以及新兴市场增长等因素，全球保险市场已逐步恢复增长。中国再保险企业将抓住机遇，进一步前瞻谋划国际业务发展战略，着力提升国际化经营管理能力；把握国际市场周期性变化规律和全球宏观金融周期，积极研究、稳妥推进海外布局，持续优化境外机构管理模式和管控机制，提升全球资产投研和配置能力，不断提升全球竞争力。同时，中国再保险企业将以上海国际再保险中心建设为契机，积极把握新机遇，不断加强境内外协同联动，提升跨境服务能力，更好参与国际市场竞争，为畅通国际国内双循环作出积极贡献。

当前，高质量共建“一带一路”重点聚焦在构建立体互联互通网络、推动科技创新、促进绿色发展、开展务实合作、完善国际合作机制等方面。中国再保险企业将积极发挥再保险在全球化、平台化和专业化方面的优势，强化风险保障机制，推动完善服务网络，提升风险保障水平和综合服务能力，为高质量共建“一带一路”作出新贡献。

与此同时，中国再保险企业将统筹好发展与安全，积极稳妥推进国际化发展。主动应对“走出去”过程中面临的地缘政治、气候变化、资本市场波动等风险，加强风险研判，完善风险管理体系和应对机制，持续提升风险管理能力，有效防范跨境风险。

第五章 2023年中国再保险行业监管回顾及展望

2023年，中国再保险行业监管坚持金融工作的政治性、人民性，统筹做好防风险、强监管、促发展各项工作，引导保险再保险业不断提升保障能力和服务水平。2023年，国家金融监督管理总局揭牌，我国金融监管领域机构改革迈出重要一步，为防范化解金融风险、推动高质量发展提供有力保障。

一、再保险行业监管体系总体架构

（一）保险行业监管“三支柱”架构

中国保险及再保险行业经过数十年的经营发展，目前行业监管已形成以偿付能力监管为核心、公司治理监管为基础、市场行为监管为抓手的“三支柱”监管架构。

具体而言，偿付能力监管是现代保险行业监管的核心，通过全面评价和监督检查保险公司偿付能力充足率、综合风险及风险管理能力等，确保保险公司偿付能力满足承保需求，维护保险市场稳定。2021年，原中国银行保险监督管理委员会（以下简称原中国银保监会）顺利完成“偿二代”二期工程建设，陆续修订发布《保险公司偿付能力管理规定》（中国银行保险监督管理委员会令2021年第1号）以及《保险公司偿付能力监管规则（Ⅱ）》（银保监发〔2021〕51号），明确第一支柱定量监管要求、第二支柱定性监管要求以及第三支柱市场约束机制的偿付能力监管“三支柱”框架体系，确定核心偿付能力充足率、综合偿付能力充足率以及风险综合评级三个有机联系的偿付能力监管指标，进一步收紧和细化对直保及再保险公司的偿付能力监管要求，提升对保险公司偿付能力监管的科学性、有效性和全面性，引导中国保险市场整体稳健发展。2023年，国家金融监督管理总局发布《关于优化保险公司偿付能力监管标准的通知》（金规〔2023〕5号），进一步完善保险公司偿付能力监管标准，促进保险公司回归本源和稳健运行，更好服务实体经济和人民群众。

公司治理是现代企业制度的基石，通过建立包括股东（大）会、董事会、监事会、高级管理层（以下简称“三会一层”）等治理主体在内的公司治理架构，明确各治理主体的职责边界、履职要求，完善保险机构风险管控、制衡管制及激励约束机制，助力提升公司治理水平，保障保险机构健康稳健运营。2006年1月，原中国保险监督管理委员会（以下简称原中国保监会）发布《关于规范保险公司治理结构的指导意见（试行）》（保监发〔2006〕2号），正式将公司治理监管引入中国保险行业监管体系。此后十余年，中国公司治理监管实践经验和理论逐步积累完善，监管机构陆续发布《银行保险机构公司治理准则》（银保监发〔2021〕14号）以及《银行保险机构大股东行为监管办法（试行）》（银保监发〔2021〕43号）等公司治理监管细分领域多项监管政策，细化明确保险机构“三会一层”组成设置、职责分工及运作机制，特色化地将党的领导融入保险机构公司治理各个环节，全面系统规范保险机构公司治理要求，不断优化完善保险行业公司治理监管体系。

市场行为监管是保险市场有序运行的重要保障，主要包括对保险条款与费率制定、保险销售行为、保险中介行为、保险服务行为以及保险欺诈行为等方面的监管，以保险消费者权益保护为核心，强调通过规范保险机构市场行为维护保险市场正常秩序。市场行为监管具体政策措施与被监管主体的市场行为特点紧密联系，因财产保险、人身保险以及再保险行业在交易主体、经营模式、业务性质以及风险特征等方面存在一定差异，监管机构通常会采取分类监管方式，针对不同类型的保险机构和保险业务制定不同的监管政策。其中，针对再保险领域，原中国银保监会于2021年7月修订发布《再保险业务管理规定》（中国银行保险监督管理委员会令2021年第8号），加强对保险机构再保险顶层战略制定、再保险业务安全性管理及再保险业务经营管理规范等方面的监管，强调保险公司应正确使用再保险工具，促使再保险回归“保险的保险”的核心定位。

（二）再保险行业监管政策体系

在法律层面，中国保险及再保险行业均由《中华人民共和国保险法》进行规范。

在行业监管机构发布的政策层面，国家金融监督管理总局对再保险行业的监管政策主要分为两类。（1）适用于保险行业整体的监管政策，如对偿付能力、公司治理以及保险资金运用等方面的监管政策。此类监管政策基于再保险和直保行业的共同特点制定，通常同时适用于再保险公司和直保公司，或者适用于直保公司，参照适用于再保险公司。（2）适用于再保险行业的特别监管政策，主要体现在再保险市场行为监管领域，以及针对再保险行业的国际化特征所做的特别监管，包括规范再保险公司的设立、明确再保险业务管理规范以及通过建立再保险关联交易信息披露机制、再保险登记机制、要求离岸再保人提供符合要求的担保等措施来加强再保险业务安全保障等。为保障上述监管政策的有效施行，国家金融监督管理总局将现场监管与非现场监管相结合，对保险机构采取制定管理标准、开展能力评估以及对违法违规行为实施行政处罚等监管方式，促使保险机构维持合理的偿付能力，提升公司治理水平，规范市场经营行为。

在其他相关监管机构发布的政策层面，中国保险及再保险行业除接受国家金融监督管理总局“三支柱”体系下的行业监管以外，在反洗钱、反恐怖融资、财务会计、国有资产管理及网络安全和个人信息保护等领域同时受到中国人民银行、财政部及国家互联网信息办公室等监管机构的专业监管。此外，党中央、国务院以及相关监管机构关于国家经济金融工作的指导意见和发展规划对中国保险及再保险行业的经营发展及监管政策也会产生深远影响。

二、2023 年再保险行业重要监管政策出台情况

2023年，国家金融监督管理总局在中国银行保险监督管理委员会基础上组建。国家金融监督管理总局和原中国银保监会在2023年发布的再保险行业相关重要监管政策主要涉及保险机构操作风险管理、涉刑案件风险防控、系统重要性保险公司识别评估以及偿付能力监管标准优化等方面，有效支持再保险行业高质量发展。

（一）金融监管领域机构改革——组建国家金融监督管理总局

2023年3月，《党和国家机构改革方案》正式印发，明确在原中国银保监会的基础上组建国家金融监督管理总局，统一负责除证券业以外的金融业监管。2023年5月，国家金融监督管理总局正式揭牌。2023年11月，《国家金融监督管理总局职能配置、内设机构和人员编制规定》正式发布，确定了国家金融监督管理总局的主要职责、机构设置和人员编制。

主要职责方面，国家金融监督管理总局在原中国银保监会职能的基础上，扩大至统一监管除证券业以外的金融业，纳入中国人民银行对金融控股公司等金融集团的日常监管职责以及中国人民银行有关金

融消费者保护职责和中国证券监督管理委员会（以下简称中国证监会）的投资者保护职责，强化机构监管、行为监管、功能监管、穿透式监管、持续监管，统筹负责金融消费者权益保护，加强风险管理和防范处置，依法查处违法违规行为，作为国务院直属机构。

机构设置方面，国家金融监督管理总局对原中国银保监会内设机构做了保留、撤销和合并，并根据职能需要新设数个机构。一是保留原办公厅（党委办公室）等17个内设机构的设置和基本职能，将其中部分局、部更名为司。二是撤销原重大风险事件与案件处置局（银行业与保险业安全保卫局）。三是合并原政策性银行监管部等内设机构，成立新内设机构承接原机构职能，包括撤销原政策性银行监管部、国有控股大型商业银行监管部，成立大型银行监管司；撤销原全国性股份制商业银行监管部、城市商业银行监管部，成立股份制和城市商业银行监管司；原财产保险监管部（再保险监管部）更名为财产保险监管司（再保险监管司），将原保险中介监管部并入财产保险监管司（再保险监管司）；撤销原创新业务监管部、保险资金运用监管部、信托监管部，成立资管机构监管司。四是新设金融机构准入司、科技监管司、机构恢复与处置司、稽查局、行政处罚局、内审司（党委巡视工作领导小组办公室）、党建工作局（党委宣传部）和稽查总队，承接从原内设机构划出的职能和国家金融监督管理总局新增职能。

保险行业监管方面，国家金融监督管理总局公司治理监管司、财产保险监管司（再保险监管司）、人身保险监管司、资管机构监管司等四个司分别负责保险集团、财产保险机构/再保险机构/保险中介机构、人身保险机构、保险资产管理机构的非现场监测、现场调查、风险分析、监管评价、采取监管措施以及个案风险处置等工作，其中公司治理监管司新增对保险集团的主要机构监管职责，财产保险监管司（再保险监管司）、人身保险监管司、资管机构监管司等原来对相应保险机构的准入、退出管理职能被剥离，分别纳入新设的金融机构准入司、机构恢复与处置司的职能中。同时，保险和非银机构检查局继续保留对保险机构的现场检查职能，新设的稽查局、稽查总队和行政处罚局负责包括保险机构在内的违法违规金融事件的调查取证工作和行政处罚案件审理工作。

（二）完善银行保险机构操作风险管理要求

操作风险是银行保险机构经营管理中面临的主要风险之一。此前，保险机构操作风险管理规范主要是原中国银保监会于2021年10月发布的《保险公司偿付能力监管规则（Ⅱ）》（银保监发〔2021〕51号），银行机构操作风险管理规范主要是原中国银监会于2007年5月发布的《商业银行操作风险管理指引》（银监发〔2007〕42号）。但随着操作风险防控形势日益复杂，原相关监管规则或因年代久远不能体现最新变化趋势，或因不够具体细化而难以满足银行保险机构操作风险管理的现实需求，因此国家金融监督管理总局于2023年12月修订发布《银行保险机构操作风险管理办法》（国家金融监督管理总局令2023年第5号）[①]，完善统一银行保险机构操作风险管理要求。

新办法规定了银行保险机构在操作风险管理中的基本原则、责任分配、基本要求和流程方法。其中，在责任分配方面，新办法强调了操作风险管理三道防线机制，银行保险机构各级业务和管理部门、操作风险管理和计量牵头部门、内部审计部门分别履行相应的操作风险

① 原《商业银行操作风险管理指引》（银监发〔2007〕42号）、《中国银行业监督管理委员会关于加大防范操作风险工作力度的通知》（银监发〔2005〕17号）自《银行保险机构操作风险管理办法》施行之日起废止。

直接管理、指导监督以及监督评价职能。在基本要求方面，新办法要求银行保险机构制定与自身机构特性相适应的操作风险管理基本制度、操作风险管理考核评价机制、操作风险偏好，并持续监测、预警操作风险，建立具有操作风险管理功能的信息系统等。在流程方法方面，新办法明确银行保险机构应根据操作风险偏好开展操作风险识别、评估、控制和缓释工作，制定并有效执行业务连续性计划等管理制度，建立操作风险内部定期报告机制等工作机制，并建议银行保险机构恰当运用操作风险损失数据库等管理工具。同时，新办法也兼顾不同类型机构的实际情况，区分银行机构和保险机构、规模较大的机构和规模较小的机构实施差异化监管，如新办法虽适用于保险公司，但保险集团（控股）公司、再保险公司和保险资产管理公司属于参照适用；保险公司不适用新办法关于风险计量、计提资本等方面的要求；分别给予规模较大、规模较小的银行保险机构一年、两年的过渡期等。

（三）加强银行保险机构案件风险防控

为规范银行保险机构案件管理工作，原中国银保监会于2020年6月印发《银行保险机构涉刑案件管理办法（试行）》（银保监发〔2020〕20号），规定了银行保险机构案件管理的基本工作原则、责任分配以及案件处置机制。此后为推动银行保险机构前移案件风险防控关口，国家金融监督管理总局于2023年11月印发《银行保险机构涉刑案件风险防控管理办法》（金规〔2023〕10号）[①]，进一步提升银行保险机构案件风险防控的规范性、科学性和有效性。

该办法强调银行保险机构的案件风险防控工作应做到“预防为

① 原《中国银监会办公厅关于印发银行业金融机构案防工作办法的通知》（银监办发〔2013〕257号）同时废止。

主、关口前移，全面覆盖、突出重点，法人主责、分级负责，联防联控、各司其职，属地监管、融入日常”，构建各方联动、齐抓共管的案件风险防控格局，要求银行保险机构应建立健全案件风险防控机制、监督检查案件风险防控相关机制、内部问责机制、案件风险线索发现查出机制、案件风险防控绩效考核机制、案件风险防控评估机制等工作机制，制定案件风险排查与处置制度、从业人员行为管理制度，定期开展案件风险防控培训以及案件警示教育活动，加大相关信息化建设力度，从而构建案件风险防控的全链条治理机制。

（四）建立系统重要性保险公司评估与识别机制

系统重要性金融机构的稳健经营对维护我国金融体系和实体经济稳健发展具有重要作用。2018年11月，中国人民银行、原中国银保监会、中国证监会联合发布《关于完善系统重要性金融机构监管的指导意见》（银发〔2018〕301号）[①]，建立了系统重要性金融机构的识别、监管和处置机制。为落实该意见，打好系统重要性保险公司的差异化监管基础，国家金融监督管理总局于2023年10月发布《系统重要性保险公司评估办法》（银发〔2023〕208号），进一步明确了系统重要性保险公司的评估识别机制。该办法详细规定了对系统重要性保险公司的评估流程与方法，采用定量评估指标计算参评保险公司的系统重要性得分，并结合其他定量和定性信息作出监管判断，综合评估参评保险公司的系统重要性。该办法在《关于完善系统重要性金融机构监管的指导意见》确定的机构规模、关联度、复杂性、可替代性、资产变现等一级评估指标的基础上，细化明确了二级定量指标及其权重（见表1）。

① 《关于完善系统重要性金融机构监管的指导意见》（银发〔2018〕301号）自发布之日起施行。

表1 系统重要性保险公司评估指标

单位：%

一级评估指标	二级定量指标	权重
规模（20%）	总资产	10
	总收入	10
关联度（30%）	金融机构间资产	7
	金融机构间负债	7
	受第三方委托管理的资产	7
	非保险附属机构资产	7
	衍生金融资产	2
资产变现（30%）	短期融资	10
	资金运用复杂性	10
	第三层次资产	10
可替代性（20%）	分支机构数量和投保人数量	6.67
	赔付金额	6.67
	特定业务保费收入	6.67

数据来源：国家金融监督管理总局。

（五）优化保险公司偿付能力监管标准

为完善保险公司偿付能力监管标准，促进保险公司回归本源和稳健运行，更好服务实体经济和人民群众，国家金融监督管理总局于2023年9月发布《关于优化保险公司偿付能力监管标准的通知》（金规〔2023〕5号），在保持综合偿付能力充足率100%和核心偿付能力充足率50%监管标准不变的基础上，根据保险业发展实际，优化了保险公司偿付能力监管标准。一是实施差异化资本监管。对不同规模的保险公司进行差异化管理，计量最低资本时，中型公司按照95%计算，小型公司按照90%计算。二是优化资本计量标准，引导保险公司回归保障本源，鼓励保险公司发展长期保障型产品、审慎计提准备金，引导保险公司提升资产负债匹配管理能力。三是优化风险因子，引导保险公司服务实体经济和科技创新，更新科技保险最低资本计量方法，鼓励保险公司开展长期价值投资（见表2）。

表2　保险公司偿付能力监管标准优化前后风险因子

投资标的	原风险因子	新风险因子
沪深300指数成分股	0.35	0.30
科创板上市普通股票	0.45	0.40
REITs未穿透部分	0.60	0.50
国家战略性新兴产业未上市公司股权	0.41	0.40

数据来源：国家金融监督管理总局。

三、再保险行业监管趋势展望

2024年，中国再保险行业保持良好发展态势，面对宏观经济、地缘政治、气候变化、人口老龄化等挑战，再保险行业将保持强监管严监管态势，根据宏观导向和行业发展新形势不断优化调整监管政策，推动再保险行业高质量发展，有效服务国计民生。

一是将不断加大再保险行业监管力度，完善风险防控机制。习近平总书记指出"要着力防范化解金融风险特别是系统性风险""金融监管要'长牙带刺'、有棱有角""在市场准入、审慎监管、行为监管等各个环节，都要严格执法，实现金融监管横向到边、纵向到底"。未来，再保险行业强监管严监管趋势不会改变，金融监管机构将进一步提高监管的前瞻性、精准性、有效性和协同性，加强与其他监管机构的监督合力，在金融风险处置和金融犯罪治理领域继续加大对违法违规行为的打击力度和对相关责任人员的追责问责力度。

二是将持续推动再保险更好服务实体经济和民生保障。保险再保险业作为重要的金融细分领域，在分散经济社会运行风险、保障和改善民生、防灾减损、服务实体经济等方面发挥了重要作用。中央金融工作会议指出，金融行业应当做好“五篇大文章”，发展科技金融、绿色金融、普惠金融、养老金融和数字金融。保险再保险业监管将继续鼓励和引导保险业发挥好经济减震器和社会稳定器功能，大力提升保险保障能力和服务水平，推进金融强国建设，服务中国式现代化大局。

三是将鼓励和引导再保险业创新发展。推动再保险业加快数字化转型，提升经营管理效率。鼓励运用人工智能、大数据等技术，提高营销服务、风险管理和投资管理水平。鼓励再保险机构提升风险管理专业能力，加强对电子信息、先进制造、生物医药、现代农业、智慧交通、新型能源、航空航天等高精尖技术领域新型风险、特殊风险的保险定价、承保和理赔的专业技术支持，助力提升保险业整体服务保障实体经济、特别是服务新质生产力的能力。鼓励再保险业在建立健全国家巨灾保险保障体系中发挥更大作用，有效分散转移巨灾风险，研发运用巨灾风险模型，提升风险减量服务能力，支持防灾减灾救灾。

专题报告

专题一

全球视野下商业长期护理保险发展经验及对中国的启示

商业长期护理保险（以下简称商业长护险或长护险），是指由保险公司经营，为部分或完全生活不能自理、需要被长期照护的人提供保险金支持的保险产品。其中，“长期”是指所需要护理的时限较长甚至是终身需要护理；“护理”侧重于生活类护理，即由于生活无法自理而需要的涉及衣食住行的护理活动。

商业长护险在我国起步较晚，目前仍处于初期探索阶段，保险行业对于长护险在中国市场的发展前景、发展策略和实施思路等方面缺乏规律性认识。为了帮助人身险行业积累长护险领域的专业知识，促使行业在长护险的发展前景和发展规律方面达成一定共识，赋能行业转型，本文将深入探究分析美国、法国、日本等主要商业长护险市场的差异和共性，提炼底层核心规律，并基于我国保险市场现状，提出发展建议。

一、海外主要商业长护险市场概况

（一）美国

美国商业长护险起源于20世纪70年代，美国护理院井喷式发展的年代，Medicare针对出院病人入住护理院提供短期的医疗护理保障，商业护理险定位为Medicare的延续保障。后来其定位从短期医疗护理向长期生活照护转变，并将保障范围扩展到包含居家护理、日间照护等多种形式的护理服务。

美国社保长护服务属于Medicaid的保障范围，仅向低收入人群提供，美国大部分民众社保长护保障缺失。商业长护险面向社保未覆盖的中高收入人群。为了推动商业长护险的发展，1996年美国国会出台HIPPA法案，予以支付指定的护理服务且触发定义符合要求的长护险税优政策。

美国是覆盖人群最广、保费规模最大的长护险市场，长护险在20世纪80年代到21世纪初期迅速发展，增长高峰期（2002年前后）以独立型产品为主流，年新单件数约75万件，新单保费约14亿美元，总保费约52亿美元。之后因为定价不足，保险公司普遍亏损，独立型长护险供给收缩导致新单规模下降，2010年新单销量下滑至23.5万件，新单保费下滑至5.25亿美元。组合型长护险在2010年前后开始流行，2022年，独立型长护险新单销量仅约3.4万件，组合型产品的新单销量约40万件。在美国长护险近50年的发展历程中，客群年龄以50~70岁为主，超过80%的客户年收入在5万美元以上，客群为中产偏富裕人群。

美国长护险的经营主体是寿险公司，主力渠道是代理人渠道，保单数占比近75%，其余主要来源于团险渠道。销售理念主要有两点：一是形成资产保护，避免因护理支出消耗资产；二是长护险的高杠杆，以低成本享受更高品质的护理服务。

产品设计方面，产品定位为高保费产品，件均保费从1990年的1 071美元增长到2022年的3 618美元。产品结构分成独立型和混合型，保险期间是终身，缴费期和保险期间等长且费率可调，通常不提供现金价值。责任触发定义由保险公司自行设计，当前主流触发定义是基于卡式量表的六项日常生活活动中不能独立完成至少两项（以下简称不能独立完成2/6ADLs，六项日常生活活动包括洗澡、穿衣、进食、如厕清洁、排便控制和移动）。产品的给付形式从定额给付型演变为费用报销型。

运营管理方面，美国长护险的鉴定依赖医疗体系的支撑，由美国的医生或注册护士作为护理状态鉴定和需求评估的主体，护理服务方案需与保险公司达成一致才能得到理赔。理赔阶段则综合病情、诊断、鉴定和需求评估结果等形成判定意见，且保险公司保留核验调查护理状态和服务使用情况、调整护理服务计划、重新选择评估机构进行鉴定的权利。

（二）法国

法国长护险起源于20世纪80年代，商保源于补充社保的不足。之后公共长期护理保险制度持续演进，于2002年升级为“护理津贴保险制度”（以下简称APA），并沿用至今。法国政府和社会对于长期护理保险制度的探索和变革引起了公众对于长护风险和商业长护险的关注，推动了商业长期护理保险的发展。

APA为60岁以上人群提供了广覆盖、保基本的长期护理保障，以中重度失能为保障标的，提供津贴式给付，家庭护理和商业护理均在补贴范围内，与法国的家庭护理文化相匹配。APA津贴支付水平由失能程度和护理计划的成本决定，并随着退休金进行调节（退休金越高，APA津贴越低）。在居家护理的补贴方面，退休金以法国养老金平均水平1 500欧元为例，该收入水平的重度护理患者的平均自付金额为760欧元，超过养老金的半数，再考虑其他生活开支，APA的补贴无法保证收支相抵。APA对于机构护理的补贴较低，仅补贴护理费用，昂贵的食宿费用由个人支付。大众群体根据退休金水平而面临不同程度的保障缺口，大部分人对长期护理的风险感知较强，商业护理险定位为APA津贴的补充，面向中等收入水平的大众客群。

长护险规模在1999—2007年以年化15%的速度增长，2010年总保费规模约5亿欧元，总保单件数约550万件，2019年，长护险总共覆盖740万人，总保费规模达到8.1亿欧元，其中，6.8亿欧元来自商业保险公司，以个人产品为主，40%的承保客户贡献了80%的保费。其余保费来自社会保险公司和互助保险社，主要提供雇主团体保险计划，虽然承保人群规模大，但保费占比仅为20%。

长护险的经营主体是寿险公司，其中银行渠道和代理人渠道的保单件数占比分别为34%和30%，是最主要的两大分销渠道，寿险公司定位长期护理保险为赋能主力储蓄产品销售。互助保险社是承保人群最大的经营主体，其本质是员工团体保险计划，长护险通常作为附加险来丰富保障内容。

产品设计方面，法国长护险的定位是面向大众客群的普惠型产品，个人长护险件均保费约400欧元，互助团体长护险的件均保费为几十欧元；个人产品的产品结构是均衡保费的终身保险产品，缴费期终身且费率可调；产品的触发定义由保险公司自行设计，核心责任的主流触发定义是五项日常生活活动中不能独立完成至少四项（以下简称不能独立完成4/5ADLs，五项日常生活活动包括洗澡、穿衣、进食、如厕排便和移动）；给付形式是定额给付型，一旦触发护理状态，产品都持续给付护理金直至身故；产品为痴呆类疾病和其他疾病分别设置了三年和一年等待期；迭代升级幅度相对平稳，始终以重度失能为核心。

运营管理方面，核保流程相对简化；理赔时的生活能力鉴定由被保险人的主治医师完成，再由保险公司的专业核赔人员调查医生诊断和病历资料。保险公司保留核验调查、指定机构重新鉴定的权利。

（三）日本

日本长护险起源于20世纪90年代，在当时低利率环境下，传统储蓄型产品的利差损风险暴露，保险公司调整产品结构，加强保障型产品销售，同时考虑人口老龄化程度较高，保险行业开始推广长护险。

日本政府在2000年建立了40岁以上公民强制参保的长期护理保险制度，其保障水平较高，且覆盖了机构护理、居家护理等大部分护理场景，民众的自费水平通常在总护理费用的10%以下。商保主要覆盖社保不覆盖的护理机构费用和费用项目，如非社保机构的入住费用、昂贵护理设备购买费用、心理咨询和聊天陪伴服务等，给高收入客群提供更优质的护理服务和更广泛的服务供应选择。

日本长护险的市场规模持续增长，2022年市场存量保费达6 610亿日元，占寿险27.7万亿日元总保费收入约2.4%，占Third Sector业务（包括医疗险、长护险、失能险和癌症保险）总保费收入约10%。寿险公司是主要的经营主体，主要通过自有代理人进行销售。

产品设计方面，因其中高端的产品定位，件均保费约18万日元

（折合人民币约9 000元）；产品结构上主流设计为类似美国市场的组合型产品，不同的是日本多采用普通型而美国多采用指数型或变额型；触发定义通常跟随社保长护制度；定额给付，既有一次性支付，也有持续终身给付。

运营管理方面，日本长护险的管理比较简单，在护理鉴定方面，可参考社保的鉴定结论形成理赔意见，且产品是定额给付形式，无须运营服务网络。

二、海外商业长护险市场发展规律

（一）市场供求

1. 长护险的主要购买人群具有明显的年龄特征，是寿险行业应对人口结构老龄化的重要产品线

从美国、法国看，长护险主要面向40岁以上客群，且主要分布在50~70岁区间：美国平均投保年龄57岁，50~70岁的保单占比约78%（见图1）；法国个险长护险平均投保年龄60岁，50~70岁的保单占比约80%。主要原因：一是导致长期护理状态的疾病多数是老年疾病，如脑中风、阿尔茨海默病等；二是50岁以上人群因父母健康问题很可能已经成了照护者，对护理风险的感知更强烈。

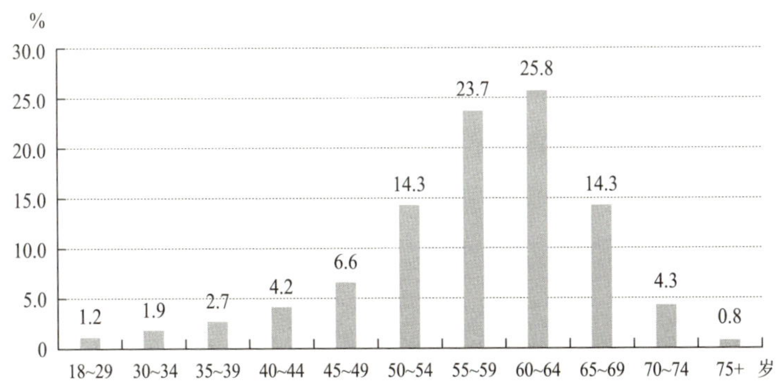

图1　2022年美国长护险投保年龄分布

基于以上年龄特征，长护险在发达市场通常被当作客户的第三张或第四张保单（在医疗险和寿险之后）、作为一种退休规划方案销售给客户，是寿险公司实现“全生命周期客户经营”的重要产品。此外，海外市场认为随着人口结构的老龄化，大量客群已经进入中老年阶段，既往的产品线已不再适配，代理人要掌握长护险的销售技能以获取规模越来越庞大的40岁以上客群。

2. 长护险的风险特征和经营特点与寿险类似，这决定了其经营主体是寿险公司

在风险特征方面，长护险和寿险有以下相似点。第一，长护险保障的长期护理状态和寿险保障的身故状态一样均是不可逆的状态改变。第二，长护险和身故都属于老年人高发、年轻人较少发生的风险，长期护理的发生率曲线规律（见图2）与死亡高度相似。第三，对被保险人的主动干预对于长护险和死亡的风险发生影响较小，长期护理的状态随年龄增长、机体功能退化而产生，某种程度是疾病进展或身体老化的必然结果，无法通过管理去干预，与寿险类似。第四，长护险多采用定额给付型设计，与实际损失金额无关，风险变量仅有发生率，与寿险一致。

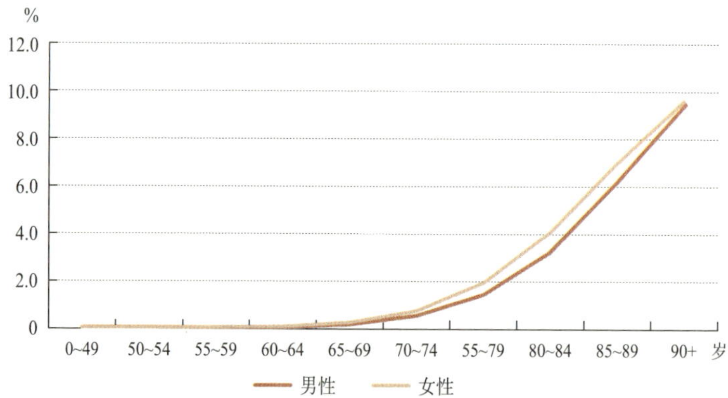

图2 美国长期护理保险护理责任发生率

长护险和寿险类似的风险特性决定了两者具备类似的经营特点，即二者本质都是一种低频交互的业务，承保阶段筛选健康体，确保实际发生率在定价水平内是经营关键。

综上所述，寿险公司更熟悉长护险的风险特性，其经营特点符合寿险公司的经营习惯，因此大部分是由寿险公司经营。寿险公司出于丰富产品线、辅助促进储蓄类寿险销售等目的积极经营长护险。

3. 社保体制决定了商业长护险的产品定位：社会保障空缺的市场，商业长护险提供全面的护理保障，价格较贵且客群偏中高端；社保有保障基础的市场，商业长护险在社保基础上进行补充，产品定位可更多层次

美国社保对中高收入人群保障完全缺位，商业长护险提供全面保障，产品聚焦中高端客户。美国的公共保障体系里，Medicaid仅向低收入人群提供长期护理保障。由于没有社会保险的“打底”，商业长护险需要从“0”起保，即保险责任触发门槛低，被保险人不能独立完成2/6ADLs或严重认知障碍即可获得保障，对标了Medicaid。美国商业长护险的件均保额较高，3 000~6 000美元/月，显著高于法国，2022年独立型长护险的件均保费3 618美元。

美国长护险主要吸引中等偏高收入人群，满足这部分人群保护家庭资产不被护理支出所侵蚀，帮助被保险人享受更优质的护理服务等需求，市场覆盖率也因此相对低，在25岁及以上人群中的持有率比例不超过3%。

法国社保广覆盖但有缺口，商业长护险在社保基础上提供补充，产品根据不同客群提供不同层次的保障水平。法国的公共失能保障制度APA主要保障中重度失能，且制度的设计逻辑是让所有法国民众共担护理成本，实现方式是嵌入收入调节机制，APA津贴数额与收入成反比，让家庭的老年收入加上APA津贴能够支付护理成本。

法国长护险主要解决重度失能下APA津贴的缺口。个人产品件均保费300~400欧元，增加了轻中度失能责任等可选责任。法国互助和团险市场非常发达，为提高长护险覆盖率作出了主要贡献，这些保单仅保障重度责任，投保金额较低，件均保费仅10~20欧元。依赖于多渠道共同发展，25岁及以上人群中覆盖率达到14.3%。

（二）产品设计

1. 家庭护理功能强的国家，商业长护险的功能主要是补贴家庭成员，给付形式是定额给付；家庭护理功能弱的国家，商业长护险与护理服务产业融合，长护险具备服务和支付的双重功能，给付形式是费用报销型

长期护理保险的给付形式主要有费用报销型（Reimbursement）和定额给付型（Cash Benefit）两种，对于达到条款定义的长期护理状态，费用报销型报销实际发生的、符合条款约定的护理服务费用（报销金额不超过每日给付上限）；定额给付型直接按约定的固定金额给付护理金，无论被保险人是否发生了护理费用。

法国文化注重家庭凝聚的观念，且劳动力紧缺，政府对发展家庭护理出台了多个支持政策，比如，向家庭护理成员提供现金补贴等。根据OECD的报告，在法国50岁以上人口中，15%~20%的人为亲人提供护理服务。家庭护理并非“免费”的护理，机会成本较高，因此，法国长期护理的保障设计需要考虑覆盖家庭护理的成本。由于家庭护理难以量化其市场公允价格，在给付形式方面，定额给付更加适配。法国社保长期护理制度APA便是以津贴形式给付，75%的APA津贴受益人接受了家庭成员提供的护理服务，商业长护险定位是补充社保，也是定额给付形式。

美国流行个人主义文化，家庭护理功能相对弱化：50岁以上人口中，仅有7%的人为亲人提供护理服务，该比例远低于法国。美国在社会层面更倡导民众使用商业护理服务而非家庭护理，解放失能老人的家属投入工作来创造社会价值。基于此，美国的商业护理产业发达，商业护理机构是美国长期护理服务的主要提供方，这也使得美国社保和商保长护险均强调保险金对护理产业的定向支付。美国Medicaid给付形式是费用报销型，商业长护险主要保障中高收入客群，在责任设计和运营管理方面与护理服务高度融合，其给付形式从早期的定额给付型演进为当前的以费用报销型为主。这种演进的内生动力是美国鲜明的“护理服务商业化”的价值观和高度发达的商业护理产业，向费用报销型演进也是满足客户需求和市场竞争的结果。美国商业长护险在20世纪90年代之前采用定额给付型，但暴露出客群缺乏护理服务触达通路、定额给付的保障效率不能达到最大化两个问题。之后保险公司开始通过TPA链接护理机构网络，为被保险人提供有管理的护理服务（Managed care），和护理机构进行商保价格谈判，最终降低长护险产品价格。1996年，美国国会出台了HIPPA法案，形成了标准化形态，并为符合条件的产品赋予税收优惠资格，长护险核心竞争力是高效护理服务网络带来的保费价格优势，费用报销型产品成为主流。

从全球商业长护险市场来看，费用报销型并不是主流，除美国外大部分市场选择定额给付型设计。原因如下：一是大部分市场无法忽略家庭护理的重要性；二是构建和管理护理服务网络是一个系统且复杂的工程；三是费用报销型进一步提高了销售难度和理赔难度。

表1　　定额给付型长护险和费用报销型长护险的对比

对比要素	定额给付型（Cash Benefit）	费用报销型（Reimbursement）
所适配的养老文化	家庭护理不可或缺，强调子女对父母的赡养义务	鼓励商业护理取代家庭护理，强调对于提供照护的家庭成员的解放
所适配的社保制度	广覆盖，政府提供护理服务渠道	覆盖部分人群，未覆盖人群缺少护理服务通路
产品复杂度	保额确定、给付责任简单	·产品责任复杂：覆盖居家、机构、日间照护、生活照护等各类服务场景 ·定义项目较多：可保项目、理赔流程等
成本	按照保额定价，同等保额下价格更贵	按照使用率和护理费用定价，平均护理费用通常低于保额
风险	·发生率风险 ·道德风险 ·长寿风险	·发生率风险 ·使用率风险 ·长期护理成本通胀风险 ·长寿风险
服务	部分产品提供增值服务，实际上也需要客户自行遴选服务商	保险公司制订服务计划、联系服务商、直接报销服务
运营管理重点	护理状态的认定和理赔调查	·服务网络的构建与管理 ·服务成本控制，为客户提供成本最优的护理供应商和护理方式
销售难度	销售难度相对较低，主要宣导长期护理的概念、触发定义	·产品设计复杂，销售难度较高 ·解释产品的触发条件 ·解释各类服务的含义、场景、费用、使用条件 ·解释产品的理赔流程

2. 商业长护险赔付触发条件由保险公司自行定义，而非跟随社保，由此商保掌握了理赔权，加强了对业务的管控

美国和法国拥有世界上长护险最大的市场，商保自定产品触发标准。法国社保统一将AGGIR分级体系作为护理支付的触发标准，而商保大多将“不能独立完成4/5ADLs”作为触发定义，并通过行业协会推动行业形成GAD标准条款。在美国，社保Medicaid在不同州的触发标准不同，商保在HIPPA法案下，以“不能独立完成2/6ADLs或严重认知障碍”作为统一触发标准。

采用社保触发标准可以提高产品理赔判定方面的公信力，但商保难以形成独立的理赔决议，本质上让渡了理赔管理权，所以长护险的触发定义通常由保险公司自定。

日本市场相对特殊，商保通常跟随社保的护理触发标准设计护理的触发定义，理赔实务也参考社保的鉴定结论执行，这主要是因为日本具有高保障、广覆盖的公共长护制度，因此商业长护险在日本存在感偏弱。

3. 长护险精算假设较复杂，隐含系统性风险，且利源是“三差”，经营主体需通过费率可调、长期缴费、严格化产品设计等方式应对风险

长护险的精算风险主要体现在：第一，长护险发展初期，产品定价通常会受到数据缺失、颗粒度不足等问题的制约，尤其是高年龄段发生率假设的数据基础往往不充分。第二，长护险隐含了死亡率改善这一系统性风险。

由于定价难度大，且长护险的盈利模式也是传统的“三差”，各地市场的产品设计都具有很强的风险管理特征：第一，缴期与保期等长、费率可调。主流产品设计是终身保障搭配终身缴费和费率可调。

第二，严格化产品设计、降低定价难度。法国采用定额给付的方式，以避免护理费用、使用率这一类非传统精算假设的预测风险。在触发标准设计时，采用“重度失能”的定义，降低状态变化的复杂度。法国长护险近30年的稳定运行验证了“定额给付、重度失能”是可保的风险。

（三）运营管理

1. 长护险的鉴定有赖于医疗体系的支持，且长护险核赔不依赖单一证据，而是靠体系化的综合判定路径

在海外医疗体系下医生是商业主体，在理赔鉴定上相对客观。医生是护理状态认定的关键角色，长护险的理赔流程也比较一致。海外的医疗体系对于提高商业长护险的理赔客观程度有更强支撑作用。长护险的理赔是体系化的工作，保险公司形成理赔结论并非仅依赖失能鉴定。在实务操作中，理赔人员还会采用结合病历资料、实地走访调查、参考社保的鉴定结论等方法。

2. 由于护理服务的复杂性，商业长护险通常作为护理相关服务的聚合主体，满足了以居家护理服务为主、兼具机构护理服务的客户一站式护理需求

护理服务具有复杂性，对民众而言搜索、遴选和使用门槛较高。首先，护理服务不像医疗服务一样供给集中。其次，护理服务往往缺乏方案指导。最后，护理服务相比医疗服务的信息更加不透明。因此，长期护理的保障需求不仅包括护理的资金支持，还需要提高护理服务的可及性。

三、中国商业长护险的市场现状与发展建议

（一）中国商业长护险市场现状：机遇和挑战

1. 在“未富先老”的严峻挑战下，社会各界对老年失能风险关注度极大提高，建立全国的长期护理保险制度已提上日程，长期护理的基础设施建设不断完善

“未富先老”使我国面临严峻的挑战。国家、个人、护理机构、评估机构和保险公司等社会多方对老年失能风险充分关注。

在制度方面，2024年1月9日，全国医疗保障工作会议指出，2024年医保工作将推动建立长期护理保险制度；2024年7月，《中共中央关于进一步全面深化改革、推进中国式现代化的决定》也指出要加快建立长期护理保险制度。同时，长期护理保险制度地方性试点工作已发展约8年，随着地方性试点的经验积累、筹资和运营管理的持续完善，我国正逐步建立起全国性的长期护理保险制度。从试点情况来看，由于筹资的主要来源是医保基金，长护存在较大的保障缺口，有较大的社会需求。

标准和鉴定的基础设施建设也在不断完善。2021年，国家医保局办公室联合民政部印发了首个全国统一的评估标准《长期护理失能等级评估标准（试行）》；2023年，国家医保局相继发布《长期护理保险失能等级评估管理办法（试行）》和《长期护理保险失能等级评估机构定点管理办法（试行）》，进一步完善了政策性护理评估鉴定的管理。一系列的政策支持为商保的运营创造了更好的生态环境，增强了商保在产品宣传、评估鉴定方面的公信力。

2. 养老意识不足，护理尚未从潜在需求转化为现实需求

社会对于养老、长期护理的需求引导不足，民众对养老护理的认

识还不够深刻、不够具象化。一方面，对于“谁来养老”的问题，长期以来传统式的“养儿防老”、家庭式护理仍然为主流；另一方面，社会对护理风险的科普宣传仍然不足，民众对养老、护理的成本缺少理性和具象化的认知。

3. 养老金融的主力客群风险保障供给缺位，保险公司战略上重视程度较低

随着老龄化发展，50岁以上客群占比将持续提高，寿险公司客群结构尤为显著，对于50岁客户来说，养老还需要补充保障型产品。这是长护险发展的重要机遇，行业应将长期护理保险定位为50岁客户的主力保障型产品，但目前对于发展长期护理保险的尝试大多仅停留在完成产品开发上，较少从公司战略层面予以重视，实质性投入较少。

4. 产品开发和运营层面基础薄弱

在产品设计层面，目前市场上主流的长护险（不包括增额护理险）大多以重疾确诊拟合护理状态，这虽然解决了在基础设施欠缺情况下的理赔鉴定难题，但特定重疾确诊与真正的护理需求仍存在偏差。在数据层面，行业内外部数据均比较薄弱，制约了长护险的定价和开发。在运营层面，行业既往经营的健康险均是以客观指标作为赔付标准，行业缺乏以状态认定作为理赔条件的运营经验和理赔人才，也尚未形成有权威性的鉴定网络。

（二）发展建议

1. 倡议社会加强对养老、护理的宣导教育，加强对于长期照护的风险和成本的科普

建议通过出台相关政策和指导意见，树立养老理念，构建政府、社会、市场等协同推进的养老科普教育机制。在教育内容方面，一是

使人民群众认清养老和护理保障的现实需求，包括退休后的日常生活支出和失能导致的额外康复和护理支出；二是使人民群众对养老和护理的成本有明确认知，了解其对于家庭负担的影响程度。

2. 中国长期护理保险体系应将社保和商保统筹起来，社保长护险和商保长护险协同一体推进。商业护理险要依赖社保长护险发展，建议社保加快明确自身定位，推动商保明确自身保障空间

从顶层设计角度，中国长期护理保险体系应该将社保与商保统筹起来，协同一体推进。社保长护险是基础，商保长护险是补充。中国商业医疗险的发展路径是先将保障范围和社保取齐，保障医保内医疗费用，在社保报销后进行二次报销；然后将保障范围扩展至社保外自费项目；最后是在院外责任和健康管理服务上做文章。相类似的，在商保长护险发展前期，其对护理的保障程度应与社保保持一致，保障重度护理状态，补充社保给付金额的不足。下一步随着业务发展和经验数据积累，商业长护险可以提供轻中度护理保障；最后在预防性的保障、和社保有差异化的护理服务方面进行突破。总之，只有社保明确自身的保障定位，商保长护险才能进一步明确补充边界和产品定位。另外，商业长护险的赔付标准设计与理赔鉴定实施均非常依赖有社会公信力的基础设施建设支撑，这也要求社保形成一套完整的基础设施。

3. 建议加大税优相关的政策支持，一方面将长护险纳入和补充医疗保险有同等待遇的企业税前列支保险范畴，另一方面加大个人长护险税优政策的力度

税优政策是激发商业长护险发展的有效手段，建议放宽税优政策范围并加大支持力度。随着保险代理人数量的萎缩，代理人越来越倾向于经营中高端客户；从海外经验看，团险渠道是提高保障类产品覆

盖率的重要途径。建议将商业长护险纳入和企业补充医疗保险享有同等待遇的企业税优优惠保险范畴，引导并鼓励国内相关企业将长护险纳入团体补充保险。另外，建议加大个人长护险的税优政策力度并明确对个人税优型长护险产品的保障属性要求。

4. 保险公司战略层面，应明确长护险是养老产品体系中的核心保障类产品，定位是赋能主业发展

长护险应是大养老市场下养老产品体系中的核心保障型产品，在养老储蓄、养老投资等养老泛金融领域体现保险独特的风险保障功能。借助长护险，保险公司可以丰富代理人队伍的服务内容，使其在销售储蓄产品的同时能给客户补充风险保障功能。此外，长护险可以提升储蓄型产品尤其是养老年金的产品吸引力。

长护险的定位是赋能核心业务的抓手，无论是赋能长期储蓄、年金产品的销售，还是作为团体保障，在增强养老金融服务的大趋势下，都可以支持保险行业发挥独有的保障功能。

5. 保险产品设计层面，定额给付型产品和商保自建的定义标准应该是中国市场的主要选择，产品应定位大众客群

受传统观念影响，家庭护理在我国难以替代，对提供护理服务的家庭成员进行补贴是我国商业长护险的重要功能。在给付形式方面，费用报销型产品对保险公司的运营管理和护理服务基础设施建设有较高要求，当前我国商业护理产业成熟度较低，保险公司建立服务网络的难度较大，难以形成产业融合。因此，我国更适合采用定额给付方式。

在定义标准方面，各地政策性护理保险会根据社保基金的充裕程度调整给付标准或者理赔尺度。商保长护险保险期间较长，若跟随社保给付标准和鉴定结论，则会面临难以预知的政策风险，因此建议自建标准。在量表使用上，建议和国际市场主流保持一致，以实操简

单、内容聚焦的卡式量表作为基础。

6. 监管政策层面，建议开展对长护险的费率可调、长护险保障身故责任等政策支持的研究

长期护理的需求随年龄增长而提高，且护理时长随技术进步、寿命延长而延长，终身保障、发生护理后终身赔付是市场当前对于长期护理保险的普遍期待和诉求。但长期护理保险隐含了给付期死亡率改善的系统性风险，以及80岁以后阿尔茨海默症等疾病的定价风险。从美国和法国经验来看，费率可调是重要的活跃长护险产品供给和维护产品长期运营的手段，建议国内市场探讨并推动形成长护险的费率可调机制，降低长护险的承保难度，市场可以提供真正可终身保障、终身给付的长期护理产品。

7. 行业层面，建议推动定义标准、权威专家库、鉴定机构认证等基础设施建设，建立健全商业长护险的服务运营体系

医生属于我国公共服务体系中的一员，定位是服务广大人民群众，与保险公司基本没有商业合作。医疗工作主观判定性质较强，医生判定尺度较大，且大部分会作出利于患者的判定。因此，在长护险这类主要依靠医生鉴定的理赔实务中，经常出现医生支持客户利益出具有利于被保险人的鉴定意见。建议监管、行业协会组织推动与社保鉴定网络的合作和认证，形成一套具有公信力和行业共识的护理鉴定体系，包括定义标准、医生网络、认证鉴定机构等，推动行业在发展初期可以共用鉴定的基础设施。

8. 第三方平台机构和再保险公司应重点聚焦居家护理服务，加强产品与服务的生态融合

提供服务是长护险的重要价值，从海外经验看，居家护理是主要的服务需求。《国务院办公厅关于推进养老服务发展的意见》明确指出

“完善居家为基础、社区为依托、机构为补充、医养相结合的养老服务体系，建立健全高龄、失能老年人长期照护服务体系”，居家护理也是国内市场护理服务的重点领域，市场需要保险公司、再保险公司围绕居家护理的场景和需求，共同推进与护理服务机构的合作，遴选优质护理服务商、构建服务网络。

专题二

保险（再保险）助力应对人口老龄化：现状问题与发展建议

养老金融是中央金融工作会议提出的“五篇大文章”之一。当前，中国老龄化呈现总体规模大、低龄老人占比高、高龄化增长速度快、未富先老四大特点。保险（再保险）如何发挥风险管理职能作用，助力应对老龄化挑战，本文从需求和供给两侧出发，分析保险（再保险）应对老龄化的痛点和难点问题，总结在保障时间、对象和方式三个方面存在供需错配，并提出五个方面建议。一是构建与基本社会保障相配合、经纬互补的养老保险体系；二是确立以“长期、普惠、服务”为宗旨的养老保险发展方向；三是依托数字技术提升养老保险服务能力；四是优化养老保险的监管和税优环境；五是发挥再保险的机制优势，推动养老保险行业的供给侧结构性改革。

一、保险（再保险）应对老龄化的痛点与难点

（一）中国老龄化的四大特征

我国的老龄化呈现总体规模大、低龄老人占比高、高龄化增长速度快、未富先老四大特点。

1. 总体规模数量巨大

从总体规模来看，庞大的人口基数决定了我国老年人口的总体数量巨大。截至2022年底，我国60岁及以上老年人数量增长至2.8亿人，65岁及以上老年人2.09亿人。我国65岁及以上老年人口数量是美国的3.8倍，是日本的5.8倍，占世界老龄人口总量的20%左右。

2. 低龄老人占比高

当前我国60~69岁老年人在所有老年人中占比超过一半，70~79岁老年人在所有老年人中占比在1/3左右。据预测[①]，2050年以前，我国80岁以下低龄老年人在老年群体中占比都将维持在70%以上。

3. 高龄群体增长速度快

我国老年群体以低龄老人为主，高龄群体的增速更加明显。据统计[②]，我国80岁及以上高龄老人数量在2000年为1 199万人，2020年已超过3 500万人。根据预测，我国80岁及以上高龄老人数量将在2050年超过1.3亿人，在老年群体中的占比将从2020年的13%增长到26%。

4. 未富先老

美日等国家在进入老龄化时人均GDP达到1万美元，而我国2000年进入老龄化社会[③]时人均GDP不足1 000美元；美日进入深度老龄化时期人均GDP为3万~4万美元。2021年我国进入深度老龄化时人均GDP为1.23万美元。相较于发达国家，未富先老、未备而老带来了前所未有的挑战，一方面是支付能力的问题，养老和医疗保障水平都较低，由

---

① 资料来源：https://www.populationpyramid.net。

② 全国第五、第六、第七次人口普查年鉴。

③ 根据联合国老龄化的相关标准，一个地区60岁以上老人达到总人口的10%，或者65岁老人占总人口的7%，即该地区视为进入“老龄化社会”；65岁以上人口占总人口的比例超过14%，则进入“深度老龄社会”，比例达20%，则进入“超老龄社会”。

国家、社会、家庭和个人构成的多层次社会保障体系尚未完善；另一方面是服务的问题，医养服务、社会服务等仍较为欠缺。

（二）从供给侧看，保险（再保险）探索多种方式助力应对老龄化，但仍存明显短板

1. 在养老金方面，保险机构参与方式多样

第一支柱基本养老保险方面，保险机构参与业务经办及投资运营。在全国社会保障基金理事会评审21家基本养老保险基金投资管理机构中，保险背景的有华泰资管、泰康资管、人保资管、平安养老、国寿养老、长江养老等6家养老保险公司和保险资产管理公司。

第二支柱企业年金方面，保险机构主要在受托和投管方面发挥重要作用。在企业年金四类管理资格[①]中，有9家保险机构参与受托人、账户管理人和投资管理人三类业务。其中企业年金受托业务由保险机构主导管理，受托管理企业占总量的84%，覆盖职工占比75%，受托资产规模超过2万亿元，占74%的市场份额。

第三支柱个人养老金方面，商业保险主要承担产品开发运营。主要发挥在精算定价方面的优势，开发具有养老属性的保险产品。目前积累了约5万亿元的养老责任准备金。专属养老保险试点以来，投保人数超过25万人，其中包括4.7万新产业、新业态的劳动者和各类灵活就业人员，养老理财产品已经发行49只，规模超过1 000亿元。

2. 在养老服务方面，保险机构探索不同模式

（1）保险机构投资建设养老社区

近年来，商业保险大量投资建设养老社区，成为机构养老的组成

① 根据人社部《企业年金基金管理办法》，企业年金共有受托人、投资管理人、账户管理人和托管人四类管理资格牌照。各类业务的参与主体有银行、信托、保险、基金等。

部分。据统计，以泰康、国寿、太平等为代表，目前有近30家保险公司投资了养老产业、50多个养老社区项目，分布在全国24个省市地区，总投资规模超过1 400亿元。

在投资模式选择上：一类是重资产模式，以泰康为代表，将养老产业作为公司主营发展方向之一，建立品牌效应及服务标准，多数大型保险集团以重资产模式进入；另一类是轻重资产并举模式，其中太平保险通过与第三方合作互换资源、建立独家合作获取项目资源，借助第三方专业优势进行开发和运营。总之，这些“保险+养老社区”①创新方式，在一定程度上推动了高档养老产业发展。

表1　主要保险机构参与养老社区投资情况

保险机构	进入时间	布局城市及规模	投资模式
泰康保险	2009年	32个城市，37个项目	重资产
中国人寿	2013年	8个城市，9个项目	重资产+轻资产
新华保险	2012年	2个城市，3个项目	重资产
太平人寿	2014年	27个城市，32个项目	重资产+轻资产

数据来源：根据公开资料整理。

（2）保险机构探索“保险+居家养老服务”模式

以平安集团为例，平安自2021年开始启动居家养老服务业务，通过“医、食、住、行、财、康、养、乐、护、安”十大服务场景，为长者提供一站式居家养老解决方案。截至2023年9月，平安居家养老已覆盖全国50余个城市，累计超7万名客户获得服务。2023年10月，平安联合40多家康复护理服务商及行业内产学研专家，打造居家养老“护联体”，建立“标准—系统—服务—履约”闭环。

① 这一模式的概念是保险公司销售保险产品，并向购买相关产品累计缴纳保费达到一定金额的投保人，提供入住养老社区权益等增值服务的业务。

（3）延伸产业链，打造“养老+医疗”，构建康养生态

国寿2016年出资设立总规模500亿元的国寿大健康基金，战略性布局大健康主要赛道的龙头企业，覆盖生命科学、医疗科技、医疗服务和数字医疗等多个领域，提供多样化健康养老服务。泰康在布局养老社区的同时，投资医院和专科医疗机构，依托南京、武汉、成都、深圳和宁波五大医学中心，搭建自有医疗服务体系。

3. 在医疗保障方面，适合老年人的保险产品较少

目前，商业健康险对老年人群保障程度较低。2013年保险机构首推老年防癌产品，成为国内首个面向老年人群的商业健康险产品。根据中保协统计，老年防癌产品已为超过140万老年人提供约1 560亿元的癌症保障，平均保额10.84万元，累计向1.7万人赔付8.66亿元。此后相关产品赔付经验不理想，推广程度不高。

近年来，惠民保通过代际转移支付，为老年人群健康提供了有力保障。根据中再寿险经验估算，惠民保对60岁以上老年人群的覆盖程度约10%，且绝大多数赔付流向了老年人群。

4. 在长护险方面，保险机构既承办社保型试点，又探索商业型产品

长期护理险，简称长护险，是对失能老人的照护服务。一是关于社保型长护险试点。目前有18家保险公司参与承办，以太平洋人寿、国寿、太平养老和泰康为主。以太平养老为例，截至2022年6月底，经办长护险项目已达36个，覆盖辽宁、山东等12个省份，服务人群2 600万人，协议筹资金额超过40亿元[①]。二是关于商业型长护险。目前该市场规模小、产品价格高、保障功能弱、产品特色不鲜明，整体发展仍处于初步探索阶段。2023年5月开始试点将寿险保单责任转换为长护险

---

① 澎湃新闻：《长护险试点六年：18家险企参与、覆盖1.45亿人，投标管理等多重问题待改善》。

责任，已有保险公司与护理院开展长护险转换业务试点。

（三）从需求侧看，满足养老需求仍存明显痛点和难点

1. 未富先老，养老金制度安排不足以支撑长期需求

（1）第一支柱养老金替代率低，支付能力不足

主要存在三个方面问题：一是养老金替代率低。养老金替代率是指退休时的养老金领取水平与退休前工资收入水平之间的比率。国际劳工组织将55%作为养老金替代率的警戒线，而我国近十年养老金替代率在45%以下，最近几年呈下降趋势。二是结构性矛盾突出。首先城乡水平差异大。十年来城镇职工和城乡居民养老金差距由27倍缩小到18倍，但差异仍然巨大；其次区域差异大，东北等地区经济增长乏力，养老基金缺口日益严重。三是养老金支付压力持续增加。过去10年，老年人口抚养比不断上升，养老金征缴差额不断扩大，需各级财政资金持续投入。长期来看，随着老龄化不断加深，财政补贴负担日益加重，未来基本养老金规模出现缺口难以避免。

（2）第二支柱企业年金自主需求不强，覆盖率低

企业年金覆盖人数整体较少。截至2022年，我国共有12.8万户企业建立了企业年金，参加职工有3 010万人，不足参加城镇职工基本养老保险人数的6%，仅占全部就业人口的4%。目前企业年金主要为大中型央企、国企建立，中小民营企业参与意愿低。

（3）第三支柱个人养老金仍处于起步阶段

个人养老金采取完全积累制，通过被保险人年轻时为养老做准备，实现个体全生命周期的财富储备和平滑，包括税优个人养老金保险以及其他具有养老属性的保险产品。目前，此类产品累积约有5万亿元养老责任准备金，但发挥作用有限，原因主要有两个方面：一是不

享受税优政策的普通养老金产品特色不突出。当前市场销售的产品以期限较短的储蓄型产品为主，且领取设计多采用一次性或固定次数，缺乏长寿风险保障功能，导致客户简单地将其与基金、理财、存款进行收益率和安全性比较，处于竞争劣势。二是专门的税优个人养老金保险提供长期养老保障，但推广效果不及预期。相关产品推动力主要来自银行，银行平台通过开户引流。保险等机构的个人养老金产品难以直接触达客户，加之产品具有普惠性质，保险公司销售费用相对较低，渠道拓展意愿不足。

2. 老年人群体医疗需求大，但医疗保障水平不足

（1）基本医保对老年人实现全覆盖，但保障水平有限

近年来中老年人医疗保障覆盖率一直稳定在98%以上[①]。但是在老年人实际医疗费用支出中，医保报销比例不足50%[②]，自付费比例较高，成为老年人日常开支的大项。老年人就医过程中产生的交通费、陪护费等间接费用高，进一步加重老年人经济负担。此外，仍有少量老年人没有被医疗保障覆盖，因病致贫的风险高。

（2）商业健康险对老年人群保障程度较低

商业健康险产品投保年龄多限制在60岁左右，且存在“保健康体，不保非标体”“保短期，不保长期”等错配现象，商业健康险未能较好满足老年人群的健康保障需求。个别公司推出的面向老年群体的专项产品，如骨折险，因定价或承保责任等原因并未在市场引起广泛关注。

（3）惠民保为老年人群提供医疗保障，但存在可持续性风险

近几年，各地陆续推出惠民保，通过不限定投保年龄和既往症将

---

① 第四次城乡老年人生活状况调查。

② 2018年民生调查。

老年人群纳入参保体系。从运行结果看，惠民保理赔的年龄结构集中在高年龄段，如A市惠民保理赔成本中，50岁以上理赔额占总理赔的73%，B市为78%[①]。惠民保实现了中青年人和老年人之间的代际补贴，对老年人医疗保障作出贡献。由于惠民保没有强制性，未来可能会出现年轻人购买意愿下降而退出计划；老年人受益，购买意愿提升；易造成补贴和被补贴群体结构失衡，从而陷入“死亡螺旋”。因此，需要多方努力共同完善惠民保相关机制。

3. 高龄照护压力巨大，长期护理保险试点有待推广

（1）长护险试点尚处于初级阶段

2016年起开展社保长护险试点，目前在49个城市试行，其中，吉林和山东全省推开。截至2022年底，长期护理保险参保人数达到1.69亿人，累计有195万人享受待遇，累计支出基金624亿元，年人均支出1.4万元[②]。长护险试点初步建立了失能老人照护制度体系，对减轻失能老年人家庭负担、促进养老照护及老年用品行业发展、拓展就业渠道、提升医保基金支出绩效有显著成效。以上海市为例，经评定老年人得到长护险服务，长护基金支付90%费用，个人自付比例仅10%。居家失能老人只需支付少量费用，即可享受足不出户的专业照护服务。江苏省南通市长护险试点以来，享受此待遇超过7.5万人，居家上门服务人次超过300万人，辅具服务人次超过28万。长护险定点机构达380家，社会资本投入超过30亿元，吸纳就业人员超过万人[③]；长期住院的失能人员中近3 000人转入照护机构，减少了60%的医保基金支出。南通是第一个将康复辅具购买、租赁服务纳入长护待遇补偿范围的试点

① 中再寿险《惠民保的内涵、现状及可持续发展报告》。

② 2023年5月18日，国家医疗保障局在国务院新闻发布会介绍。

③ 南通市医保局网站，2023年7月28日，长护险“南通模式”为失能人员构筑“生命驿站”。

城市，解决了失能人群生活必需品置办困难的问题。

（2）长护险推广面临挑战

由于目前筹资渠道较单一，长护险实施给医保带来较大压力。长护险发展还面临四个方面挑战：一是覆盖面不广，参保人口占总人口的12%，相比德国、日本等国家全覆盖尚有差距。二是保障程度不足，以保障重度失能老人为主，对于中度和轻度失能老人普遍不赔付，相比其他国家，保障还不充分。如德国强制型长护险对轻度失能人士可以赔付约43%的费用。三是待遇支付标准低，提供的每周几个小时上门护理，对于很多长期家庭照护来说杯水车薪，被照护人无法得到持续的专业照顾。四是服务能力和技术水平还比较低。当前长护险多由家政服务人员提供，除大型机构外，多数服务机构没有应用权威培训标准。

二、养老需求与供给之间存在三大错配问题

上述分析表明，助力应对老龄化，现有保险（再保险）供给难以满足保险需求，主要原因是产品服务供给体系与现实需求主要在时间、对象和方式三个方面存在错配。

（一）时间错配：缺乏长周期的养老金融创新

应对未富先老问题的关键是在做好已退休人群养老保障基础上，为现有中年人群提前储备未来长期养老资金。但当前行业提供的主要是中短期年金，不能支持长期养老需求。保险业在个人养老金领域开拓力度不足，老年人支付能力难以提升，养老金体系未发挥应有作

用。一是专属个人税优养老金保险产品开发数量少、客户开发力度不足、积极性不高，在银行拥有流量端口的情况下，保险业务开拓难度大，积极性远不及银行等渠道；二是企业年金管理方面可以挖掘的业务机会没有受到重视，如被保险人达到退休时点之后，美国一般会将第二支柱产品购买转换为分期年金，而中国年金分期领取的保险产品设计很少；三是保险公司主要提供流动性的短期产品，缺乏从保险长期主义角度综合评估全生命周期下的疾病、意外、责任、养老、教育、资产等保障需求，尤其是针对老年生活的资金安排的保险产品设计和养老金融创新较少。

（二）对象错配：忽视带病群体和低收入群体

一是保险行业面向老年带病群体的商业健康险产品有限，作为医保的补充作用比较薄弱。保险公司仍以经营寿险的理念经营商业医疗险。在客户对象的选择上倾向于健康群体而把超过60岁、患有“三高”等慢性病的群体排除在外，而最需要保障的老年群体很难得到保障。二是普惠性不足，保险机构重视通过资产投资建设养老社区，忽视了以低龄老人为主的社区和居家养老大市场的普遍需求。

（三）方式错配：重产品而轻服务

一是重视养老硬件建设，但软件服务不足。目前养老机构投资旺盛，但配套的康养服务不足，入住率不高，真正社区/居家养老服务供给与需求相差甚远。二是尚未搭建起以服务为给付形式的商业长护保险机制。以2022年长护险人均支出1.4万元的水平为基础，如按照

4 800万[①]失能人数计算，长护险需求总量约为6 720亿元，占当年GDP的0.56%。以国际成熟经验来看，目前德国、日本等长期护理支出均超过其GDP的2%，由此来看，我国长期护理需求缺口巨大，亟待形成商业保险参与的、多层次支撑的长期护理保险体系。三是老年医疗服务不足。老年人相关医疗服务需求与年轻人存在较大差异，需要"防健诊治康养"全流程手段。当前保险产品以定额给付为主，重金融、轻服务；少数医疗产品还与基本医疗形成重叠。如图1所示，保险公司尚未充分发挥作用，在预防和保健环节，支付体系尚未成型，也是商业保险的空白地带；在诊断和治疗环节，已形成较完整的医疗供给和支付体系，但尚无老年人专属的商业健康保险；在康复和养护环节，供给体系还处于发展初期，相应的支付体系不完善、保障水平有限，商业康复保险和商业护理保险也处于发展初期。

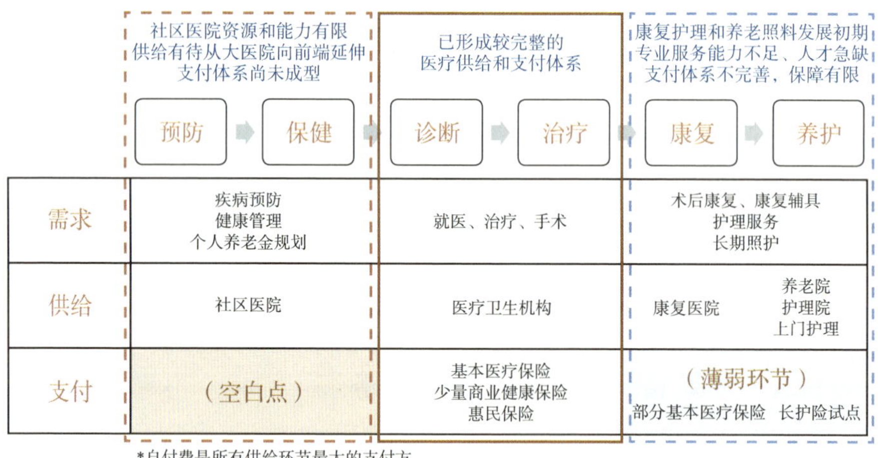

图1　从"防健诊治康养"链条看保险保障的空白点和薄弱环节

① 国务院发展研究中心《健康老龄化：政策与产业双轮驱动》。

三、保险（再保险）应对老龄化相关建议

（一）高度重视商业保险在应对老龄化中的独特作用，构建与基本社会保障相配合、有效互补的养老保险体系

当前，我国基本社会保障的筹资方式以现收现付为主，尤其是基本医疗保险和试点的长期护理保险，均依靠现收现付机制运转。现收现付的互助共济社会保障模式有助于维护社会公平和效率，但是在人口结构变化、老龄化加速的趋势下，社会保障基金支出将快速增长，将导致入不敷出的问题。

从国际经验来看，社会保障筹资方式可以分为政府、市场以及政府市场相结合三种模式，单一政府筹资和单一市场筹资模式都具有局限性，“政府+市场”双轮驱动正成为主要趋势。“政府+市场”能够实现时空两个维度分散风险，在保持政府公信力的同时，发挥商业保险跨周期的优势。

商业保险作为社会保障体系的重要支柱，可充分发挥其跨周期优势，向老年人群提供养老、医疗和长期护理等保障，为社会发展提供长期稳定的资金来源，推动养老服务体系建设完善。

我国已初步构建覆盖广泛、保障适度的多层次养老保障体系，商业保险能够与基本社会保障形成经纬互补的机制，社会保障是“纬”，商业保险是“经”，即以横向的公共代际转移为基础，大力发展纵向个人生命周期的基金积累制度，推动实现社会保障总体平衡和个体效用最大化。

（二）做好养老金融大文章，以“长期、普惠、服务”为宗旨推动商业养老保险发展

1. 坚持长期主义：扎实发展真正意义的长期商业养老金保险产品

培育壮大个人养老金市场，有利于解决中国人口不同年龄段变化给社保带来的压力。一是鼓励发展长期限、稳定保底、可以覆盖退休后整个生存期的保障领取年金（DB型年金），稳定被保险人未来养老收入预期，促进社会当期消费，缓解社保压力。同时，将商业保险与养老基金、理财区分开来，发挥保险保障特色。二是推动税优养老产品普及。当前税优个人养老金有优势，但消费者对其了解不足，要打通银行与保险间的壁垒，在利润薄、销售费用不足时，国有企业积极宣传推广，从服务国家战略角度率先垂范、培育市场。

2. 强化普惠特性：完善适老、友好的商业保险产品和服务，推广面向普通老人的普惠型保险产品

一是积极推动突破现有年龄和既往症限制，推进针对以慢病、共病为主的老年人群保险保障普惠化，大力开发针对60岁及以上老年人的商业健康保险产品。二是推广客户群体普惠化。对于活力老人客户群体，推动面向一般工薪阶层的居家和社区养老服务的产品创新。三是拓展保障内容，为老年人提供有能力支付的普惠型商业保险产品。

3. 增强保险服务：打通服务“最后一公里”，加大对健康产业和银发经济的支持力度

商业保险应从老年人的客观需求出发，转变一次性给付的强金融属性，提供养老、医疗及相关产业链的全方位服务。一是优化产品责任设计，加大产品服务属性。一方面，在老年人需要，但基本医保不

能覆盖的预防、康复等疾病管理流程上做文章，让老年人健康全链条有保障；另一方面，对于失能、失智老人，探索改变当前商业长护险仅提供现金给付的问题，未来逐步加强产品设计，以基本生活照料和医疗护理等服务作为给付。二是转变经营逻辑。商业保险公司应转变传统少赔、不赔才算盈利的寿险经营思维，逐步建立健康险经营新逻辑，通过整合产业链、提升医疗运行效率、提供风险减量管理服务来盈利。三是培育满足老年人需求的医疗、健康管理网络。针对老年人的医疗体系以基层社区医疗机构、药房等小型机构为主。因此，要强化商业保险与相关医疗机构的合作，有助于做强医疗服务体系，也一定程度上解决商业保险的控费和服务网络难题。

（三）依托数字化新技术提升商业保险服务能力

一是运用大数据提高精准识别风险的能力。突破可保风险界限，将传统模式下保险不愿保、不敢保的风险逐渐转变为可保风险，例如，通过大数据分析，保险可以拓宽业务边界，为多数老年人非标体人群提供风险保障。二是依靠数字化运营提升全流程风险管理能力。促进保险模式由“承保+理赔”，扩展到“承保+运营+服务+理赔”全流程服务，从简单赔付升级为全流程健康风险管理，真正成为客户的健康守护者。三是在大数据、人工智能、物联网等新技术的支持下，赋能康养业务提质增效。利用科技化手段，补齐单纯依赖人力提供服务的短板，实现客户触达精准化、运营服务智慧化、保险服务品质化。四是利用数字化手段降本增效，通过搭建信息化平台，统一产品和技术路线，实现总体降本增效。

（四）推动完善养老保险监管和税优政策

一是支持和引导商业保险加强产业融合创新。养老产业是典型的综合型产业，商业保险要做好养老金融大文章，必须通过跨行业合作，加强产业融合，推动产品及服务创新，加强保险与养老、医养、医药等各领域资源协同，提供专业精准的养老产品和服务。二是支持普惠保险创新和可持续发展。国家顶层设计中明确支持惠民保发展，明确惠民保衔接基本医保的重要补充作用。进一步优化惠民保产品设计，支持使用个人医保账户资金购买惠民保。三是鼓励加快养老、护理等领域的基础设施建设。对于民众需要、社会效应突出的社区及居家养老服务产业等给予政策支持，如降低资本要求、加大税收优惠、提升可投资资产上限等，引导保险业建设民生需要的养老服务业态。

（五）有效发挥再保险专业优势，推动养老保险供给侧结构性改革

再保险在数据、技术、产品创新等方面具有专业优势，要着力发挥再保险在风险分散、资本优化、经验技术分享、行业互通方面的重要作用，引领行业创新发展。一是加大相关基础设施建设，夯实长命风险数据定价基础。发挥再保险数据分析优势，编制更新行业生命表，对平均寿命、死因分析、生命改善等核心数据做好定期检视和回顾，摸清精算定价底数，总结老年人群发生率经验基础，聚焦老年险、慢病险、长护险等民生保障类险种，积极开展面向银发人群的产品服务创新。二是学习借鉴国际经验，推动本土化创新。商业养老金是欧美等国最重要的人身险产品，有着较长的发展历史和丰富的产品形态。再保险公司要发挥国际化优势，积极研究总结国际经验，推动

中国养老保险市场发展。三是为直保提供多样的风险解决方案。再保险积极研究和运用国际成熟的解决方案，为直保公司提供转移单一长命风险、单一投资风险或两种风险同时转移的不同风险偏好的解决方案，为保险公司参与商业养老年金业务提供再保险综合保障和服务。

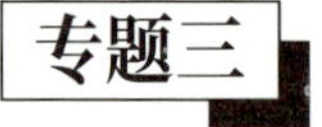

2023年全球自然灾害概况与降低灾害风险探讨

一、2023 年全球自然灾害损失回顾

（一）自然灾害长期损失趋势再次得以确认

2023年自然灾害事件造成的保险损失达1 080亿美元，再次印证了自1994年以来自然灾害保险损失年均5%~7%的增长趋势。[①]土耳其和叙利亚的破坏性地震、强对流风暴和大规模城市洪水是造成损失上升的主要灾害事件。2023年成为连续第四个保险损失突破1 000亿美元的年份，且高于此前5年（1 050亿美元）和10年（890亿美元）的平均水平。2023年全球范围内的自然灾害造成的经济损失高达2 800亿美元，意味着约62%的损失未投保（见图1）。受灾最严重地区的保险深度相对较低，因此全世界很多地区依然存在巨大的保障缺口。

① 如无特别说明，本文有关自然灾害保险损失的数据均来源于瑞士再保险sigma数据库。

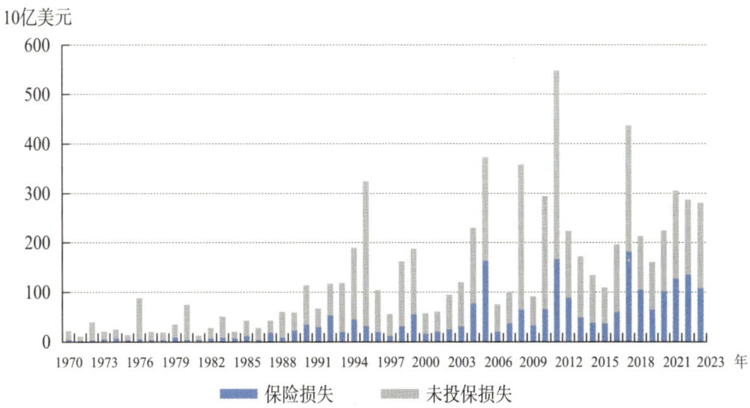

注：经济损失 = 保险 + 未投保损失。

图1　全球自然灾害保险和未投保损失（10亿美元，按2023年的价格）

（资料来源：瑞再研究院）

2023年破坏性最大的自然灾害是2月份发生在土耳其中南部的地震，土耳其大部分地区和叙利亚西北部都受到地震影响，受灾地区大量建筑倒塌，约58 000人死亡或失踪。这次地震造成的保险损失估计高达62亿美元，是有记录以来土耳其最严重的保险损失事件①。在该事件中，地震灾区的保险深度较低，约90%的经济损失没有保险覆盖，存在巨大的保障缺口。

此次地震成为2023年全球保险业损失最大的灾害，显示出灾害潜在后果存在巨大的不确定性。过去10年因地震导致的年均保险损失低于上一个10年的平均水平，但不能将过去的损失经验视为未来的趋势。地震存在巨大的长尾风险，如果受灾地区保险深度较高，导致的损失可能使行业承受极大的理赔压力。例如，2011年东日本大地震和2010—2011年新西兰克赖斯特彻奇地震导致的保险损失总额分别达到470亿美元和360亿美元。

① 损失最高纪录是指根据sigma记录，因自然灾害事件导致的最高保险损失（经通胀调整后）。下文同。

2023年，强对流风暴造成的保险损失达640亿美元，创下新纪录，几乎是过去5年和10年平均水平的两倍（见图2）。大部分强对流风暴损失发生在美国，但其他国家也遭到侵袭，尤其是意大利北部，风暴和冰雹灾害导致高达55亿美元的保险损失。

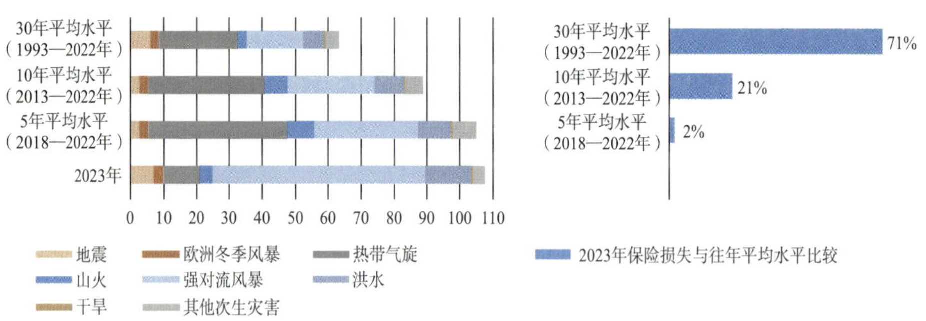

图2　2023年全球自然灾害保险损失和历史平均水平（10亿美元，按2023年价格）

（资料来源：瑞再研究院）

热带气旋仍是第一大损失灾害风险类型，占过去10年保险损失的38%，及过去40年保险损失的37%（见图3）。热带气旋和强对流风暴两种灾害保险损失合计占比从20世纪80年代的60%上升至过去10年的70%。而且，热带气旋损失占比波动较大，仅一次极端事件，如2005年的飓风卡特里娜（保险损失1 020亿美元，经通胀调整）或2022年的飓风伊恩（保险损失620亿美元），就可能使其占比大幅上升。

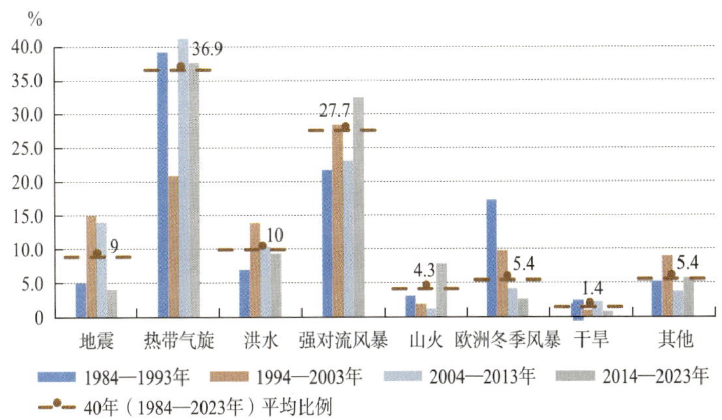

图3　10年间各灾害类型保险损失比例和40年平均水平

（资料来源：瑞再研究院）

2023年，世界各地的洪水事件导致的保险损失总额为140亿美元，高于5年（100亿美元）和10年（90亿美元）平均水平。2023年还是有记录以来最热的年份[①]，约1/3的天数全球平均气温至少比工业化前的气温高1.5℃。尽管2023年与山火有关的损失低于10年平均水平，但是北美、澳大利亚和其他地区的火灾威胁仍持续存在。随着林野与城市交界处人口增长、气温持续上升，未来几年的损失可能进一步上升，加剧山火相关风险。

（二）自然灾害损失上升的驱动因素

灾害频发是2023年损失的主要驱动因素。2023年共发生142起导致保险损失的自然灾害事件，为灾害数量最多的一年。尽管未发生像

① “世界气象组织确认2023年打破全球气温纪录”，世界气象组织，2024年1月12日。

2022年飓风伊恩那种强度的极端损失事件，[①]但灾害频发是造成全年保险损失的主要原因。

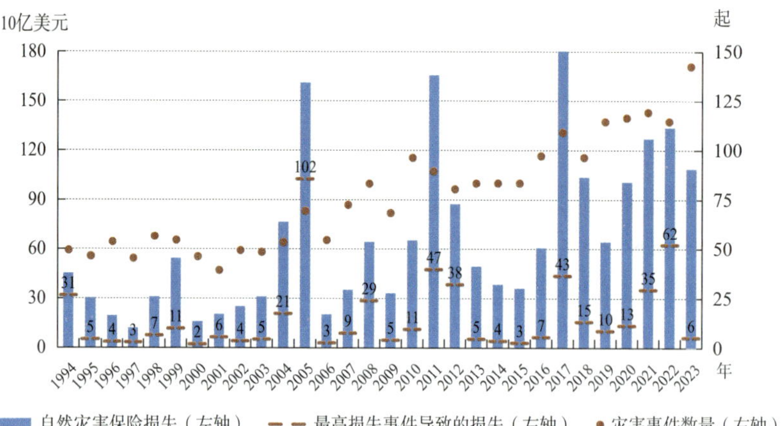

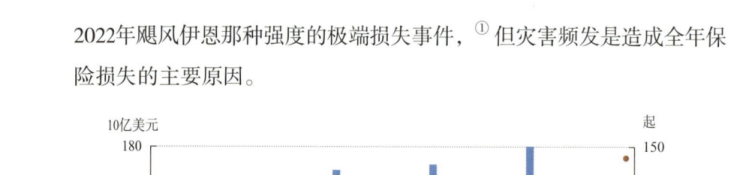

图4　1994—2023年各年度保险损失总额、最高损失事件（10亿美元，按2023年价格）和各年灾害事件总数

（资料来源：瑞再研究院）

中等损失灾害，尤其是强对流风暴，是导致损失的最主要因素。很多中等损失灾害（我们将其定义为导致10亿~50亿美元保险损失的事件，经通胀调整）的发生是2023年损失超过1 000亿美元的主要因素。2023年至少发生了30起中等损失灾害（远高于过去10年17起的平均水平），其中包括21起强对流风暴事件，创历史新高，是过去10年平均水平（8起）的两倍多。自1994年以来，中等损失灾害的数量年均增长7.5%，几乎达到自然灾害总数增幅（3.9%）的两倍（见图5）。

① “经济洞察”（Economic Insights）2022年第29期，“飓风伊恩加剧了再保险硬市场环境面临的压力”，瑞再研究院，2022年。

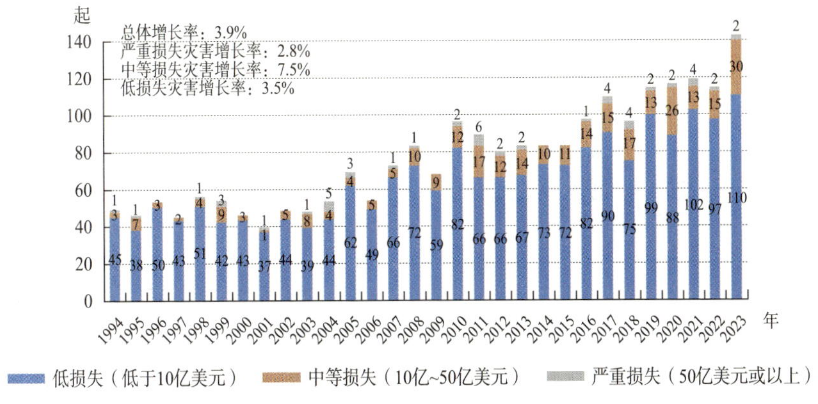

图5　1994—2023年按损失严重程度划分的自然灾害事件数量

（资料来源：瑞再研究院）

经济发展和人口增长以及城镇化导致风险格局不断变化，财富和有形资产的积累增加了对保险的需求。①这是多年来因自然灾害导致的保险损失呈上升趋势的主要原因。近几年，通胀压力，包括建筑成本上升，使风险敞口扩大②，造成损失结果进一步加剧。城市的扩张和大都市人口密度的提升，可能导致中等严重程度灾害造成的损失增加。

（三）聚焦强对流风暴

强对流风暴是一系列自然灾害的总称，包括龙卷风、直线风和大冰雹。这是一种常见的气象事件，当暖湿气流从地表上升至对流层上方时可形成强对流风暴，产生高耸的云层和雷电。与此同时，冷气团下沉到地面，带来强劲的阵风、雨水甚至冰雹。

2023年，全球因强对流风暴导致的保险损失总额为640亿美元，占去年全部自然灾害保险损失的一半以上。强对流风暴已日益成为仅次

① 见sigma 2022年第2期，“2021年自然灾害——洪水泛滥”，瑞再研究院。

② 见sigma 2023年第1期，“2022年自然灾害和通货膨胀：一场完美风暴”，瑞再研究院。

于热带气旋的第二大损失灾害风险类型，在过去10年的保险损失中占比超过32%。与强对流风暴有关的大部分（85%）损失发生在美国，但是欧洲和世界其他地区的损失增速快于美国。冰雹是威胁最大的风险，在各年度强对流风暴引发的保险损失总额中占比达50%~80%。

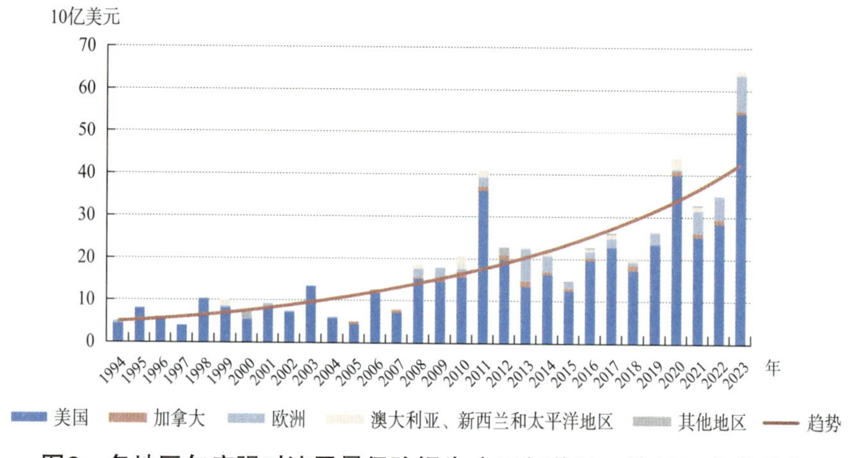

图6　各地区年度强对流风暴保险损失（10亿美元，按2023年价格）及全球趋势

（资料来源：瑞再研究院）

在欧洲，过去3年每年因强对流风暴导致的保险损失都超过50亿美元，尤其是冰雹风险呈上升趋势。2023年7月，意大利受到了严重的冰雹侵袭，该国北部人口密集地区遭受一系列强对流风暴的侵袭。冰雹导致意大利遭受55亿美元的保险损失，成为sigma有记录以来欧洲损失最大的强对流风暴事件。灾害严重性同样创下纪录，记录到的冰雹直径超过16厘米，甚至达到19厘米，是欧洲有史以来报告的最大冰雹①。此次保险损失成为意大利新的冰雹风险基准，表明调整相关风险评估的必要性。考虑到家财险深度依然相对较低，损失的严重性会对行业

① “2023年的冰雹风暴”，欧洲强风暴实验室，2024年1月23日。

造成冲击。与法国在2022年发生的情况类似，最近几年，由于缺乏细化风险敞口数据和准确的强对流风暴/冰雹风险模型，风险敞口扩大等影响天气风险格局变化的重要发展趋势在很大程度上未被有效识别。

通胀与风险敞口变化趋势是影响美国强对流风暴损失的主要因素。基于对2008—2023年美国强对流风暴损失驱动因素的分析，我们发现通胀是主导因素。强对流风暴保险损失合计8%的增长中，一般通胀贡献了2.2个百分点，建筑材料、建造和维修成本上升对保险损失增长的贡献为1.2个百分点。经济发展和人口增长、城镇化以及财富积累导致的风险敞口扩大约贡献了2.3个百分点，依然是导致强对流风暴相关损失上升的主要因素，大约占过去15年间美国相关保险损失增长额的1/3。

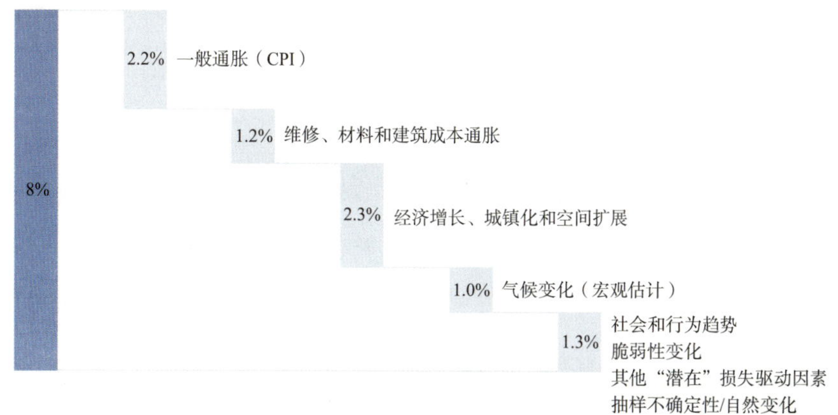

图7　美国2008—2023年强对流风暴保险损失合计年增长率（深蓝色）和每个驱动因素导致的增长率（淡蓝色）

（资料来源：瑞再研究院）

气候变化对强对流风暴损失的影响仍存在争论。越来越多的证据显示一些地区的强对流风暴活动呈上升趋势，最近的研究表明，严重冰雹事件的数量（在本文中将其作为气候变化影响的代表）每年上升约

1个百分点，但仍存在很多不确定性。此外，剩余的影响主要由于社会和行为趋势、脆弱性等方面的变化。

脆弱性的变化尤其体现在住宅建筑上。2022—2023年，美国由强对流风暴导致的保险损失中，约70%来自住宅部分，远高于60%的历史平均水平。冰雹可能严重损坏屋顶、建筑物外立面、外部保温层、太阳能面板和房屋其他部分，如天窗和百叶窗。如果进水，还可能影响内部结构和建筑物部件。屋顶损坏是冰雹造成保险损失的主要因素，尤其是老旧屋顶；而安装于屋顶的太阳能面板增多是脆弱性增加的另一个因素。此外，冰雹可能导致车辆凹陷和结构变形，因此导致昂贵的维修费用、车险理赔费用上升以及转售价值下降。

综上所述，强对流风暴导致的损失增速已超出通胀、风险敞口趋势和气候变化影响的解释范围。其他社会经济和行为趋势也在发挥作用（其中有些因素的影响尚不明了），同时风险资产的脆弱性也在变化。在风险评估和承保中，需要考虑这些因素的影响。相对而言，仅把握历史趋势但忽略该趋势的持续性，会低估风险并高估利润。由于获取与强对流风暴相关的细化风险敞口数据的渠道受到限制（包括时间和地理空间的限制），保险行业的建模能力受限。保险公司、行业协会和政府机构需要更好地监测强对流风暴事件和相关损失。此外，制定并遵守建筑规范以降低面对强对流风暴灾害时的脆弱性，有助于提升社会韧性。

二、2023 年中国自然灾害损失回顾及巨灾保险发展

（一）中国自然灾害损失回顾

2023年，中国自然灾害较2022年严重，以洪涝、台风、地震和地质灾害为主，其他如干旱、风雹、森林草原火灾等也有不同程度发生。全年各种自然灾害共造成农作物受灾面积10 539.3千公顷，死亡失踪691人，倒塌房屋20.9万间，直接经济损失3 454.5亿元（见图8）。与近5年均值相比，倒塌房屋数量、直接经济损失分别上升96.9%、12.6%。[①]

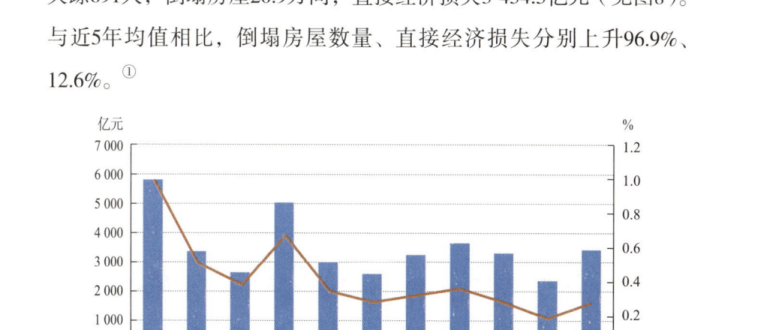

图8　中国自然灾害直接经济损失及占该年GDP比重

（资料来源：中国应急管理部，瑞再研究院）

洪涝灾害依然是造成直接损失最大的自然灾害类型（见图9），受台风“杜苏芮”影响，华北、东北相继出现极端暴雨天气，海河发生流域性特大洪水，松花江流域发生严重汛情，西南、西北等局地山洪地质灾害多点散发。全年洪涝灾害共造成直接经济损失约2 445.7亿

① 数据来源：中国应急管理部，《2023年全国自然灾害基本情况》。

元，占全年自然灾害直接经济损失的71%。单次事件造成严重保险损失的趋势依然持续，京津冀暴雨洪涝灾害造成保险损失超过75亿元。[①]

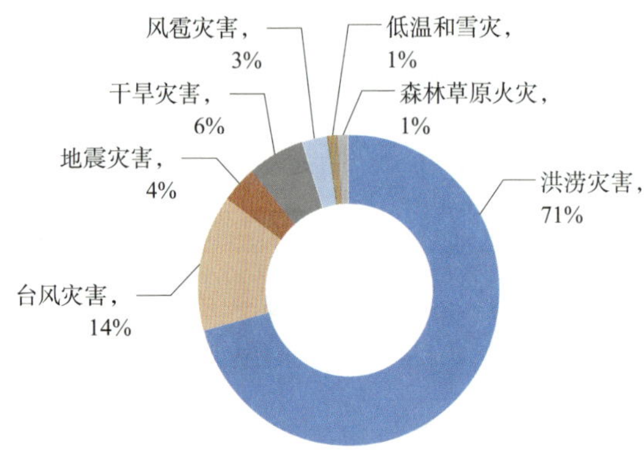

图9　各类型自然灾害占全年自然灾害直接经济损失的比重

（资料来源：中国应急管理部，瑞再研究院）

（二）保险再保险行业为中国自然灾害提供保障

中国保险再保险业在提供自然灾害保障方面继续发挥积极作用。据中国保险行业协会统计，2023年保险业涉及重大自然灾害的赔付约252.59亿元，投入防灾减灾资金约6.61亿元，投入防灾减灾人力约11.31万人次，发送预警信息约1.3亿人次，排查企业客户风险约17.14万次，预计减少灾害损失约37.09亿元。在灾害救援方面，协助救援受灾人员约9.26万人次，协助救援受灾机动车19.02万辆次，捐赠资金约4 681.41万元，捐赠物资折算金额约619.96万元，捐赠保险的保险金额约3 000.55亿元。总体而言，保险再保险业在应对自然灾害风险中起到“安全网”与“稳定器”的作用。

与此同时，再保险行业不断更新迭代自然灾害风险量化模型，在

① 16个受灾地区保险预赔付金额达75.82亿元 进度超七成 央地联合 首都之窗 北京市人民政府门户网站（beijing.gov.cn）。

防灾减损和灾后救援方面发挥重要作用。中再研发迭代首个拥有自主知识产权的中国巨灾模型，覆盖地震、台风、洪涝三大主要灾害。截至2024年6月，地震模型更新至3.5版本，台风模型更新至2.4版本，洪涝模型更新至1.5版本，2024年将完成洪涝模型2.0商业化版本的开发。[①]瑞再发布的“信瑞智农”2.0实时风险分析模块，以其实时灾害分析功能，对2023年“杜苏芮”台风影响的省份进行强降水灾害全程跟踪监测及风险评估。平台能够实时评估灾损严重程度，且分析县乡四级灾害结果。巨灾模型的不断突破能够帮助政府部门、保险行业和企业家庭更主动地、更有针对性地进行防灾减损和灾后救援工作，基于大数据、人工智能和农业风险管理模型推动农业风险减量服务。

近年来，中国在推动巨灾保险发展方面也取得了积极进展：

完善巨灾保险制度建设，加快推动巨灾保险高质量发展。2024年3月，国家金融监督管理总局、财政部联合印发《关于扩大城乡居民住宅巨灾保险保障范围进一步完善巨灾保险制度的通知》，完善巨灾保险制度建设，加快推动巨灾保险高质量发展。其内容包含以下三个方面：扩展巨灾保险责任，在现有的破坏性地震的基础上，保险责任增加台风、洪水、暴雨、泥石流、滑坡等自然灾害；提升基本保险金额，扩展巨灾保险的基本保险金额至城镇居民住宅每户10万元、农村居民住宅每户4万元；支持商业巨灾保险发展，对于现有保障内容之外的保险责任和保障对象，可以提供商业保险补充，充分满足各地区差异化风险保障需求。

第一次全国自然灾害综合风险普查取得丰硕成果。2024年5月，《第一次全国自然灾害综合风险普查公报》发布，本次普查明确了全

① 科技赋能巨灾模型建设，中国银行保险报。

国高灾损区、高隐患区、高风险区和低减灾能力区“三高一低”的自然灾害综合风险区域。建设了国家自然灾害综合风险基础数据库（以下简称“国家基础数据库”），包括23种致灾因子数据，27种承灾体数据，以及灾害风险评估、风险区划、防治区划成果数据等。除了为各地和有关部门提供数据服务外，还同时对科研教学工作者和社会公众开放使用。

各地巨灾保险创新发展步伐持续加快。据国家金融监督管理总局统计，全国已有15个省份74个地市开展了不同形式的综合性巨灾保险试点，保障的灾因除地震之外，还扩展到台风、洪水、泥石流等，部分地方巨灾保险也为人身伤亡提供责任保障。①浙江省宁波市多灾因巨灾保险试点多年，同时创新推出普通国省道营运期巨灾风险保险等，保障范围不断延伸；广东省采用双重触发条件的参数保险（即针对气旋风险，考虑台风路径和风速；针对暴雨风险，则考虑降水量），保险公司不需查勘定损即可赔付，支持灾害救助和重建；2024年2月，全国首单全灾种、广覆盖、长周期综合巨灾保险在河北省落地，全省7 400多万群众有了“人身+住房+财产”三层巨灾保险保障。

三、结构性降低灾害风险，保障中国经济社会韧性

（一）结构性降低灾害风险

降低天气相关的财产风险需要考虑三个关键因素（见图10）：风险因素、风险敞口和脆弱性。因此，需要采取结构性措施降低灾害风险：（1）通过减缓气候变化应对风险加剧（频率和严重性）；（2）最大限

① 城乡居民住宅巨灾保险保障范围、基本保额提升，巨灾保险保障体系已初步建立，澎湃新闻，2024年3月16日。

度地减少生命、生活和资产的风险暴露程度（如通过改变土地使用方式、防范洪水等措施避免潜在损害）；（3）降低风险脆弱性（如采取措施限制或更好地应对灾害影响，以及减轻潜在损害）。

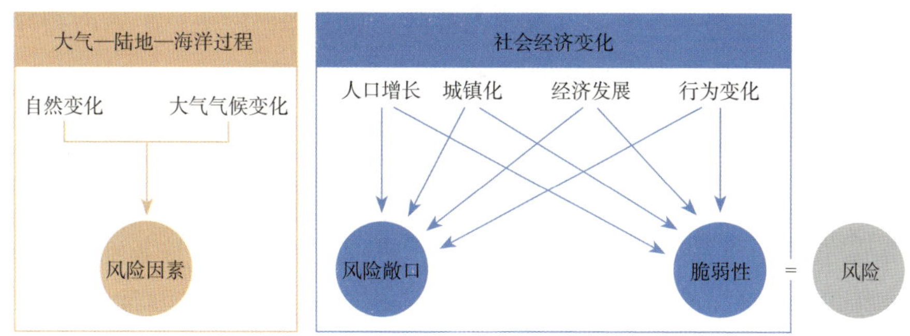

图10　天气相关风险的三个组成部分和驱动因素

（资料来源：瑞再研究院）

减缓气候变化是最为根本的风险应对措施，旨在从根源出发延缓灾害加剧。减少温室气体排放是抑制气候相关物理风险加剧的关键，这涉及重塑全球能源体系：能源的生成、使用、运输和储存方式。此外，需要改革农业生产过程，加快碳捕捉和封存。国际货币基金组织指出，如果到2050年实现净零排放的有序转型，对全球GDP的净贡献接近7%（与现行政策相比），其中一半以上来自避免因恶劣天气风险（如洪水、热浪和干旱）导致的损失①。

应对恶劣天气影响的下一道防线是减少风险敞口和/或脆弱性，包含损失降低、防范和适应措施，与保险、减缓气候变化共同组成应对天气相关风险的三大措施。具体来看，降低建造环境的风险敞口和脆弱性有多种方式，包括损失防范（如更新/扩展建筑规范，以及采用更

① 其他贡献来自避免因气温的逐渐上升引起的慢性物理风险，如海平面上升以及热应激和传染病流行的加剧。见“加速气候转型的益处远超成本”，国际货币基金组织，2023年12月5日；以及“气候变化经济学：不采取行动是行不通的”，瑞再研究院，2021年。

可靠的建筑材料和技术，以提高建筑的韧性）、损失降低（如现有建筑的翻新或改造）以及更广泛的适应措施（如增加和/或加强应对风暴潮/海平面上升的防洪基础设施）。随着经济发展水平提升，城镇扩张使高风险地区人口活动和建设开发逐渐增加，短期内风险敞口扩大的趋势将持续。这使关注财产和基础设施的脆弱性更加重要。

2023年的损失经验就体现了降低脆弱性的必要性。在2月份发生在土耳其的地震中，按照最新建筑规范建造的很多建筑成功抵抗了冲击[①]，但没有按照建筑规范建造的老旧房屋大量倒塌。韧性基础设施的建设同样重要。当前，很多水利基础设施的设计标准是按照历史极端降雨数据制定的。在快速变化且复杂的城市环境中，短时间的高强度降雨事件就可能击溃排水基础设施，如去年发生在北京、香港、奥克兰和纽约的洪水事件。另外，由于风险格局不断变化且日趋复杂，需要采取综合措施降低脆弱性。例如，考虑将风险加剧的概率分布变化等因素纳入不同灾害模型，以提高风险定价的准确性。

（二）解决激励错配和信息壁垒问题是未来降低脆弱性的关键

2023年的经验证明，尽管采取了针对各类资产的降低脆弱性措施，但实际执行的措施依然有限。例如在美国，仅31%的司法管辖区采用了适用于新建筑的更严格的现代化建筑规范[②]。脆弱性的降低面临各种阻碍，首先是错配的激励措施。即使成本收益分析显示将产生净收益，但对于业主和房地产开发商而言损失降低措施通常需要高昂的前期投入，但未来的收益却并不确定。另外，由于收益通常较低，对

① “更安全、韧性更强的学校如何经受住土耳其地震的冲击”，世界银行，2023年。

② 资料来源：“建筑规范采用跟踪”，FEMA.gov；“自然灾害缓释措施减少了损失：2019年报告”，美国国家建筑科学研究院，nibs.org。

现有的老旧建筑和基础设施进行改造面临阻力。因此，在提升公共基础设施韧性方面政府应发挥更大作用。

降低受灾脆弱性还需要打破信息壁垒。除了激励措施，提升透明度可以帮助业主和开发商更好地了解其可能面临的风险的性质和概率，并促进基于风险的保险定价。例如，应将有关风险和风险缓释措施投资的信息，充分披露于房地产经纪、评估师和抵押贷款机构收集的资料中。政府和监管机构也可以发挥积极作用。例如，使降低脆弱性的措施扩展为公共物品，包括有关安全特性和改造收集的数据；或鼓励保险公司采用透明且基于风险的定价，以提升信息对称性。

四、总结

2023年，自然灾害导致的全球经济损失估计达到2 800亿美元，保险理赔约1 080亿美元，即62%的损失未投保。年度保险损失超过1 000亿美元已成为常态，我们预计实际保险损失将保持年均5%~7%的增长趋势。在过去30年间，全球自然灾害保险损失增速已超过了全球经济增速：1994—2023年因自然灾害保险损失年均增长5.9%，而同期全球GDP年增长率为2.7%。换言之，过去30年，相对于GDP的自然灾害保险损失负担增长了两倍多。

全球自然灾害损失的迅速增加凸显了加强风险应对能力的重要性。为更好地应对当前损失风险并为未来做好准备，需要依靠三大措施：适应措施、保险和减缓措施。当前，由于存在投资不足、激励错配和信息壁垒等问题，风险应对能力还有待提升。因此，各类主体需要共同行动，采取长期的风险减缓和适应方法，提升应对自然灾害的韧性，并帮助保险业继续发挥风险保障作用。

专题四

气候相关风险对保险再保险业的冲击与应对

近年来，高碳行业的转型风险、极端天气以及公司治理风险等ESG风险不断冲击着金融机构原有的风险管理框架。国际能源署（2020）预测，全球碳密集行业资产搁浅规模到2050年和2100年将分别达10万亿和28万亿美元。若各类金融机构不能以恰当的方式及时防范和处理ESG风险，长期来看可能对整个金融体系的安全和稳定造成重大影响。

《2023年全球风险报告》显示，未来十年内与气候变化相关的风险占全球十大风险的50%，且前三大风险均为气候相关风险，气候变化成为影响人类生产生活方式的严峻挑战之一。气候风险作为ESG风险的重要组成部分，受到越来越多金融监管部门和交易所的关注。比如，近年来，港交所不断提高上市企业ESG披露标准。2023年4月，港交所建议所有发行人在其ESG报告中披露气候相关信息，以及推出符合国际可持续发展准则理事会（ISSB）气候准则的新气候相关信息披露要求。2022年6月，原中国银保监会发布的《银行保险业绿色金融指引》中指出，银行保险业金融机构应当有效识别、监测、防控业务活动中的ESG风险，将ESG要素纳入全面风险管理体系。

将气候变化要素融入企业经营，尤其是风险管理当中，是我国金融机构面临的崭新课题。面对这一时代课题，我国金融机构不仅要从满足监管要求的角度贯彻气候相关风险管理要求，更要深入探究气候风险因素究竟会给企业经营带来哪些风险，从市场层面深入理解气候相关风险管理要求，从而及时规避气候相关重大风险事件，实现自身的可持续发展。

一、气候相关风险对宏观金融稳定的影响

气候变化是金融稳定的重要威胁，当下大量证据表明，气候变化会给宏观金融稳定带来大量直接或间接影响，引发系统性金融风险。如全球气温升高将明显提高极端天气的发生频率和强度，各类极端天气会直接给经济社会造成损失，而在这个过程中，房地产价值锐减、企业生产经营受到影响，盈利能力下降，居民财富遭到损失，这些经济恶化会直接传递给宏观金融体系，导致通胀上升，资产价值下降，引发系统性的金融风险。

已有研究认为，整体上看，气候相关风险主要通过两个渠道影响金融稳定，即间接的资本收益变动和直接的资产贬值（Weitzman，2009；Carnevali等，2021）。具体来看，气候风险又被分为物理风险（Physical Risks）和转型风险（Transition Risks）（见表1）。物理风险是指极端天气事件导致的财产损失或对生产生活产生干扰，进而对保险责任以及金融资产价值产生影响；转型风险是指人类社会在向低碳经济转型过程中产生的经济金融风险，主要包括政策转变、技术或商业模式的颠覆式创新以及消费者观念和情绪的转变，这将导致原有资产价值的大规模重估（资产搁浅风险）。

表1　　气候相关风险类别划分

物理风险	示例
极端天气事件	热带气旋/台风、洪水、冬季风暴、热浪、干旱、野火、冰雹
生态污染	土壤污染和退化、空气污染、水污染、海洋污染、环境事故
海平面上升	长期海平面上升或海浪
水资源短缺	干旱或供水不足
沙漠化	森林砍伐导致物种灭绝、气候条件变化、荒漠化和人口迁移
转型风险	**示例**
公众政策转变	能源转型政策、污染控制法规、资源保护法规
技术改变	清洁能源技术、节能技术、清洁交通和其他绿色技术
情绪改变	消费者对某些产品的偏好变化，投资者对某些资产类别的情绪变化
商业模式颠覆式改变	经营企业的新方式可以从传统企业快速获得市场份额

资料来源：NGFS（2020）、公开信息整理。

虽然金融机构可能直接面临环境与气候相关风险（例如，一些金融机构的总部位于沿海地区，可能受海平面上升带来的直接影响），但大多数风险都是间接的，来自其客户和被投资方对这些风险的敞口。从具体传导过程看，物理风险以两种方式影响经济。一种是极端天气事件可能导致业务中断、财产损失以及建筑物重建等。从历史经验看，这些影响被认为是暂时的，但随着全球变暖的加剧，这种情况将变得更为常见。这些事件会增加保险公司的承保风险，并损害资产价值。另一种是气候的渐进变化带来的长期影响，特别是气温升高、海平面上升和降水，可能会影响劳动力、资本和农业生产率。这些变化将需要公司、家庭和政府的大量投资和适应。上述两种风险将直接降低实体资产的价值，导致家庭财富受损，企业经营受到冲击，进而引发金融系统的市场风险和信用风险以及运营风险，造成金融不稳定（见图1）。

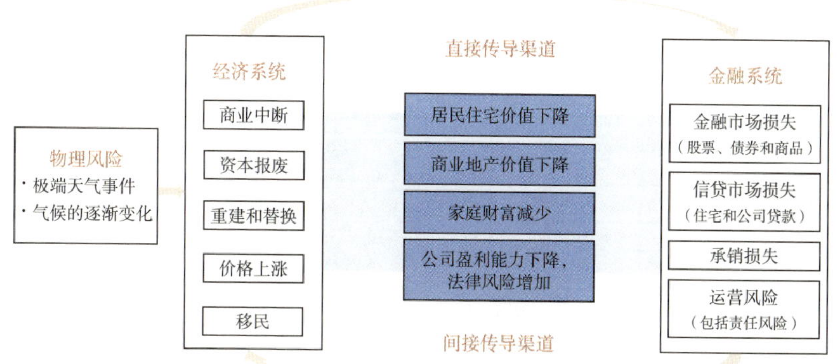

图1　物理风险向金融风险的传导机制分析

（资料来源：根据公开资料整理分析）

转型风险中政策改变、技术突破以及消费者偏好改变都会对经济发展带来影响，转型风险将直接冲击传统的碳密集行业，造成资产搁浅。例如，低碳政策的突然收紧可能给传统能源行业造成致命打击，化石燃料的价值将会突然下跌，在碳排放的约束下，“将化石燃料留在地下”的呼吁可能让超过14万亿美元的资产面临搁浅风险。而投资于碳密集行业的金融机构若不提前进行资产配置规划、防范风险，将使自身面临严重的投资损失，进而提高金融系统整体的市场风险和信用风险（见图2）。另外，无论是物理风险还是转型风险，都会间接带来更大范围的经济恶化，进而传递给金融系统，影响整个金融体系的稳定。

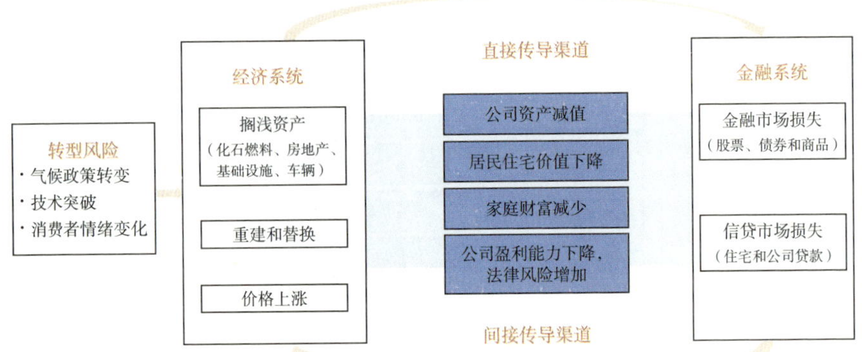

图2 转型风险向金融风险的传导机制分析

（资料来源：根据公开资料整理分析）

二、气候相关风险对保险再保险业的影响

作为市场化的风险管理机构，保险业可以分散投保人风险，为各类建设提供保险资金支持，助力金融体系的多元化发展。保险机构在维持各类经济主体发展韧性方面发挥了重要作用。气候相关风险的覆盖范围广、影响大，保险企业若不能提前以适当方式加以考虑，可能会导致保险业无法生存，风险将影响整个经济金融体系。因此，在分析气候相关风险如何影响保险业活动时，要从承保端、投资端以及运营端综合考虑气候变化带来的影响，并从更长的周期考虑保险业在应对气候相关风险时所能发挥的作用。

整体上看，气候变化中的物理风险和转型风险给保险公司带来了严峻挑战。比如物理风险让保险公司面临高于预期的理赔支出（保险风险），还可能直接损坏保险企业的办公场地，影响正常经营（运营风险）。而转型风险则给保险公司带来投资损失和资产减值（市场风险），给保险公司对新产品的定价带来困难（保险风险）。

表2　物理风险和转型风险对保险业的影响

风险类型	保险风险	市场风险	信用风险	运营风险	流动性风险
物理风险	高于预期的保险理赔支出	实物资产损失和业务中断导致股票价值下降	再保险公司信用评级下降，损失风险增加	保险公司处所受到损坏，影响正常运营	为弥补收入损失，保单取消增加
转型风险	新保险产品定价困难（或偏低）	投资损失和资产价值	公司债投资受损	网络风险上升	面临投资长期绿色基础设施项目的压力

资料来源：根据FSI（2019）内容整理。

另外，从英国审慎监管局（PRA）的一份对保险行业的调查数据也可以看出，气候变化带来的物理风险及转型风险将对保险公司的资产负债表带来巨大影响（见表3、表4）。在A、B、C三种不同的情景下，可以发现气候相关风险呈现显著的非线性特征，在情景C状态下，物理风险对保险公司资产负债表的影响呈现指数型增长。

表3　物理风险对保险公司负债端的可能影响

行业	假设条件	物理风险情景		
		A	B	C
美国受飓风影响的行业	大型飓风发生频率增幅	5%	20%	60%
	大型飓风风速整体增幅	3%	7%	15%
	热带气旋引起的降水增加导致地表径流增幅	5%	10%	40%
	美国得克萨斯州和北卡罗来纳州之间海岸线风暴潮海平面平均升幅	10cm	40cm	80cm
英国受天气影响的行业	降水增加导致地表径流增幅	5%	10%	40%
	英国大陆海岸线风暴潮海平面平均升幅	2cm	10cm	50cm
	以有记录以来最糟糕的一年为基准，地表下陷相关财产索赔频率增幅	3%	7%	15%
	以有记录以来最糟糕的一年为基准，与冰冻有关的财产索赔频率增幅	5%	20%	40%

资料来源：根据FSI（2019）内容整理。

表4　　气候风险对保险公司投资端的可能影响

单位：%

受影响行业	以下行业的投资组合	假设：投资组合中包含以下能源部门风险敞口的部分股票价值变化	物理风险情景			转型风险情景		
			A	B	C	A	B	C
燃料开采	煤/石油/天然气	煤				-45	-40	
		石油				-42	-38	
		天然气				-25	-15	
				-5	-20			
发电	电力传输和天然气、可再生能源输送	煤				-65	-55	
		石油				-35	-30	
		天然气				-20	-15	
		可再生能源（包括核能）				+10	+20	
				-5	-20			

资料来源：根据FSI（2019）内容整理。

在讨论气候相关风险对保险业的冲击时，再保险的作用显得尤其重要。再保险可以有效分散保险业面临的极端风险，为提高保险公司应对极端情况时的韧性保驾护航（Upreti et al.，2015）。整体上看，气候相关风险将从两个方面对再保险公司产生影响：一是巨额索赔，极端气候事件的影响往往巨大，这将在短时间内产生大量的索赔费用，保险和再保险公司在这一过程中面临严峻的财务考验；二是声誉风险。再保险公司的一个重要职能就是为直保公司提供承保、定价等一系列咨询服务，如果再保险公司没有及时跟进研究，没有将气候相关风险纳入再保险业务范畴，就会导致其无法为直保企业提供有效的气候风险解决方案，进而损失客户资源。

以上从理论角度分析了气候相关风险对保险业发展的可能影响。从实际影响看，物理风险对保险业的资产负债表都可产生直接或间接的损失。《2023全球保险业展望》显示，2018—2022年，保险公司支付的自然灾害理赔数以千亿美元计，而未投保的损失更大，这仅是承保端的直接损失。从投资端来看，物理风险的影响较为间接，物理风险对资产业务的影响主要体现为因持有房地产、基础设施等项目股权而遭受的间接损失。相关数据显示，2020年，纽约可能遭受严重风暴潮侵袭的住宅重建价值高达3 340亿美元（王信等，2021）。

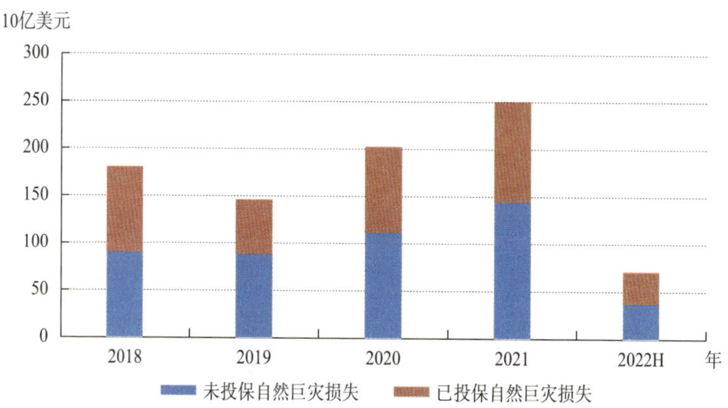

图3　2018—2022年上半年自然灾害（巨灾）造成的经济损失

（资料来源：《2023 全球保险业展望》，安永）

三、金融机构应对气候变化风险的经验借鉴

（一）德国安联集团

作为全球重要保险集团，德国安联集团不仅是市场化的风险管理者，也是重要的机构投资者。安联集团高度重视ESG相关问题，积极将ESG要素纳入其业务中，无论是承保端还是投资端，都积极融入ESG要素，并针对非上市资产类别制定了ESG风险管理流程和ESG敏感业务指南。德国安联集团ESG风险管理流程包括三部分：第一步，筛选业务类型，按照敏感业务指南判断该业务是否属于本企业认定的13个敏

感业务领域[①]（敏感业务指南均根据国际公认标准进行设定）；第二步，按照敏感业务指南中标准对筛选出的业务类型进行评定，这一步是决定该项目是否纳入集团ESG评估的重要参考；第三步，已纳入ESG评估的项目需提交一份ESG评估报告，作为最终是否进行交易的决策依据。另外，安联集团还将企业所有运营实体进行ESG整合，通过将ESG要素纳入核心业务、与非政府组织对话、鼓励内部利益相关者参与等形式，不断提高其ESG风险管理的透明度。

（二）中国工商银行

中国工商银行在应对ESG风险、尤其气候相关金融风险方面走在国内金融业的前列，其通过积极参与国际组织（TCFD）、修订企业风险管理制度、组织力量进行气候风险压力测试等方法，积极应对ESG风险，为我国金融机构将ESG风险纳入全面风险管理流程做出了有益探索。具体做法有：一是积极参与国际组织，中国工商银行是气候相关财务信息披露工作组（TCFD）发起成员中唯一来自中国的金融机构，金融稳定委员会发布的《2022年TCFD现状报告》中指出，按照TCFD建议框架进行信息披露的公司由2017年的45%上升至2021年的70%，100家全球最大的上市公司中有92家支持TCFD，或者已经根据TCFD建议发行报告；二是修订自身《全面风险管理规定》，将气候风险融入其中，明确了风险管理的三道防线在应对气候风险时的职责、偏好、限额和制度流程；三是率先构建了国内适用于银行业的气候风险压力测试体系，为行业应对气候风险提供行业标准和基础设施；四是不断完善气候风险信息披露体系建设，逐步形成了以绿色债券年度

① 安联集团涉及敏感业务的领域包括农业、采矿业、水电、博彩业、人权以及动物试验等13个影响社会和公共环境的重要行业和事项。

报告、社会责任报告以及绿色金融专题报告为主体的信息披露框架。

（三）中国太平洋保险集团

中国太平洋保险集团建立较为完善的ESG管理体系，把ESG全面融入公司的经营管理。首先，董事会负责全面监督ESG规则、实施与管理，评估ESG对公司整体策略的潜在影响。其次，由专门的战略与投资决策及ESG委员会依据相关ESG报告指引，识别ESG风险，制定应对策略，优化运营体制。再次，集团成立ESG办公室，具体进行ESG关键议题和绩效的识别和披露，推动相关制度和指引在集团全系统地落地执行。最后，推动各个职能部门将ESG相关指标整合融入日常运营中，推进中国太平洋保险成为“行业健康稳定发展的引领者”。

（四）中国再保险（集团）股份有限公司

再保险是“保险的保险”，被称为保险业的“安全阀”和保险市场的“调控器”，在分散市场尾部风险和巨灾风险等方面具有重要价值。中国再保是目前国内唯一国有再保险集团，近年来在服务国家“双碳”战略方面作出了积极贡献。一是深耕环境污染责任保险、绿色能源保险、绿色交通保险、绿色建筑保险、农业保险、巨灾保险及核保险等领域，积极开展绿色保险创新研究，加快构建产业融合生态圈，推动行业绿色保险发展。2023年服务绿色发展领域保额3.1万亿元，同比增长26.8%，助力科技创新领域保额超过4 300亿元，同比增长16.4%。二是积极应对气候变化，推动巨灾保险发展。2023年承担国内地震、洪水和台风风险责任25.8万亿元，同比增长11%；参与全部19个省市巨灾保险试点项目并在80%的项目中担任首席再保人。2023年全年服务社会治理领域有关险种保额9 607.2亿元，同比增长33.6%。发挥专业技术优势，聚焦巨灾科技研发与创新，持续迭代研发巨灾模型，提高巨灾风险量化管理能力水平，为国家风险治理体系及治理能力现代化建设提供关键技术支撑。三是积极履行环境责任，深入践行责任投资和绿色金融理念，持续强化绿色投资管理体系，将ESG责任投资理念纳入投资分析和决策考量，促进投融资结构的绿色转型。

四、气候风险要素纳入保险再保险业风险管理框架的思考与建议

气候相关风险系统复杂、与多方关联、难以预测和评估，气候风险事件一旦发生会给金融机构甚至宏观金融稳定带来巨大威胁，这给金融机构、特别是保险再保险业的风险管理工作带来了不小挑战。将气候风险要素融入风险管理框架和流程是保险再保险业面临的崭新时代课题，行业也正在不断摸索适应自身发展和风险管理需要的气候风险管理框架、制度和流程。基于前文分析和对相关经验的总结，对未来发展提出如下建议。

（一）完善保险再保险企业气候风险管理框架和流程，建立有效的气候风险管理考评体系

建议保险再保险公司从战略高度推进气候风险管理体系建设，将气候风险嵌入公司治理架构和流程。搭建气候风险管理架构，明确职责分工。将气候风险嵌入公司风险管理三道防线当中，即前端业务部门承担气候风险的首要责任（第一道防线），风险管理部门统筹协调本公司气候风险管理活动（第二道防线），内部审计部门负责检查监督自身气候风险管理贯彻情况（第三道防线），公司董事会承担气

候风险的最终责任。另外，建议探索将公司管理层薪酬与气候风险管理工作挂钩，完善激励约束措施，建立有效的气候风险管理考评体系。

（二）将气候风险要素融入保险再保险企业风险管理体系，丰富气候风险管理工具

建议保险再保险公司将气候风险要素融入自身风险管理全流程中，包括气候风险识别、风险评估、风险承担战略以及制定风险减缓措施。一是对气候相关风险进行识别。对可能导致财务损失的气候因素进行战略评估，如极端天气、海平面上升、碳定价提升等，可以实行“风险清单”制；衡量对上述风险的敞口规模（风险评估），用于风险定价以及风险对冲参考。二是制定气候风险承担战略。如确定风险偏好，在战略层面评估风险应对的各类选择。三是采取减缓气候风险冲击的举措。例如，可以逐渐减少对碳密集行业企业的投资比重，避免可能面临的碳锁定和资产搁浅风险；通过积极参与公司治理，要求被投资企业按照国际框架披露气候风险相关信息，提供气候相关风险管理产品，在降低自身气候变化相关风险影响的同时，引导经济社会向低碳转型发展。

（三）积极对接符合国际标准的气候风险信息披露制度，释放气候风险管理的增量价值

在气候相关风险管理实践中，发布报告是最为普遍的信息披露方式。香港特区政府承诺在2025年或之前强制实施符合ISSB要求的披露规定，港交所也正在积极修改上市规则，要求上市企业按照ISSB标准，从管治、策略、风险管理、指标及目标四个维度披露气候信息，

经修订的港交所《上市规则》及附录27于2024年1月1日生效。2022年，我国上市公司中34%的企业发布了独立ESG报告，银行、非银金融等行业ESG相关报告发布率超过80%。建议我国保险再保险企业积极对接符合国际标准的气候风险信息披露制度（如积极参与ISSB披露框架），在年度社会责任报告中开辟专门板块披露气候风险相关信息。另外，相关信息沟通和披露可以采取媒体宣传、互动平台等多种方式，形成立体化的气候风险信息沟通与披露网络，展示企业气候风险管理的负责任形象，传递气候风险管理工作成效，释放气候风险管理的增量价值。

专题五

保险业应对气候变化背景下巨灾风险上升的挑战

近年来全球自然灾害频发，洪水、干旱、台风、野火等事件形势复杂，极端天气气候事件的程度之强、频次之高十分罕见，除短期的直接气象因素之外，有大量证据表明极端事件的发生与长期的气候变化（主要为变暖）关系密切。气候变暖加剧了地球气候系统的不稳定性，大气环流的持续异常通过海洋—大气、陆地—大气之间的相互作用又进一步影响局地气候，使得极端天气气候事件呈现出频发、广发、强发和并发的趋势。

同时，随着经济的快速发展，全球主要国家的城市化率也在不断提升，资本及劳动力不断向大城市圈聚集，人口及社会经济在面对自然灾害时，风险暴露概率大大增加，自然灾害尤其是极端天气和气候事件造成的复合型灾害损失和影响日益增加。中国作为全球气候变化的敏感区和影响显著区之一，气候变化引起的巨灾风险对经济发展和人民生命财产安全构成了严峻的威胁。近十年，我国各地在政府的主导下与商业市场相结合，陆续尝试建立了不同形式的巨灾保险制度以防范、分摊和转移风险。但是，当前巨灾保险市场仍不健全，制度设计也亟待完善，积极探索建立符合中国国情的巨灾保险制度以防范和应对各类巨灾风险刻不容缓。

一、引言

气候变化是指在经过一段长时间的观察，在自然气候变化之外由人类活动直接或间接地改变全球大气组成所导致的气候改变[①]。近几十年，随着超级计算机算力的进步、气象等卫星和地面观测技术的完善，以及地球系统领域综合科学研究的深入，关于气候是否发生变化的争议正逐步减少并逐渐形成共识。2022年，政府间气候变化专门委员会（IPCC）正式发布了第六次评估报告（AR6）[②]，报告指出气候变暖趋势仍在持续，目前全球平均温度较工业化前水平（1850—1900年平均值）高1.2摄氏度，尤其是近50年全球变暖正以过去2000年以来前所未有的速度发生。

我国地处东亚季风区，气候类型复杂多样且气候波动性强，与其他国家相比，我国受到全球变暖的影响程度较高。根据《中国气候变化蓝皮书（2021）》，中国正处在20世纪初以来的"最暖时期"。1961—2020年，全球平均气温上升速率为0.15摄氏度/10年，中国地表年平均气温上升速率为0.26摄氏度/10年，明显高于全球同期水平，中国对气候变化的敏感性更高（见图1）。

① 资料来源：《中国极端天气气候事件和灾害风险管理与适应国家评估报告》。

② 资料来源：The Working Group I contribution to the Sixth Assessment Report, Climate Change 2021: The Physical Science Basis was released on 9 August 2021.

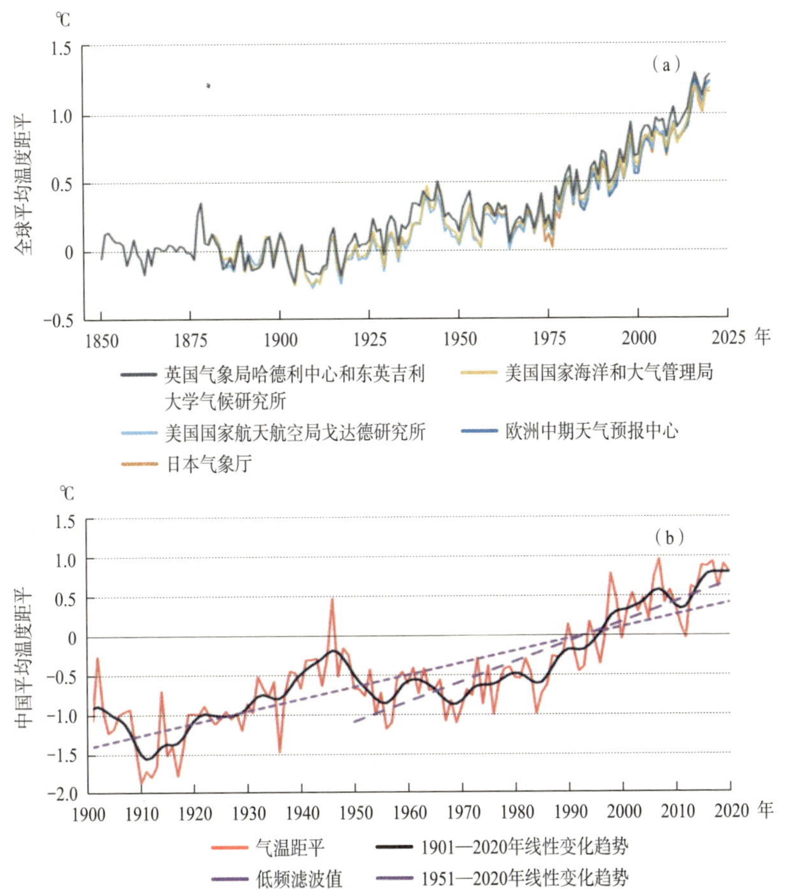

图1　全球及中国年平均气温距平的变化趋势（相对1981—2010年的平均值）

（资料来源：《中国气候变化蓝皮书（2021）》）

气候变化已经在全球和区域产生了很多影响，其中最引人注意的是天气气候灾害，这一种类是频次最多、影响最广泛、总体损失最严重的自然灾害。

二、气候变化引起巨灾发生的风险增加

气候变化在全球不同的地区有多种组合性变化，而这些变化都将随着进一步升温而增加，大大加剧各地区的气候风险，进而造成极大的经济损失。瑞再研究院对灾害损失的统计显示，2020年自然灾害造成的全球经济损失共计2 700亿美元，自然灾害造成的保险损失为1 110亿美元，主要的经济和保险损失来自台风、洪涝以及强对流风暴。通过对灾害流行病研究中心（ORED）的自然灾害数据（EM-DAT）进行分析，显示1970—2020年的50年间，由于气候变化的影响，全球灾害发生的次数增加了近5倍，灾害损失增加了7倍多（见图2）。

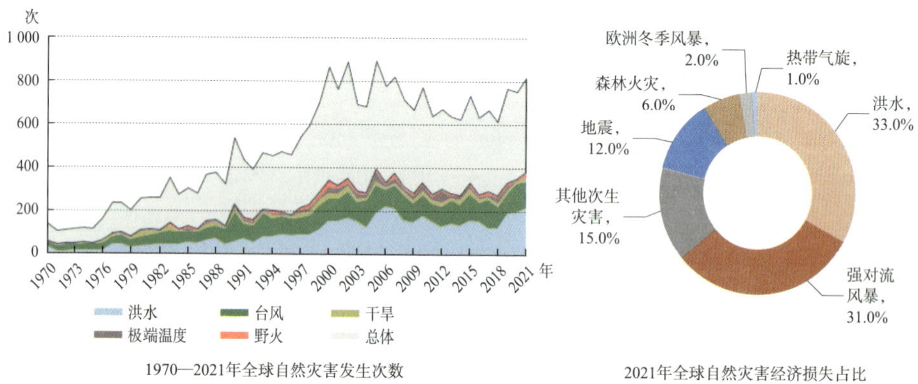

图2　1970—2021年全球气候相关灾害发生次数及2021年全球自然灾害经济损失占比

（资料来源：EM-DAT）

中国位于北半球中纬度环球自然灾害带与环太平洋灾害带交汇位置，自然灾害发生广泛、灾种多样、灾情严重，是世界上自然灾害最严重的国家之一。在不稳定季风的大气环流控制下，季风到来的早晚和强弱、太平洋和东亚大陆间强烈的海陆相互作用、复杂的三级阶梯地形条件，导致我国极易发生台风、旱涝、极端温度等水文气象和气候相关的灾害。

《中国气候变化蓝皮书（2021）》显示，1960年至今，观测到的极端天气气候事件的发生频率以及气候风险都有显著增加（见图3）。极端高温事件明显增多，区域性干旱事件上升，极端强降水平均每10年增长3.8%，这导致了更高的气候风险。

具体来说，气候变化背景下我国季风降水的变化季节性明显，区域差异大，影响范围广（高信度）：在高纬度地区，降水可能会增加，带来更强的暴雨和洪水；北方和西南地区预估的降水量可能会减少，部分地区甚至可能发生更严重的干旱；对于城市来说，由于城市“热岛”“雨岛”效应的存在，气候变化的影响会被放大，造成更极端的高温热浪、更极端的暴雨洪水等；而对于东南沿海地区，登陆的台风强度可能增大。

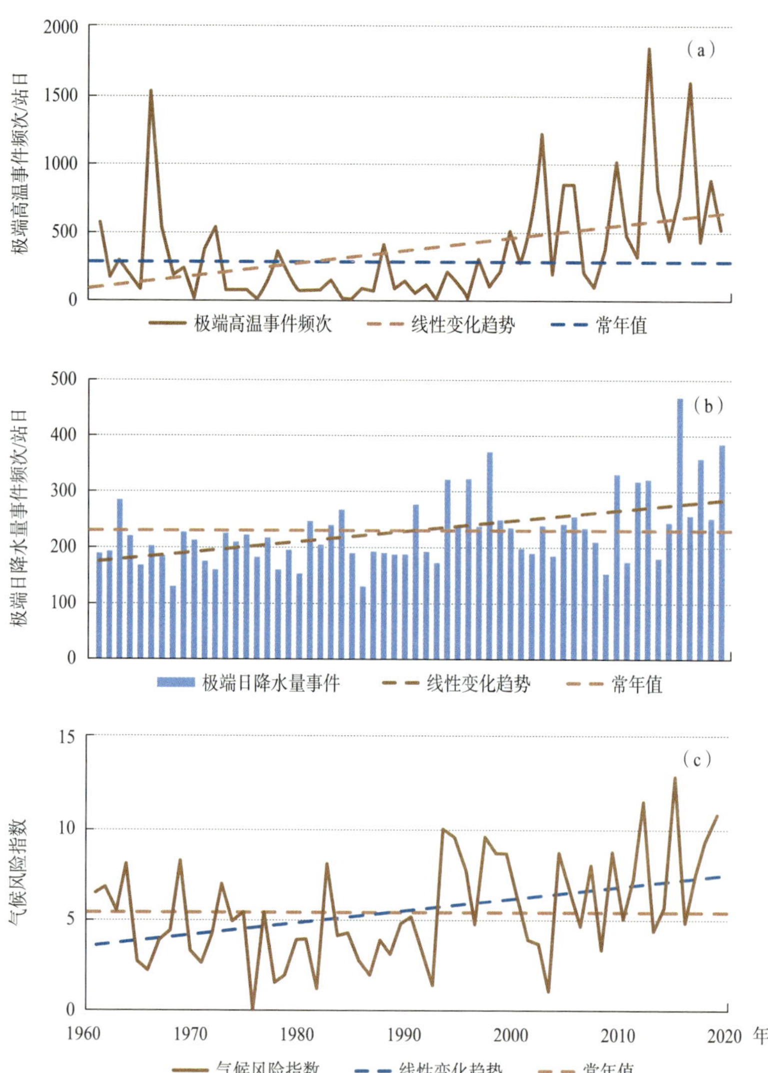

图3　1960年以来我国极端天气和气候风险的上升趋势

（资料来源：《中国气候变化蓝皮书（2021）》）

三、城镇化及经济发展导致巨灾风险暴露增加

除了上述气候变化这一自然驱动因子导致的灾害增加，近二十年我国的城镇化率也在快速提升，内陆省份的人口大量向东南沿海及主要的大城市群迁移，城镇化配套建设了大量的基础设施和公共设施，引起了陆地表面物理性质的剧烈改变，导致了陆地和大气间的相互作用加强，城市群所处区域的气候风险进一步增大，对气候灾害的发生风险有叠加和放大效应。

在推进城镇化进程中，沿海及大城市群的人口和国内生产总值增长迅速，人口和经济增长推高了资产价值，产生了经济资产（人员和财产）高度集中的区域，也使得风险暴露增大。同时由于人口高密度化、高流动性以及老龄化，加之社会财富的快速积累和防灾减灾基础仍较薄弱，导致各类气候灾害承灾体的脆弱性增大，这也是我国灾害损失持续上升的主要社会经济驱动因素。

四、巨灾风险应对及风险分担

气候变化和社会经济变化导致的自然巨灾损失上升，给我国政府社会治理、人民的生命财产安全和防灾减灾带来了极大的挑战。

面对灾害风险，我国政府实施了诸多防灾减灾措施，实行了相关的生态环境保护政策，完善了防灾防损的法律法规，很多地方政府也将防灾防损纳入地方重大建设项目。防灾工程的建设有利于提升自然灾害的防御能力，降低灾害的损失程度。虽然我国的灾害管理已经取

得了一定的成效，但目前还不能完全降低其整体的脆弱性。

我国“十四五”规划纲要明确提出“发展巨灾保险”，确立巨灾保险在国家防灾减灾体系建设中的重要功能。面对灾害风险时，保险业正在发挥越来越重要的救助和补偿功能，保险赔付占损失的比重从2007年不到5%提升至目前已超过8%。从国内外的巨灾保险实践来看，巨灾保险在应对气候变化、减轻灾害风险等方面均可发挥积极的作用。

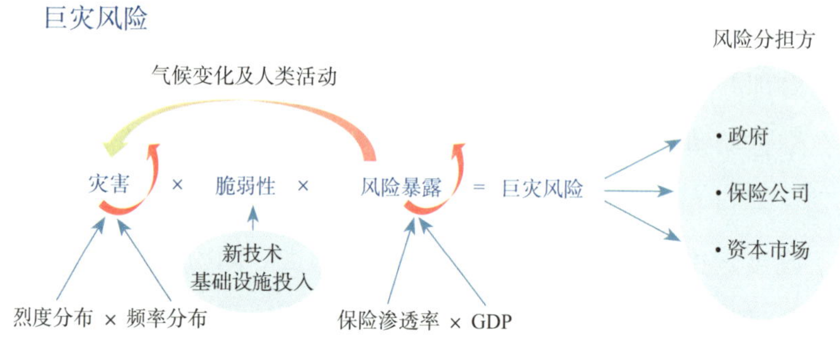

图4　气候变化导致巨灾风险上升及风险的主要分担方构成

近年来，中国保险市场从高速增长步入高质量发展阶段，精耕细作式的差异化发展越来越重要。而直保公司财产险保费费率呈下降趋势，这给保险公司和再保公司的经营和风险管理都带来挑战。因此，市场主体应该意识到，一味降低保费费率的做法将不可持续，财险公司需要调整经营思路，回归可持续增长和获得稳定承保利润的模式上来。

自然灾害定价模型是再保险公司对巨灾损失进行定价的重要工具，也是再保险公司巨灾风险量化管理的核心。目前，我国学术界和保险公司在这方面的研究已经有了初步基础，但仍存在很多不足亟须进一步提高。低频高损是巨灾风险的特性。能否科学准确地对巨灾风险进行定价和管理，是巨灾保险持续发展的关键。但目前对巨灾的定价还存在一定的困难和不足，主要由于对自然灾害建模的困难大，灾害发生的物理过程十分复杂，影响因素及不确定因子较多，且很难直接与保险经济损失建立物理联系。大部分保险公司对自然灾害的发展和未来的气候变化风险认识不足、历史风险累积数据不清晰；巨灾保险的渗透率不高、保险损失数据不充分也对巨灾风险建模有一定的阻碍。因此，提高对气候相关巨灾风险的认知、建立合理的可信度高的巨灾模型，进而科学准确地对巨灾风险进行定价和管理是亟须解决的问题。

五、总结和思考

全球及区域气候变化对我们的社会经济系统提出了挑战，尤其是对保险行业的影响日益显著。我国气候类型复杂多样，气候波动性强，未来可能受到气候变化的影响更高，这意味着更多的自然灾害可能会在中国发生。在这样的背景下，巨灾保险的发展显得尤为重要。

（一）直保公司的角色与策略

直保公司作为保险业务的前线，承担着直接为客户提供风险保障的重要职责。在气候变化加剧巨灾风险的背景下，直保公司面临的挑战尤为严峻。为了有效应对这些挑战，直保公司必须采取一系列综合性措施，以增强自身的风险资本和偿付能力，提高资本效率，并创新巨灾保险产品与定价策略。

在增强风险资本和偿付能力方面，直保公司需要进行资本规划和资本管理的全面审视。这包括对现有资本结构的评估，确定是否需要增加额外的资本以应对潜在的巨灾损失。同时，公司可以通过优化资产负债管理，提高资本的使用效率，确保在巨灾发生时迅速动员足够的资金来满足赔付需求。此外，直保公司还可以通过再保险安排，将部分风险转移给再保市场，从而降低自身的风险暴露。

在产品设计和定价策略上，直保公司需要深入理解气候变化对不同地区和行业的影响，以便开发出更加精准和适应性强的保险产品。例如，公司可以与气候风险研究机构合作，利用先进的气候模型来预测未来可能发生的极端天气事件，从而为产品设计提供科学依据。同时，直保公司可以开发包含气候风险缓解措施的保险方案，如提供防灾减灾咨询、技术支持和财务援助，帮助客户提高对气候变化的适应能力。

直保公司还可以探索引入基于气候模型的动态定价机制。这种定价机制可以根据气候变化的趋势和实时数据，动态调整保险费率。例如，对于位于高风险区域的客户，公司可以在台风季/汛期提高保费，而在风险较低的季节适当降低保费。这种灵活的定价策略不仅可以更好地反映实际风险，还可以激励客户采取风险缓解措施，从而降低整体的保险赔付成本。

直保公司还需要加强对气候变化和巨灾风险的宣传教育。通过提高客户和公众对气候变化影响的认识，提高保险产品的接受度，并鼓励采取更加积极的防灾减灾措施。同时，公司还可以与政府、非政府组织和其他利益相关方合作，共同推动气候变化适应和减缓措施的实施。

综上所述，直保公司在面对气候变化带来的巨灾风险时，需要采取一系列综合性措施，包括增强风险资本和偿付能力、提高资本效率、创新产品设计与定价策略，以及加强宣传教育。通过这些措施，直保公司不仅能够提高自身的风险管理能力，还能够为客户提供更好的保障，同时为社会的可持续发展作出贡献。

（二）再保公司的风险管理与创新

再保行业在保险市场中发挥着至关重要的作用，尤其是在当前气候变化加剧巨灾风险的背景下。再保公司通过分散和转移直保公司的风险，帮助整个保险行业增强对巨灾事件的抵御能力。

再保公司首先要提高对极端天气事件频发带来的财务影响的认识。这不仅意味着再保公司需要增加资本储备以应对可能的巨额赔付，还需要对现有的资本管理策略进行重新评估和调整。再保公司可能需要探索新的资本来源，如发行新股或债券，以确保在面对巨灾时有足够的财务资源。

其次，再保公司需要对传统的风险评估模型进行更新和优化。气候变化带来的不确定性要求再保公司采用更为动态和灵活的风险评估方法。这涉及引入气候科学、地理信息系统（GIS）、大数据分析和人工智能等技术，以提高对巨灾风险的预测和评估能力。通过这些技术，再保公司可以更准确地模拟和评估气候变化对不同地区和行业的潜在影响，从而为风险管理和产品设计提供科学依据。

再保公司在策略制定和产品设计中也必须考虑长期气候变化的影响。这就意味着再保公司需要对气候变化趋势进行深入研究，并将其纳入产品设计和定价策略中。例如，再保公司可以开发包含气候变化适应措施的保险产品，如提供气候风险咨询、技术支持和财务援助，帮助直保公司和客户提高对气候变化的适应力。

同时，再保公司需要不断创新风险分散机制。与资本市场合作为再保公司提供新的风险分散渠道。通过发行巨灾债券和其他衍生金融产品，再保公司可以将风险转移和分散给更多的市场参与者。这不仅有助于减轻再保公司的直接风险暴露，也有助于为应对巨灾提供更稳定的资金来源。

最后，再保公司在应对气候变化带来的挑战时，还需要加强与政府、科研机构、保险公司和其他利益相关方的合作。通过建立合作网络，再保公司可以共享数据和资源，共同研究气候变化的影响，并开发适应性强的保险产品和风险管理工具。这种多方合作不仅可以提高整个保险行业的风险管理能力，还可以促进社会对气候变化的集体应对。

综上所述，再保行业在应对气候变化带来的巨灾风险时，需要采取一系列综合性措施，包括提高资本充足性和财务稳定性、更新和优化风险评估模型、考虑长期气候变化影响的策略制定和产品设计、创新风险分散机制，以及加强与各方的合作。通过这些措施，再保行业不仅能够提高自身的风险管理能力，还能够为客户提供更好的保障，同时为社会的可持续发展作出贡献。

（三）政府与行业的协同合作

政府与行业的协同合作对于有效管理巨灾风险至关重要。在这一合作框架下，政府、保险公司、再保险公司、科研机构和教育机构等各方需要共同努力，以构建一个全面、高效且适应性强的巨灾风险管理体系。

1. 政府的角色与措施

在立法和政策支持方面，政府可制定和完善与巨灾风险管理相关的法律法规，确保巨灾保险制度的建立和运行有一个清晰的法律框架。这包括对巨灾保险产品的监管、风险评估标准、赔付机制等方面的立法工作。

在财政支持与激励方面，政府可以通过财政补贴、税收减免等措施，鼓励保险公司和再保险公司参与巨灾风险的管理和保险产品的开发。同时，政府可以设立巨灾风险基金，为巨灾赔付提供额外的资金保障。

在公共教育方面，政府可积极开展公共教育活动，提高公众对气候变化和巨灾风险的认识。通过媒体宣传、学校教育、社区活动等多种途径，普及气候变化知识，增强公众的风险防范意识。

此外，政府可建立跨部门的协作机制，协调气象、民政、财政、农业等相关部门的资源和信息，共同应对巨灾风险。

2. 行业内部的合作与创新

加强数据共享与研究合作。保险公司、再保险公司和科研机构可建立数据共享平台，共同收集和分析气候变化和巨灾风险数据。通过合作研究，开发更为精确的风险评估模型和预测工具。

推动产品与服务创新。行业可根据气候变化的影响，开发新的保险产品和服务。例如，推出基于气候风险的个性化保险方案，提供灾害预防和减灾咨询服务，以及开发与气候变化适应相关的保险产品。

拓展教育培训与能力建设。教育机构可与行业合作，开展保险和气候变化相关的教育培训项目，提升从业人员的专业能力和公众的风险管理意识。

探索和应用新技术。行业可积极探索和应用新技术，如物联网、大数据分析、人工智能等，以提高风险评估和管理的效率和准确性。

总的来说，随着气候变化影响日益显著，保险再保险行业可以通过加强资本管理、创新产品服务、提升风险评估技术，以及与政府和科研机构的紧密合作，更有效地应对巨灾风险。同时，政府在立法支持、公共教育和跨部门协作等方面发挥积极作用。只有多方共同努力，才能不断强化社会经济系统的韧性，以适应和抵御气候变化带来的不确定性和潜在风险。未来，我们期待看到一个更加强大、灵活且可持续的保险行业，为经济社会的稳定发展提供坚实保障。

专题六

气候变化风险及巨灾保险发展探讨

近年来，气候异常事件的频率逐渐增加，全球气候风险明显增高，未来可能将更加复杂且难以管理，应对气候变化已成为全球共识。2020年以来，全球经济论坛发布的《国际风险报告》中，极端天气、气候行动失败等环境方面的风险一直位于高风险的位置。2024年我国政府工作报告多次提及对自然灾害的防范，提出要“提升防灾减灾救灾能力”，凸显了政府对应对气候变化的重视。

2024年政府工作报告提出，回顾过去一年，多重困难挑战交织叠加，其中包括我国部分地区遭受洪涝、台风、地震等严重自然灾害。气候异常带来的灾害天气使农业、工业及服务业均遭受巨大损失，我国是世界上极端天气多发的国家，随着全球变暖加剧，高温干旱、洪涝暴雨等自然灾害层出不穷，保险业作为经济“减震器”和社会“稳定器”，在应对气候风险、推动社会低碳转型等方面发挥着独特而重要的作用。

一、当前巨灾风险的特点

（一）短期特点

2023年我国自然灾害呈现以下特点。一是台风灾害强度大，2023年西北太平洋和南海共有17个台风生成，较常年偏少，其中6个登陆我国，虽然数量较少，但登陆我国的台风强度较大，其中第5号台风“杜苏芮”于7月28日以强台风级强度登陆，是1949年以来登陆福建第二强的台风，福建5个国家气象观测站日降水量突破历史极值，造成直接经济损失149.5亿元，受其影响，北京、天津、河北、山西、山东、河南等省份大范围地区遭遇了极端强降雨天气，累计雨量远超2012年“7·21”特大暴雨，其后续影响东北地区时，30个气象站中有37站次突破了历史单日降雨量极值，五常单日最大降雨量达145.3毫米，大大超过了单日降雨量49.9毫米的历史最高纪录。第11号台风“海葵”于9月5日先后登陆福建和广东沿海，多省共有6站降水量突破历史极值，造成直接经济损失166.6亿元。气温方面，中国气象局发布的《中国气候公报（2023年）》显示，2023年全国平均气温10.71摄氏度，较常年偏高0.82摄氏度，为1951年以来历史最高。公报显示，2023年全国平均高温日数较常年偏多4.4天，极端高温事件为历史第四多，127个国家站日最高气温突破或持平历史纪录。二是灾害影响范围广，台风“杜苏芮”登陆后，海河流域性特大洪水、松辽流域严重暴雨洪涝等重大灾害相继发生。首先，受其台风残余环流影响，7月底至8月初，京津冀等地区遭受极端强降雨，引发严重暴雨洪涝、滑坡、泥石流等灾害，造成直接经济损失1 657.9亿元，接下来，台风残留云系继续北上，叠加西风槽影响，东北地区多地出现强降雨，引发洪涝灾害，造成黑龙江、吉林受灾，直接经济损失215.2亿元。三是地震灾害造成重大损失，12月18日甘肃临夏积石山县发生了6.2级地震，造成甘肃、青海两省151人死亡，983人受伤，倒塌房屋7万间，直接经济损失146.12亿元。

不仅我国巨灾损失严重，从世界范围来看，2023年也已被认为是极端天气事件多发的一年。欧盟气候监测机构哥白尼气候变化服务中心（C3S）表示，2023年可能是人类历史上最热的一年。北半球夏季气温创下新高，6月、7月和8月的全球平均气温为16.77摄氏度，超过了2019年16.48摄氏度的纪录。多国发生持续蔓延的野火，高温还导致了干旱、病虫害高发等。

（二）中期特点

中期来看，极地及高海拔的山峰上，已经显现出令人担忧的气候异常现象。据观测，2023年8月，南极海冰范围处于历史最低水平，世界气象组织称，这是“自20世纪70年代末开始卫星观测以来，迄今记录的8月最低水平”。另一方面，北极海冰范围比平均水平低10%，但仍远高于2012年8月创下的最低纪录。根据相关研究，目前南极海冰面积较1979—2022年的平均值减少了240万平方千米。海冰面积减少不仅意味着生态系统受到直接影响，还意味着南极洲反射阳光的能力减弱，而当白色冰面被深色海面取代时，地球就会吸收阳光中的热量。高海拔地区也在逐渐发生变化。我国青藏高原被誉为“亚洲水塔”，其平均海拔4 000米以上，含有10万平方千米冰川，亚洲13条大江大河皆发源于此，包括我国的长江、黄河。冰川素有“天然固态水库”之称，青藏高原冰川储量约占亚洲冰储量的29.2%，我国冰储量的81.6%，是地球上除南北极外冰储量最大的地方，被誉为“地球第三极”，它就像一座天然的高塔，将冰雪融水源源不断地向外输送。2019年，《自然》刊出一项关于全球水塔的研究成果，在全球78个水塔单元中，“亚洲水塔”（AWT）占16个，可见其地位异常重要，但也最脆弱。有研究显示，近年来青藏高原的很多冰川末端后退明显，冰量急剧减少。冰川融化带来的后果较为严峻，短期内水会增加，在第二次青藏高原科考期间就发现，近50年间，青藏高原湖泊总面积增长了20%，水量增加了约170立方千米；河流径流量由原来的5 500亿立方米增加至6 500亿立方米。而长期来看，随着冰川的持续减少，“亚洲水塔”的供水能力正在减弱，以季节性冰川融水补给为主的河流能够提供的淡水量会越来越少。

（三）长期特点

长期来看，美国国家海洋和大气管理局于2023年9月6日发表的年度气候报告显示，2022年全球温室气体浓度达到有记录以来的最高水平，全球变暖趋势加剧。欧洲环境署于2024年3月11日发布《欧洲气候风险》报告，确认并评估欧洲在生态系统、食品安全、民众健康、基础设施以及经济和金融稳定五大领域面临的36项主要气候变化风险，认为其中许多风险已经达到临界水平，政府如不立即行动，这些风险可能演化成灾难。

二、巨灾风险对保险业的挑战

在气候变化背景下，巨灾风险对保险市场产生严重影响，这种影响涉及从原保险、再保险到保险连接证券的全流程，巨灾风险的急剧增加给这些层面均带来了挑战。

首先，从致灾因子角度看，保险行业面临严重灾难损失的风险迅速增加。随着全球气温和海平面上升，严重灾难事件的频率和严重性都在增加，如穆迪公司的一项研究发现，1980—2018年全球70%以上的野火保险损失都是发生在2016—2018年。严重灾难事件所带来的风险不断变化，对行业准确评估再保险和保险连接证券交易的下行风险敞口的能力形成挑战，这些业务领域的回报可能会出现越来越大的波动。

其次，从保险标的角度看，在气候变化的背景下，很多公司从传统能源向新能源转变，与之对应，劳合社已宣布计划在2030年前停止向某些类型的化石燃料企业销售保险的计划，其他一些公司也做出了与劳合社相同的承诺，预计会有越来越多的公司效仿，这也促进了企业转型。与化石燃料开采和运输相比，虽然绿色能源通常更安全，保险损失事件更少，但是在某些方面，绿色能源也存在特别的风险，如向低碳经济转型所产生的风险，这些风险可能会影响资产价值或经营成本。在这方面，目前还没有太多的记录，由于缺乏相关数据，保险公司并未全面了解未来可能承担的所有风险。可再生能源既是能源的未来，也是保险的未来，保险公司需要更有效地理解保单、为保单建模和定价。

再次，在风险评估方面，气候异常对风险评估模型中的相关性参数设定也形成挑战。高温、干旱以及暴雨洪水，这些事件可能同时发生，也可能是连锁反应，随着每个事件的极端损失增加，事件之间的相关性也将增大，形成复合极端事件，这些新现象使得需要对原有的相关性系数进行调整。

最后，对于保险的购买者来说，他们不仅面临由于巨灾风险性质的变化导致保险公司的费率增加，而且随着索赔纠纷愈加频繁，他们还面临与此相关的费用增加。灾难事件造成的损失前所未有，行业参与者越来越多地采用法律手段来处理纠纷，这会放大波动性。这些不断变化的风险、波动性增加和再保险需求增加将导致再保险的买方成本增加。

在不断变化的环境中，需要优化完善巨灾保险保障方案，其中风险评估的准确性是当前全行业所面临的重要课题。管理灾难事件造成的损失（自然和法律损失）需要行业参与者有效评估其风险。一方面，这需要对损失风险定价的基本假设和策略进行研究。例如，虽然再保险人先前假设可以通过全球多样化分散转移灾难风险，但气候变化挑战了这一观点，因为更频繁的灾难事件在短时间内同时影响到许多地理区域。研究表明，近年来巨灾模型公司对全行业损失预测的准确性有所下降，因此可能需要采取更保守的定价策略，以避免损失暴露超出再保险人或保险连接证券参与者的预期接受水平。

对于再保险市场来说，这些挑战并非全新的，之前的一些年份中，再保险行业在经历过巨灾索赔之后，市场通过大幅提高再保险价格做出了反应，这反映了行业对损失敞口的假设发生了变化。此外，在经历了之前的巨灾损失后，再保险的需求也趋于增加，这些经历为再保险购买者提供了一个明确的信号，即随着气候变化的持续，超出现有模型和假设范围的灾难损失不断增加，鉴于气候变化带来的新风险，再保险分出人对再保险承保范围的偏好会增加，购买者可以预期，再保险的承保将面临巨大的价格上涨压力。此外，气候变化导致频繁、严重和不可预测的灾难事件的风险增加，保险连接证券的交易各方以及巨灾再保险的业务之间就灾难损失可能引发的大量索赔发生争议的风险也随之增加，这增加了在变化的环境中面对高成本诉讼的风险。

世界各地的保险公司和再保险公司都在努力解决涉及气候异常以及能源转型对其业务的影响，研究全球气候变化对于自然灾害发生、生物多样性、经济增长的影响，前瞻性地进行风险模型预测及解决方案设计。同时，保险业在研究气候变化相关风险时，也需要提升对于与气候行动有关的全球倡议的关注度，如原则签署、规范披露、目标设定以及投融资标准等。

三、基于风险成本最小原则探索巨灾风险减量模式

风险成本最小原则是指在风险管理中，应对风险的目标不是风险最小化，而是风险成本最小化。风险成本包括期望损失成本、控制型成本、融资型成本以及残余不确定型成本，风险成本最小化仅针对期望损失成本而言，显然并未考虑我们面对风险时的全部支出。从应对风险的全部成本角度考虑，从灾害风险保险的中端，即灾害保险的承保与理赔来看，保险业需要从风险减量角度寻求突破。

首先，气候异常对保险定价的基础——风险评估形成挑战。极端气候事件的不确定性和复杂性可能使风险评估变得更加困难，保险公司需要不断改进其模型和分析来更准确地估计风险，这可能需要更多的投资和资源。如果能够通过与风险减量相关的技术手段或参数化保险等创新产品降低一部分承保风险，可以在一定程度上降低潜在的风险评估模型风险。

其次，气候异常会带来更高的索赔成本。极端天气事件，如台风、洪水、野火和暴雨可能导致更多的索赔。这些事件通常会造成巨大的损失，包括房屋、商业和车辆的损害，以及营业中断等收入损失，在这一过程中保险公司需要支付更多的赔偿。这可能导致保险公

司的索赔成本上升，从而影响其盈利能力。美国《华盛顿邮报》网站2023年9月3日报道，在一连串极端天气事件过后，美国越来越多的大型保险公司不再提供易受灾害影响地区房产所有者最需要的承保服务。各大保险公司称，将把飓风、大风和冰雹引起的损失从面向沿海和野火高发区域房产的保单中剔除。这意味着这些区域的个人和家庭不仅可能失去至关重要的保险保护，而且随着全球气候变化，他们暴露于自然灾害的风险还会增加。在这样的趋势下，风险转移需求和供给的矛盾逐渐凸显。

从灾害风险保险的后端，即再保险等分散承保风险的渠道来看，保险业也需要积极探索风险减量模式。

首先，再保险分入人面临资本挑战。作为承接保险公司超额风险分散的再保险公司，也会受到极端天气事件的影响。同时，随着气候变化导致巨灾损失不断上升，与之相关的保险需求也在不断增长。根据瑞士再保险公司数据，到2040年，气候变化将使风险资产池扩大33%~41%，随着灾难损失激增，全球新增财产保费将达到1 490亿~1 830亿美元，届时财险公司尤其是再保险公司的潜在市场将扩大两倍不止。而潜在的经济增长和城镇化率提速，也将进一步推动保险需求增长。再保险市场资金供应规模需与庞大的需求相匹配，才可满足保险公司可能会逐渐增加的分出需求。

其次，保险连接证券市场扩容受阻。保险连接证券是保险公司向资本市场转移巨灾风险的重要渠道，包括巨灾债券、行业损失担保等。对于资本市场的投资者来说，由于传统的多元化策略在压力时期并不总是奏效，作为一种低相关性的资产类别，保险连接证券兼顾了多元化和稳定回报，具有一定吸引力。其中，巨灾债券市场规模在过去五年中持续增长，一直是保险连接证券市场的亮点之一。然而，这一资产类别的更高回报是否能够吸引更多资本还有待进一步观察，这主要是因为巨灾风险对于金融行业人士来说略显陌生，一些投资者可能会关注其他更熟悉的资产类别，这些资产类别也能提供较高的预期回报，且流动性更大，波动性可能更小。

基于上述分析，在前端、中端和后端的压力都增大的情况下，保险公司应积极探索模式创新，增强提供相关风险保障的能力，提高防灾减灾救灾能力，助力经济社会行稳致远。

一方面，风险减量本就是保险的应有之义。虽然这一称谓近来才在行业中广为讨论，但其具体内容对于保险来说既不陌生，也不是额外的工作，它本来就是保险对风险进行分散的机制中的重要组成部分。围绕核心的承保理赔环节，保险风险评估等都是必不可少的工作，其中也包括损失控制及安全激励，即风险减量。事实上，保险业在这一领域有很多经验，例如，承保了烟叶保险的公司和当地气象部门合作，通过人工影响天气降低冰雹灾害发生概率；又如，保险公司通过总结历史索赔数据，为社会提供风险知识培训，并向客户提出应对气候变化与极端天气灾害的防灾减损建议。类似工作看似进行了额外的支出，但却在更大额度上降低了理赔金额，由损失控制而进行的风险减量工作是服务于保险公司的，进而有助于降低价格，惠及众多投保人。风险减量有助于保险在价格上更具有可行性，以发挥经济“减震器”和社会“稳定器”的作用。

另一方面，风险减量是保险业安全激励功能的结果体现。风险减量工作并不是仅仅指控制型的技术措施，也包括费率调节和产品创新等更为专业的措施，也就是说，有一部分风险减量行动完全可以通过现有的保险业务环节来完成，而无须设立单独的环节，这些也正是保险业独特的影响投保人风险行为的途径。例如，早在几十年前，美国国家洪水保险计划就通过对不同风险区实施不同的承保条件和费率，并设置联邦灾害补偿获得条件，使得部分投保人搬离洪水高风险区，从而降低了社会所面临的洪水风险。又如，近年来一些欧洲保险公司通过提供低费率等优惠，鼓励客户在房屋中采用防洪门窗、建立天气警报系统等。再如，通过产品创新，天气指数保险极大降低了投保人的道德风险，其防灾减灾救灾的意识得到激励，这些都是保险业以其独特的行业经营机制促进安全的体现，应将这一功能发挥出来，在巨灾风险形势严峻的背景下，运用这些安全激励手段，调动和引导众多风险承担者的积极性，撬动更多的降低风险的力量。

四、基于综合风险管理视角推进巨灾保险制度安排

除了发展绿色经济、发挥各类风险管理措施的功能、减轻气候异常所造成的灾害损失之外，作为独特的融资型措施，保险无疑是重要的应对巨额损失冲击的“缓冲器”。

巨灾保险制度的推进，有赖于对综合风险管理属性的全面认识。理论上来说，能够称之为巨灾的巨额灾害损失，并不能完全满足理想可保风险的条件，因此，如果只是强调巨灾保险的灾后经济补偿作用，则难以协调供给和需求，增加巨灾保险推进的难度。综合风险管理思维的具体体现包括灾害全过程的统筹、政府与市场的统筹、保险与科技的统筹等多个方面。

（一）灾前、灾中与灾后的全过程统筹

巨灾保险制度应关注灾前、灾中和灾后的全过程。风险管理是一个系统工程，尤其对于巨灾风险来说，风险是单向的，即只可能造成

损失，不会有主体从中获益，从全社会的角度，长期来看，无论是否有保险制度，巨灾风险损失最终将由全社会承担，因此，损失融资措施和损失控制措施应紧密结合，损失控制措施包括灾前的预防和备灾，灾中的抗灾和灾后的救灾，每个环节都可在风险成本更低的条件下进行优化选择，在费率杠杆的调节机制下，保险制度可以更好地激励损失控制措施的应用。

（二）政府与市场的统筹

巨灾保险制度的推进有赖于政府和市场的有机协调。巨灾保险具有准公共产品属性，无政府支持难以推广和持续。纵观国际上较为典型的巨灾保险制度，很多都具有政府支持要素。如1996年成立的美国加州地震保险局便是政府特许经营并参与管理，且享受免税待遇；英国政府于20世纪60年代初推出洪水保险，政府主要责任是通过兴建洪水防御设施等措施不断加大防洪投入力度以尽可能降低洪水风险；隶属于土耳其财政部的土耳其国家巨灾保险运行平台——土耳其巨灾保险共同体，负责建立国家巨灾风险模型，制定地震保险精算费率体系，设计保险基金规模和风险转移机制等，开展防灾减灾研究并推动抗震标准的普及。普及抗震标准、提高承灾体的设防水平、推动巨灾模型的建立，都是成功的巨灾保险制度中政府发挥的作用，也是巨灾保险制度得以推广发展的重要前提。

政府与市场的统筹合作是近年来理论和实践领域的探索热点，政府作为巨灾保障的提供者还是保险公司作为巨灾保障的提供者，抑或是二者一定程度的合作，对应着政府和市场在巨灾保险制度运行中承担的不同责任，以及效率和公平之间的权衡。

政府与市场在应对灾害风险方面各有优势。对于政府来说，第一，降低风险是政府最重要的任务之一，它可以统筹安排灾前预防、灾中救助和灾后重建的全流程，这有助于减少损失。对于灾害风险来说，能够在成本合理的前提下降低损失，是风险管理的目标，即降低风险的成本，而不能只是关注灾后融资这一个环节。第二，风险的降低能增强保险的可用性和可负担性，这种间接效果使得保险能够触及更多风险承担主体，尤其对于中低收入群体，可以有效缩小他们的保障缺口，增强韧性，形成良性循环。第三，政府主导的保险计划，例如，针对特定行业和风险的强制性保险，以及公共保险等措施，更易于推行。对于市场来说，通过市场化的模式和产品，可以将未来的不确定性转化为一定程度的确定性。

二者的统筹协调有助于将各自优势进行整合，合作的模式可以在不同区域和不同时段进行差异化的调整，例如，建立一个有政府担保的（再）保险池，可以规划好不同层次。又如，定制的小额保险，可以在灾难后提供急需的救济。基于参数的产品和解决方案也在不断发展，其重点是降低基差风险。参数化产品可以在发生严重事件后立即提供救济，并且可以在任何层面（从宏观到微观）开发和使用，如瑞士再保险公司与墨西哥政府合作，在地震灾难发生后，墨西哥政府在两周内就收到保险公司提供的2.9亿美元赔付用于救灾。又如，为了保护州和地区的资产，作为政府建立抵御自然灾害战略的一部分，印度尼西亚于2018年启动了灾害风险融资和保险战略，这相当于一个法律框架，为国有资产提供保险。该战略旨在获得及时、有针对性、可持续和透明的灾害风险筹资计划。随后开始的国家保险试点项目就从建筑物的灾害保险计划开始，由50家直保公司和6家再保险公司组成的联合体提供了10万余亿印尼盾的保障。

（三）保险与科技的统筹

巨灾风险非理想可保的原因之一就是其厚尾特点，这对风险分散形成了挑战。巨灾“低频高损”的特性使其缺乏有效的长时间观测数据来支持基于结果的风险评估及费率厘定，而必须借助科学与工程技术，构建巨灾模型，从基于过程的角度来评估风险。由于很多巨灾损失具有大面积性，使得大数法则和中心极限定理前提难以满足，因此，对待巨灾风险业务，不能局限于传统尺度的风险个体，而应通过产品创新或制度创新，在非传统的层面加强风险分散。在地域上，可鼓励更大范围的分散，如果能实现风险的跨区域分散，精算假设的成立将更有保证，保险公司也会有更强的偿付能力。在产品方面，可以通过综合性风险保障来实现风险分散，例如，宁波的巨灾保险，就是包括自然灾害保险、突发公共安全事件（事故）保险、突发公共卫生事件保险和见义勇为保险等在内的公共巨灾保险，具有一定创新性。

五、发展展望

推动巨灾保险体系建设需要建立完善的风险分散机制，尽可能将巨灾风险在时间和空间上分散。在空间上分散风险，需要大量风险承担者的参与。在这方面，加勒比巨灾风险保险基金的经验值得借鉴。加勒比巨灾风险保险基金因其在2010年初对海地地震的巨额理赔引起关注，它是世界上第一个多国参与的国际巨灾共保体，成员国之间的风险汇聚使得整体上的期望损失趋于稳定。我国幅员辽阔，在灾害高风险区内分布有众多企业，如果能够通过一定的机制增加参与企业的数量，则可进行有效的风险汇聚。例如，洪水保险应尽可能涵盖七大江河中下游的洪水高风险区，虽然对某一区域来说，洪水发生时可能有大面积的损失，但对于众多洪水高风险区内的单位来说，在短时期内同时发生巨灾损失的概率是较低的。如果巨灾保险中包含了多个风险，如将洪水风险、地震风险和台风风险综合在一起，其风险分散的效果将更加明显。在时间上分散风险，需要巨灾保险基金、再保险、风险证券化以及国家政策的支持，以获得更多的赔付能力以及财务可持续能力。

再保险的发展与创新是巨灾保险体系的重要基石。据统计，在2024年6月的国际再保险市场续保期间，与财产保障相关的巨灾保险费率出现了一些放缓趋势，平均风险调整后的线上费率下降了5%[①]。这主要是因为资本复苏和市场容量增加，国际再保险公司在2023年的回报率较高，许多公司的股本回报率超过了20%，目前行业资本已经超过了2021年；与此同时，大量保险连接证券的发行也增加了再保险可以承载风险的容量。虽然7月和8月是热带风暴等灾害的活跃季节，预测也表明，2024年飓风季节可能会非常活跃，在此之前，厄尔尼诺现象的条件减弱，拉尼娜现象在这个季节中发展的可能性为60%，这通常预示着更强的风暴；加之其他一些市场因素仍可能给再保险行业带来挑战，但产能增加还是说明再保险市场为巨灾风险的转移提供了重要支撑。其中，保险连接证券起到积极作用。近年来市场对保险连接证券的关注增加，2024年巨灾债券市场也飞速发展，上半年发行总额就高达126亿美元，这反映了更广泛的市场趋势，即多元化的替代风险转移机制为分保人提供了更多管理其风险敞口的选择。

巨灾风险是公认的非传统风险，需要非传统的解决办法，以及创新发展方式，遵循风险管理逻辑，将损失控制和损失融资有机结合，逐步推进和完善巨灾风险管理机制。

---

① 2024年上半年线上费率仅上涨1.2%。

专题七

网络安全保险解决方案的创新探索

当前，中国已经从工业经济时代迈入数字经济时代，根据《全球数字经济白皮书》(2023年)数据，2022年数字经济规模美国居世界第1位，达到17.2万亿美元，中国居第2位，规模为7.5万亿美元，数字经济已成为中国经济增长的新引擎。数字技术正全面赋能经济社会发展的各个领域，5G通信技术、云计算、区块链、大模型等，为中国经济高质量发展提供重要支持。与此同时，数字经济时代下的网络安全威胁不容忽视。根据IBM发布的《2023年数据泄露成本》数据，2023年全球数据泄露平均成本上升至445万美元，达到历史新高，分别比2022年和2021年增长了2.3%、15.3%。可以说，网络安全风险挑战不断升级，网络安全已成为数字经济高质量发展的生命线。网络安全保险作为转移、防范网络安全风险的金融工具，逐步成为开展网络安全风险管理、降低网络安全事件损失、提升网络安全保障的重要手段。基于网络安全风险特征，探究网络安全保险解决方案，能够更好地为中国经济高质量发展保驾护航。

一、网络安全保险起源与发展现状

网络安全保险是以投保人信息资产安全性为保险标的的保险产品，通常提供第一方损失和第三方责任两类保障。其中，第一方损失是指因网络安全事件直接给投保企业自身造成的损失，主要包括数据资产重置费用、应急处置费用、营业中断损失、法律公关费用等；第三方责任是因网络安全事件对第三方造成的损失或损害，企业可能需要承担的法律责任，主要包括数据泄露责任、网络安全事件责任、产品责任等。网络安全保险是数字经济时代特定风险的新型险种，随着信息技术的发展不断演进。

（一）网络安全保险的经济学分析

面对网络风险，企业通过购买网络安全产品来加以防范。由于网络安全投入存在边际收益递减的特征，当网络安全投入超过最优投入规模后，再增加投入就是不经济的。同时，针对网络安全不存在100%的防护措施，使企业尽管进行了网络安全投入，但仍有一定的概率因网络攻击造成损失。网络安全保险成为企业化解网络安全风险的“最后一块拼图”，其本质上是一种帮助组织减轻因网络攻击或黑客入侵而带来重大损失或后果的保险策略，是为企业提供转移、分散网络“残余风险”的金融工具。通过“网络安全设备+网络安全保险”的组合，可以帮助企业化解网络安全事件带来的风险。从经济学角度看，网络安全保险具有存在的合理性。

（二）全球网络安全保险发展现状

网络安全保险起源于美国，是数字经济发展的产物。1977年AIG推出了世界上首款网络安全保险，保障范围涉及计算机病毒、黑客攻击、网络故障等网络安全风险，也被称为“黑客保险”。在美国，2003年加州颁布了第一部“数据泄露法案”，要求个人信息被泄露时要及时披露和通知用户，使得网络安全的事前保障与防护变得尤为重要，极大推动了网络安全保险的发展；2010年美国有超过50家保险公司提供网络安全保险产品，2012年美国网络安全保险保费收入突破10亿美元，2021年保费规模超过65亿美元，占到全球网络安全保险保费收入的70%。在欧洲，欧盟2018年5月发布了“通用数据保护法”（GDPR），推高了企业网络安全风险的违法成本，带动欧洲企业对网络安全保险需求不断提高。Research And Markets发布的《2022年全球网络安全保险市场报告》显示，2021年网络安全保险市场规模为92.9亿美元，2022年约为119亿美元，预计到2027年将达到292亿美元，年增长率接近20%，体现出巨大的市场需求和发展空间。

网络安全保险发展呈现以下特征：

一是网络安全事件频发使得网络安全保险需求上升。根据Allianz发布的“Risk Barometer 2023”，网络风险是企业最为关注的风险。随着人工智能、云计算的迅速普及，加之国际地缘政治形势日益严峻复杂，网络安全事件发生的频率和烈度都大幅上升，网络安全保险的重要性正在凸显。2017年，默克制药公司遭受NotPetya网络攻击，导致30 000多台笔记本电脑和台式计算机以及7 500台服务器瘫痪，通过诉讼于2022年与保险公司达成和解，将获赔14亿美元。网络安全保险正在成为保障企业网络安全，给予损失补偿的重要金融工具。

二是网络安全行业发展带动了网络安全保险增长。网络攻击、勒索病毒等网络威胁层出不穷，企业对网络安全防护产品的需求持续增长，网络安全行业市场规模逐年攀升。根据IDC（International Data Corporation）披露的信息，2022年全球网络安全规模达到1 955.1亿美元，同比增长15.8%。由于网络安全设备在实际运行中无法提供100%的安全防护，网络安全保险成为安防设备的有效补充。随着网络安全行业的快速发展，网络安全保险业呈现快速发展的势头。从现有的数据看，网络安全保险规模大约是网络安全行业规模的5%~10%。

三是网络安全相关监管制度成为网络安全保险快速发展的催化剂。信息安全保护相关的法律出台，推动了欧美网络安全保险快速发展。企业由于担心可能发生的信息泄露带来的高昂成本，将网络安全保险作为防范经营风险的重要手段，可以说，监管制度的出台间接增加了网络安全保险的购买需求。

（三）中国网络安全保险发展现状

与欧美国家相比，中国的网络安全保险尚处于起步阶段，具有较大的发展空间。2013年，苏黎世财险（中国）推出了国内市场上第一个保障网络安全和隐私保护的保险产品——苏黎世安全与隐私保护综合保险。截至2024年5月，网络安全保险备案条款数量达到258款，有36家财产险公司进行了备案。

一是国家网络安全顶层设计不断完善。我国高度重视网络安全，将网络安全作为建设网络强国的重要保障。近年来，我国针对网络安全进行了一系列立法，做好顶层制度设计，包括“三法一条例”，即《网络安全法》（2016）、《数据安全法》（2021）、《个人信息保护法》（2021）以及《关键信息基础设施安全保护条例》（2021），为做好新时代网络安全和信息化工作、扎实推进网络强国建设，提供了强有力的法律保障。

二是网络安全保险发展获得政策支持。在顶层设计下，工业和信息化部、国家金融监督管理总局加快推动网络安全产业和金融服务融合创新，引导网络安全保险有序健康发展，持续培养网络安全保险新业态。2023年7月两部门联合发布了《关于促进网络安全保险规范健康发展的意见》。为进一步推进网络安全保险落地，2023年12月工业和信息化部出台了《关于组织开展网络保险服务试点工作的通知》，2024年发布《网络安全保险服务方案目录》，全面推进网络安全保险试点落地工作，为网络安全保险高质量发展提供了有力的政策支持。

三是网络安全保险具有较大发展空间。网络安全保险作为新型险种，呈现快速发展态势。2022年我国网络安全保险保费规模约为1.4亿元，较上年翻一番。2023年根据市场各主体的信息，网络安全保险保费规模约为3亿元，保持高速增长。中国信通院预测，到2025年我国网络安全保险规模将达到5亿元左右。我国网络安全行业规模约为2 000亿元，按照国际经验，我国网络安全保险的规模潜力在100亿~200亿元，未来具有较大的发展空间。

二、发展网络安全保险面临的机遇与挑战

随着信息技术发展，近年来网络安全保险作为新型险种市场规模快速增长，未来既蕴含较大发展机遇，也面临需求和供给等多方面的挑战。

（一）网络安全保险供需面临挑战

从需求方面看，部分企业网络安全风险意识还不强，且大型企业和中小型企业网络安全保险需求分化。一方面，目前企业投保网络安全保险意愿还不高。企业普遍更加重视发展，网络风险造成的损失短期内不直接或者不明显，导致企业对网络安全的重要性认知低，保险需求尚未有效激发。2022年慕尼黑再保险全球网络风险和保险调查报告显示，全球网络安全仍存在较大的保险缺口，保险渗透率低于5%，全球83%的受访者表示他们的公司没有得到充分的保护。另一方面，大型公司与中小型公司对网络安全保险需求呈现分化态势。根据《2019年全球网络风险透视调查报告》数据，年收入超过10亿美元的公司中有57%已购买网络安全保险，而收入低于1亿美元的公司中已购买网络安全保险的比例为36%。2022年慕尼黑再保险全球网络风险和保险调查报告显示，缺乏风险转移解决方案的公司比例在中小企业领域最高，接近40%。大型企业网络风险意识更强，意味着对网络安全保险的保障范围、服务质效要求更高；中小型企业出于成本考虑，网络安全预算投入较低，保险需求也较低。

从供给方面看，网络安全保险产品和服务供给难以满足多样化的保险需求。目前网络安全保险有如下四种模式。（1）网络综合险，以第一方损失、第三方责任为主，第一方一般为财产险，第三方一般为责任险，包含应急响应费用和硬件修复费用等，本质是财产险、责任险保障范围扩展到网络安全领域。（2）场景网络保险，基于安全厂商提供软硬件的保险，以防勒索、抗DDoS攻击等为主，责任范围相对较窄；基于关键企业、重要活动的保险，如大型运动会、重点基础设施企业等。（3）供应链网络保险，保障供应链核心企业网络安全，由于面对的供应商较多，很难要求供应商达到相应的网络安全要求，需要购买网络保险作为条件，此类保险保障范围非常窄，只有供应链路径发生的风险才予以赔付。（4）政策性网络保险，对首版次产品提供风险保障，涉及公共系统软件、软件缺陷、黑客攻击损失等。在保险产品和服务上，不同行业的网络安全风险防范重点和难点差异较大，目前保险产品同质性严重，缺少对具体行业、具体场景的有针对性、多样化产品和服务，难以满足多元化需求。同时，由于网络安全专业性较高，缺乏专业机构支持也限制了网络安全保险产品的创新供给。

（二）网络安全保险核保面临挑战

一是网络安全保险开发定价缺乏数据基础。经验数据是建立风险定价模型的重要基础，网络安全风险作为新型风险，数据积累有限。从网络发展看，我国互联网发展时间较短，企业网络安全防范意识的形成更晚，缺乏像传统险种长期的数据积累。从损失形态看，网络安全损失具有隐蔽性，网络安全风险不仅限于物质损失，如数据泄露等无形资产损失在短时间内不明显，部分企业在遭受网络攻击后并不知情。从市场声誉看，企业考虑到自身声誉，在发生网络安全损失后不愿公布相关信息，数据仅是"一对一"共享。以上原因导致网络安全保险缺乏经验数据，且部分网络风险造成的无形资产损失较难量化，给网络安全保险及其细分险种的开发定价带来困难。

二是网络技术的动态演进加剧网络安全的复杂性。网络技术的动态性体现在两个方面。一方面，新的网络攻击技术层出不穷，随着网络技术的演进，网络攻击技术不断迭代升级，旧的攻击技术消失、新的攻击技术出现，攻击方式也日益灵活，加大网络风险防范和预测的复杂性；另一方面，网络系统的组织结构不断改变，网络风险防御措施不断变化，同时网络安全防御措施和标准的有效性和执行效率也存在不确定性。外部网络攻击技术演变和内部网络系统防御的不确定性使保险人较难确定风险损失概率。

三是网络风险的强相互依赖性加剧网络安全累积风险。网络风险不存在地域性，不同地理位置的计算机系统存在高度相似性，导致网络攻击可以在短时间内大面积复制，从而无差异攻击任何地理位置的网络。同时，在互联互通的全球产业链中，不同企业的网络相互依存度高，病毒可以从合作方的系统进入另一个系统，导致病毒蔓延。例如，2017年Notpetya病毒网络攻击事件，原本发生在乌克兰，但蔓延导致全球150个国家20万例病毒感染。网络风险的这一特性极易造成风险累积，为保险公司风险管理带来挑战。

四是网络安全风险专业评估具有一定难度。投保前风险评估方面，网络安全保险缺乏数据基础，且随着网络技术演进，风险持续变化，历史经验参考性低；网络安全保险缺乏统一标准的行业语言，保险范围表述不够明确，保险合同订立不够规范，加大了网络风险的评估难度。投保后理赔评估方面，网络安全损失涉及大量无形资产损失，如数据资产、声誉资产等，较难按照统一标准量化损失；保险责任较难明确，由于网络的互联互通性极高，且网络攻击往往无法及时发现，网络风险损失发生后，较难确认风险责任人。

（三）网络安全保险发展机遇

企业的网络安全策略面临着“不可能三角”难题，即价格、安全、效率三者只能得其二。价格便宜、安全性高但效率低，比如，局域网布设系统；安全性高、效率高但价格昂贵，如私有云搭建系统；价格便宜、效率高但安全性面临挑战，如公有云配置系统。对于企业来说，经济性和效率性往往是首要考虑的问题，网络安全保险能够补齐安全短板，化解“不可能三角”，实现企业经营的帕累托改进。可以说，数字经济时代的来临为网络安全保险的快速发展提供了机遇。

一是风险意识不断提升，网络安全保险保障需求持续增加。根据2022年慕尼黑再保险调查，全球范围内，购买网络安全保险的公司数量同比增长了21%，预计到2025年全球网络安全保险的保费规模将达到约220亿美元。中国网络安全保险近年来也保持快速发展势头，连续两年达到100%的增长速度，这一增长得益于网络安全保险需求的增加，以及保险产品创新和服务模式的多元化。随着风险意识的不断提升，企业在事前风险防范、事中风险监测和事后响应救助方面的需求不断提升，特别是遭受过网络攻击事件的企业对网络安全保障需求最为强烈。

二是信息技术不断进步，网络风险识别成本下降。保险科技的发展不断促进保险业加快数字化转型升级，拓宽在网络风险格局中的应用场景。无感开源扫描技术逐步成熟，能够快速探知企业暴露在公网上的端口和漏洞，判断其潜在的脆弱性，使得企业成批量、快速开展网络风险检测成为可能。人工智能和机器学习将赋能风险识别，网络风险具有动态性和复杂性，单靠人工很难进行准确高效的识别，通过机器学习模型提炼有效数据，通过人工智能进行学习分析，构建网络安全风险评价体系，形成技术闭环。区块链将助力风险管理，其去中心化分布式账本加强投保人数据保护和存储，可以安全地在保险公司及安全共享联盟中实现数据流通，有利于建立网络安全数据库，形成数据资产，也有利于通过其可追溯性特点助力风险识别和管理。

三是网络安全业务模式不断创新，网络安全生态逐步完善。目前，我国大型财产险公司在网络安全方面积极开展跨领域合作，联合网络安全企业、第三方网络技术专业机构等多方整合资源，网络安全企业及网络技术机构利用数据和技术等专业优势，通过网络风险识别、风险监测、应急响应等手段赋能保险定价、承保和理赔全流程，保险公司构建网络安全风险管理体系为企业网络安全兜底，形成“保险+科技+服务”的新业务模式。网络安全生态逐步完善，使得未来在新兴科技、新兴业态等风险场景中，将保险公司、再保险公司、网络安全企业、网络科技机构，以及法律机构、审计机构等联合起来，共同探索网络安全解决方案成为可能。

三、创新综合性网络安全保险解决方案

网络安全保险逐渐成为保障企业安全运转的重要一环，为企业的稳健经营保驾护航。但同时，网络风险的特殊性又制约着网络安全保险产品的供给，保障网络安全风险单靠保险公司难以形成可持续、可盈利的商业模式，亟待创新综合性网络安全保险解决方案。

（一）网络风险源

构建综合性网络安全保险解决方案，首先要找出“网络风险源”，分析企业面临的网络风险主要来自哪里。一般来说，企业经营面临的风险源主要来自网站、邮箱和数据库。

一是企业网站。网站是企业在网络上的门户，承担发布企业信息、提供线上交易入口等功能，容易发生DDoS网站瘫痪、网页被恶意挂马、网页被恶意篡改等攻击，对企业的经营、声誉等造成不利影响。

二是企业邮箱。邮箱是企业用于与客户进行沟通的重要方式，邮件经常会遭受钓鱼邮件、邮件炸弹等攻击，特别是社会工程学类攻击

对企业影响巨大，曾经某大型集团对内部进行钓鱼软件演练测试，结果钓鱼软件平均成功率在8%左右，有的单位高达20%。

三是企业数据库。企业数据库记录着企业的生产信息、财务信息、客户信息等，数据库经常会遇到勒索软件等攻击。数据库的损失可能对企业经营带来重大影响，严重情况下可能直接导致企业倒闭。

找到上述风险源，就可以有针对性地进行风险加固、做好风险减量，有效降低企业网络风险的暴露面，提升在网络攻击中的“存活率”。

（二）防范网络风险的关键要素

基于网络风险源，需要实施有针对性的举措来降低网络风险，同时也是网络安全保险核保的关键要素。主要从设备、制度、备份来评价。

一是设备防护。没有安防软硬件设备的加持，企业的网络安全风险将会面临巨大的挑战。在安防设备方面，关注软硬件安防设备的安装情况以及启动情况，相关安全补丁的及时更新情况。在链路方面，关注相关网络端口的开放情况、网络链路布设的情况。在系统方面，关注系统间的安全隔离情况。

二是制度建设。在硬件防护的同时，安全制度的建设和执行也尤为重要。在制度方面，人员系统权限管理情况、人员的邮件防调研管理、USB设备权限管理等，都是评判网络安全风险高低的重要制度指标。在执行方面，定期开展防钓鱼演练、网络安全教育等，提升员工的风险意识，能有效降低网络安全风险。在管理方面，第三方供应商管理、客户管理等相关制度，有效杜绝网络风险从外部传入。

三是数据库备份。数据库是企业经营的核心。在备份方面，数据库备份情况、灾害应急数据库恢复计划及演练情况等，这些措施是否完备决定了数据库能否在第一时间得到有效恢复，从而将网络攻击的风险降到最低。在加密方面，数据库的加密情况、隐私数据类型和数据等，数据库的加密能够更好地控制数据外部泄露的风险。

（三）综合性网络安全保险解决方案

尽管企业面临的网络风险十分复杂，但可以通过构建多层次的网络风险防控体系，打造综合性的网络安全风险解决方案，实现“保险+科技+服务”的网络风险减量模式，有效提升网络安全保险的可保性，优化保险供给，满足市场需求。主要包括：

第一层筛选网络风险，把控网络风险入口关，通过对企业开展网络安全扫描，进行问卷调查，对企业整体网络安全水平进行有效评估，对网络脆弱性高的企业提供提高网络安全水平的建议，促进其提高网络安全水平，筛选网络安全达标的企业提供网络安全保险服务。

第二层防护网络风险，网络安全防护设备至关重要，网络安全保险的承保是以网络安全防护为前提的。企业通过安装网络安全软件、落实网络安全策略、加强网络安全管理，有效抵御网络攻击带来的不利影响。

第三层监控网络风险，对企业的网络安全进行过程检测，通过态势感知、漏洞扫描等方式，对日常网络攻击情况以及存在的高危漏洞进行监测，同时，当发生高危攻击的时候进行必要的预警，便于企业及时采取必要的行动，降低网络攻击造成的损失。

第四层减量网络风险，开展数据库备份演练、防钓鱼演练、网络安全教育等，提升企业的应急处置能力和网络风险防护意识；在程序上，标准化应急处置程序，明确数据备份、数据恢复的流程，确保在发生网络安全事件时能从容应对；在思想上，增强全员网络安全防护意识，特别是对于防范网络钓鱼、U盘病毒等方面要着重关注。

第五层分散网络风险，通过筛选承保主体、安装安全防护、监控风险暴露以及赋能风险减量等手段，有效降低了网络安全事件发生概率，对于“残余风险”则需要通过更为经济的保险金融工具来提供保障，即网络安全保险及再保险。

通过综合性网络安全保险解决方案，能够为企业构筑起网络安全防护网，为企业安全稳健经营保驾护航。

四、相关建议

网络风险是一种新型风险，目前对其研究还处于起步阶段。网络安全保险的健康发展需要多方合作与政策支持，相关建议如下。

一是加强网络信息安全监管。工信部、网信办等网络信息主管部门应加强网络信息安全监管，建议对信息泄露事件严抓严管，进一步明确奖惩机制。从美国、欧洲的网络安全保险发展经验看，加强网络信息监管是推动网络安全保险发展的重要动力之一。通过加强网络信息监管，抬高网络信息事件的违法成本，驱动企业购买网络安全保险。同时，企业购买网络安全保险，需要接受保险公司的网络安全评估，又进一步提升了企业网络安全程度，形成良性循环。

二是建设中国网络安全事件信息库。网络安全保险定价的短板在于缺乏损失数据信息，现有网络安全数据大多是通过数据插值、数据挖掘等获得的，其精细化程度有待通过网络安全保险运行进一步校准。建议建设网络安全事件信息库，通过统一的数据平台，增加国内网络安全数据的积累，挖掘网络攻击事件的风险特征，助力中国网络安全水平的提升，增强网络安全保险定价的公允性，有效助力数字经济发展。

三是注重跨行业的业务合作。网络安全保险的开发涉及保险、信息、安全等多个行业，需要多方合作推进。建议进一步打造跨行业合作平台，打通实体企业、保险公司、再保险公司、网络服务公司、网络安全防护公司、信息安全评估公司等参与主体的合作通道，通过多方合作打造网络安全保险生态圈，共同服务数字经济高质量发展。

EMPOWER YOUR INSURANCE BY EXPERTISE

Report on the Development of Reinsurance Industry in China

(2024)

CHINA REINSURANCE (GROUP) CORPORATION

CHINA FINANCIAL PUBLISHING HOUSE

Editorial Board

Preface.

The *Resolution of the Central Committee of the Communist Party of China (CPC) on Further Deepening Reform Comprehensively to Advance Chinese Modernization*, adopted at the Third Plenary Session of the 20th CPC Central Committee has made major arrangements to further deepen the financial system reform, giving a strong impetus to building China into a financial powerhouse and pursuing Chinese modernization. The Central Financial Work Conference emphasized the five priorities of financial work, namely technology finance, green finance, inclusive finance, pension finance and digital finance, and deployed the major strategic tasks of "building the reinsurance market" and "building a sound national catastrophe insurance system" to unleash the dual role of insurance as economic absorber and social stabilizer, providing the fundamental principles for insurance and reinsurance to follow in the course of unswervingly keeping to the road of financial development with Chinese characteristics. The State Council issuing the Guidelines on Enhancing Regulation, Preventing Risks and Promoting the High-Quality Development of the Insurance Sector (the "Ten-point New Policy") devises a systematic plan for key tasks of the insurance industry reform and development in the next 5 to 10 years, sets forth specific requirements for high-quality development

of reinsurance, and points to the clear direction for the insurance and reinsurance industries to further comprehensively deepen the reform and better serve the overall economic and social development.

Since the beginning of this year, China has been the fastest-growing major economy of the world, manifesting stability and resilience with fresh energy and great potential for development. The basic trend of steady long-term growth of China's economy remains unchanged, and the necessary production factors for high-quality development remain unchanged. As an important part of the modern market economy, the insurance industry must firmly grasp the historic opportunity of high-quality development and play its part in the Chinese modernization with a pressing sense of mission and responsibility. The insurance industry will further advance the supply-side structural reform in key areas vital to national strategies, the real economy and public wellbeing, such as addressing climate change, promoting green transition, serving rural revitalization, fostering new quality productive forces, developing low-altitude economy, and pension finance. In this way, the insurance industry will help boost vitality through reform, tackle difficulties through development and overcome such challenges as slow recovery of the world economy, geopolitical tensions, increasing frequency and intensity of extreme weather and acceleration of population aging.

Reinsurance, as the "insurance for insurers", is an effective way for countries around the world to spread and tackle major natural risks, complex risks and special risks. Each of the developed insurance

markets is backed by a strong and sound reinsurance system.

Reinsurance has its unique value as a platform business. At present, addressing climate change has become the common cause of all mankind. Reinsurance can effectively promote insurance-reinsurance integration, industrial integration and government-enterprise integration. It strongly supports the development of a national catastrophe insurance system, playing a crucial role in improving the catastrophe insurance system, raising the insurance protection against catastrophe risks, enhancing the catastrophe risk management technology and introducing new ways of catastrophe risk diversification, and helping modernize the national governance system and capacity.

Reinsurance has an inherent advantage in data links. Digitalization is profoundly changing the business logic and model of the insurance industry, becoming a key driving force for industry transformation and upgrading. Reinsurance is able to pool data resources in the insurance industry and facilitate cross-industry data integration. In an ongoing effort to build a new model of "reinsurance + technology + service", reinsurers have endeavored to supply more innovative products and services and promote the positive interaction between risk reduction and insurance expansion in a virtuous circle, thereby ensuring the stability and sustainability of China's insurance market.

Reinsurance is naturally international. Opening-up is a crucial driver of the reform and development of China's financial sector. As the first financial field to open up after China's accession to the WTO, reinsurance

effectively utilizes both domestic and international markets and resources to serve China's new development pattern featuring dual circulations, with domestic circulation being the mainstay and the two circulations reinforcing each other, and contribute to the Belt and Road Initiative. As Shanghai's drive to become an international reinsurance hub gains pace, China will further expand the high-level institutional opening-up of reinsurance and raise its voice and influence in the global insurance industry.

As the national team and main force of China's reinsurance industry, China Reinsurance (Group) Corporation ("China Re") has always followed the guidance of the Xi Jinping Thought on Socialism with Chinese Characteristics for a New Era, fully put into practice the political and people-oriented nature of financial work, resolutely implemented the guiding principles of the 20th CPC National Congress, the Third Plenary Session of the 20th CPC Central Committee and the Central Financial Work Conference and thoroughly implemented the specific requirements for high-quality development of the insurance industry set forth in the Ten-point New Policy. Staying focused on reinsurance as its main responsibilities and business, China Re has been working hard to strengthen the role of reinsurance, build a reinsurance ecosphere, accelerate digital transformation and pursue international development, with the aim of serving the national strategies, spreading economic risks, assuring the people a better life and becoming a world-class comprehensive reinsurance group.

Since 2022, China Re has taken the lead in preparing the annual report for China's reinsurance industry each year under the guidance

from the National Financial Regulatory Administration and the Insurance Association of China as well as the strong support from other insurance and reinsurance institutions in China. This year, China Re has compiled the Report on the Development of Reinsurance Industry in China (2024) in collaboration with other industry players and renowned universities, providing a full picture of the new trends, new characteristics and outcomes of the industry development. We hope that this Report will provide a useful point of reference for readers to gain a full view and insights into China's reinsurance industry, and play a positive role in promoting international exchanges and enhancing the social influence of China's reinsurance industry.

On the new journey of Chinese modernization, the reinsurance industry faces important strategic opportunities alongside many difficulties and challenges down the road of reform and development, requiring pooled wisdoms and forces and shared insights to address them. China Re will shoulder its responsibility and work together with the larger community to share opportunities and pursue common development through cooperation, thus making fresh and greater contributions to high-quality development of China's insurance and reinsurance industries, building China into a financial powerhouse and serving the Chinese modernization.

He Chunlei, Chairman of China Re

November 2024

Introduction[①]

The year 2023 was the first year of fully implementing the guiding principles of the 20th CPC National Congress. In the year, China took proactive steps to deal with external risks and challenges, stepped up efforts to create a pattern of development in pursuit of high-quality development and achieved notable results in economic and social development. In the year, China's GDP exceeded RMB 126 trillion, up 5.2% over the previous year, ranking in the forefront of major economies in the world. The fundamentals sustaining the long-term growth of the Chinese economy have become more solid, shaping a favorable macro environment for the reinsurance industry. The Third Plenary Session of the 20th CPC Central Committee and the Central Financial Work Conference have set forth strategic plans to deepen the financial system reform and develop the reinsurance market, providing fundamental principles and guide to action for high-quality development of the reinsurance industry. The State Council issued the Guidelines on Enhancing Regulation, Preventing Risks and Promoting the High-Quality

① "China's reinsurance industry" or "China's insurance industry" refers to the reinsurance or insurance industry and market in the Chinese mainland, excluding Hong Kong, Macao and Taiwan. Data in this Report come mainly from the Yearbook of China's Insurance for past years, the data disclosed by the National Financial Regulatory Administration and the annual reports of reinsurance companies as well as the research and survey data for the reinsurance industry available during the preparation of this Report.

Development of the Insurance Sector, entrusting the reinsurance industry with greater responsibility, mission and development opportunities, encouraging the reinsurance industry to play a better role in bolstering economic and social development.

Following the guidance of Xi Jinping Thought on Socialism with Chinese Characteristics for a New Era, China's reinsurance industry has thoroughly implemented the guiding principles from the 20th CPC National Congress, the Third Plenary Session of the 20th CPC Central Committee and the Central Financial Work Conference and carried out the decisions and plans of the CPC Central Committee and the State Council and the work requirements of regulatory authorities. Upholding the political and people-oriented nature of financial work, China's reinsurance industry focused on the five priorities of financial work, namely technology finance, green finance, inclusive finance, pension finance and digital finance, transformed the growth model, kept optimizing the supply of reinsurance, continued with digital transformation, comprehensively strengthened risk prevention and control and took solid steps toward high-quality development. In 2023, China's insurance market registered RMB 269.42 billion in ceded premiums, the premium income of the reinsurance industry was RMB 229.61 billion, and the total assets of the reinsurance industry stood at RMB 747.15 billion. China's reinsurance industry has proactively integrated into the bigger picture of economic and social development of the country, providing solid risk protection for technological innovation, green development, rural revitalization,

disaster management and other fields and delivering positive results in serving the national strategies. China's reinsurance market has continued to expand outward opening up, with remarkable progress made in Shanghai's push for an international reinsurance center. China has increasingly integrated itself into the global reinsurance market, and the capability of its reinsurance sector for participating in global risk governance has been improving.

Based on its experience in successful compilation of the reports on development of China's reinsurance industry in 2022 and 2023, China Re continued to lead the compilation of the Report on the Development of Reinsurance Industry in China (2024) (the "Report"). Continuing with a structure of "main report + special report", the Report analyze and research on the international and domestic macro-economy, policy environment, market changes, technological innovation and other key factors influencing the industry development. It focuses on outlining the latest developments in the reinsurance industry, including market size, business structure, competition landscape, innovation practices and industry supervision. The Report also reviews the past developments and practices of the reinsurance industry, forecasts development trends and conducts studies on issues of industry concern including health and pension, climate change, catastrophe insurance and cyber insurance.

We are so grateful to Yin Jiang'ao, Head of the Property and Casualty Insurance Supervision (Reinsurance Supervision) Department

of the National Financial Regulatory Administration and Yu Hua, President of Insurance Association of China, for their valuable guidance throughout the preparation of this Report. We acknowledge support from leaders and experts from the insurance and reinsurance industries in respect of the publication of this Report. We would like to thank Wang Jun, Jin Xuequn and Zheng Wandong from the Reinsurance Regulation Division, Property and Casualty Insurance Supervision (Reinsurance Supervision) Department of the National Financial Regulatory Administration for their guidance on compilation of the Report. We extend our gratitude to Yin Bo and Fu Shenglin from the Insurance Association of China for their support and assistance.

The compilation of the Report was led by China Re, and the following organizations also participated:

China Reinsurance (Group) Corporation

China Property and Casualty Reinsurance Company Limited

China Life Reinsurance Company Limited

PICC Reinsurance Company Limited

Qianhai Reinsurance Company Limited

Swiss Reinsurance Company Limited Beijing Branch

Peking University

Renmin University of China

Qin Yueguang and Zhang Jian from China Re are responsible for overall planning of the Report. Guan Bing and Ma Xiaojing are responsible for final compilation and editing of the Report. The work on

preparation of the Report is divided as follows: The main report section was prepared by China Re, with Chapter I prepared by Dou Jian, Chapter II by Sun Tao and Zhao Xinyu, Chapter III by Jin Xiaoquan and Yu Yang, Chapter IV by Wang Hongpeng and Liu Shuang and Chapter V by Zheng Lina and Fan Lingjian. In the special report section, Special Report 1 was prepared by Zhang Chu, Wang Mingyan, Sun Xiaochen and Guo Weiqin (China Re), Special Report 2 was prepared by Jin Xiaoquan and Zou Chunyan (China Re), Special Report 3 was prepared by Dai Xin and Chen Yaxin (Swiss Re Beijing Branch), Special Report 4 was prepared by Lan Hong and Fang Yunlong (School of Ecology & Environment at Renmin University of China, China Re), Special Report 5 was prepared by Chen Si (Qianhai Re), Special Report 6 was prepared by Liu Xinli (School of Economics at Peking University), and Special Report 7 was prepared by Jiao Jian and Li Zhongyi (PICC Re).

The Report is published with the joint efforts of the reinsurers and the experts and scholars contributing to reinsurance development. We express our sincere gratitude to all the organizations and colleagues participating in the compilation of the Report. We also extend our appreciation to experts and scholars for providing professional comments, opinions and suggestions and other inputs for the Report.

China is at a critical stage of building a great country and advancing national rejuvenation on all fronts through Chinese modernization. There is an urgent need for reinsurance to unleash its unique role to provide powerful support for building China into a financial powerhouse. To

this end, with a greater sense of responsibility and mission, China Re will work with all insurers and reinsurers to deepen theoretical study and strengthen practical explorations to jointly promote high-quality development of China's reinsurance industry, take the road of financial development with Chinese characteristics and make positive contributions to building a modern socialist country in all respects.

China Reinsurance (Group) Corporation

November 2024

Contents

Chapter I

Overview of China's Reinsurance Market in 2023 and Development Outlook

I. Reinsurance Market Environment

II. Reinsurance Market Developments

III. Reinsurance Services for Economic and Social Development

IV. Reinsurance Trends and Outlook

China's reinsurance industry demonstrated strong resilience and adaptability in 2023 amid the complexities and uncertainties at home and abroad, including global inflationary pressure and geopolitical tensions. The Chinese reinsurance market saw a continued expansion in size, steady improvement in profitability, growing global influence, effective risk prevention and control as well as acceleration in technological innovation and digital transformation, making fresh headway in high-quality development. The development of the industry has showed the "4D" characteristics: The first "D" is dynamic resilience. Reinsurance became increasingly resilient to market turbulence and quickly adaptative to regulatory developments, maintaining steady growth in results and confidence in development by adjusting risk appetite, strengthening capital management and innovating business models. The second is diversified supply. Reinsurers sought to diversify the supply of products and services in response to changing market demands, including better meeting the needs for passing on emerging risks relating to cyber security, climate change, biotechnology, etc., and providing tailor-made solutions to special risks, such as the risks in large-scale infrastructure projects, so as to provide a broader range of reinsurance protection and risk ceding. The third is differentiated service. Reinsurance is shifting the service model from risk equalization to risk reduction, and gradually expanding from post-event economic compensation to services before, during and after the event, thus enhancing the anti-risk capability and reducing risk costs across the larger community. The fourth is digital advancement. Reinsurers have endeavored to develop a platform ecosystem-based new model backed by digital technology, tap the

value of data as a factor of production, and step up the business management and process reengineering using artificial intelligence, big data, blockchain and other cutting-edge technologies in pursuit of digitalization-driven transition and upgrading of operation management and service models.

I. Reinsurance Market Environment

(I) Worldwide

In 2023, the global economy struggled to recover from the COVID-19 pandemic, energy crisis, Russia-Ukraine conflict and other adversities. With the recovery seen lacking steam on a fragile footing, the world economic growth slowed down to 2.6%[①] from 3.4% in 2022 with obvious divergence among nations. The economic and trade growth was losing steam. With the supply-side problems eased and the tightening monetary policy in play, global inflation has peaked in a low-growth environment, retreating to 6.8%[②] from a multi-decade high of 9% in 2022. Major economies saw their short-term inflation expectations declining and their long-term expectations remaining well anchored. The global economy is facing increased downside risks, including rising geopolitical tensions and extreme weather shocks that continue to pose a threat, coupled by more restrictions on international trade, greater obstacles to multilateral cooperation, wide swings in commodity prices and drastic volatility in financial markets. Meanwhile,

① Source: World Economic Outlook published by the World Bank in June 2024.

② Source: World Economic Outlook published by the International Monetary Fund in January 2024.

a new wave of technological revolution and industrial transformation are advancing, expected to provide new opportunities and generate new impetus for global economic growth.

In 2023, the inflation-adjusted global premium income was about USD 7.2 trillion, and the real growth rate was about 2.8%, up by 3.9 percentage points from 2022. Specifically, the life premium income was about USD 2.9 trillion, a real growth rate of about 1.3%, up by 4.4 percentage points from 2022. The non-life premium income stood at around USD 4.3 trillion, a real growth rate of approximately 3.9%, up by 3.4 percentage points from 2022[①].

Opportunities and challenges coexisted in the global reinsurance market in 2023. In a still-turbulent world, the reinsurance market faced such adversities as geopolitical tensions, elevated interest rates, high supply costs, and deglobalization. In addition, extreme weather events have become more frequent in various parts of the world as the effects of climate change intensify. The global economic losses caused by natural catastrophes were estimated at USD 380 billion, with the insured losses exceeding USD 100 billion for the fourth consecutive year[②]. Under the combined effect of several factors, the global property reinsurance market continued to harden in 2003, with higher premium rates and attachment points, an increase in the global supply of reinsurance capital and a general improvement in the profitability of international reinsurers. The global life reinsurance market was expanding steadily on the tailwinds of technological advances, aging population and

① Source: Sigma 3/2024 - "World insurance: strengthening global resilience with a new lease of life", Swiss Re Institute.

② Source: Aon's 2024 Climate and Catastrophe Insights Report.

growing emerging markets, but also facing challenges in improving the accuracy of risk assessment and boosting the capital efficiency.

(II) China

In 2023, China's macro economy recovered with steady improvements on both supply and demand sides, manifesting advances in transformation and upgrading, overall stability in employment and prices, strong protection of people's livelihood and solid progress in high-quality development. China's gross domestic product (GDP) exceeded RMB 126 trillion, representing an annual growth rate of about 5.2%, ranking among the world's major economies.[①]

In 2023, China's insurance market kept expanding and recorded premium income of about RMB 5.12 trillion, an increase of 9.1% year-on-year and exceeding the RMB 5 trillion mark for the first time, consolidating its No. 2 position in the world[②]. The insurance density was about RMB 3,635/person and the premium per capita increased by RMB 304 over 2022, with an insurance penetration of about 4.1%, up by 0.2 percentage points[③] year-on-year. China's insurance market showed a gap with developed insurance markets, implying great potential for growth.

In 2023, the premium income of China's property insurance companies stood at around RMB 1.59 trillion, an increase of 6.7% year-on-year but a

---

① Source: Statistical Communique on the National Economic and Social Development 2022, published by the National Bureau of Statistics of China on February 29, 2024.

② Source: The 2023 insurance industry data disclosed by the National Financial Regulatory Administration.

③ Source: National Financial Regulatory Administration.

softer growth when compared with 2022. Since the shift in growth drivers of China's property insurance industry in recent years, motor insurance growth has slowed down in 2017. Thus, the premium growth is driven mainly by non-motor lines of business. The premium income of life insurance companies was about RMB 3.54 trillion, up by 10.2% year-on-year. Specifically, life insurance saw markedly faster growth, at 12.8% year-on-year, than casualty insurance and health insurance. As at the end of 2023, China's insurance industry recorded RMB 29.96 trillion in total assets, up by 10.4% year-on-year, RMB27.67 trillion in balance of fund use, up by 10.5% year-on-year, manifesting sustained momentum of development[①].

II. Reinsurance Market Developments

(I) Market size

1. Ceded premiums from primary insurers

(1) Size of ceded premiums from primary insurers

In 2023, China's insurance market recorded RMB 269.42 billion in ceded premiums, down by 3.2% year-on-year. Over the same period, the premium income of domestic primary insurers stood at RMB 5,124.7 billion, up by 9.1% year-on-year (see Figure 1 and Table 1).

① Source: The 2023 insurance industry data disclosed by the National Financial Regulatory Administration.

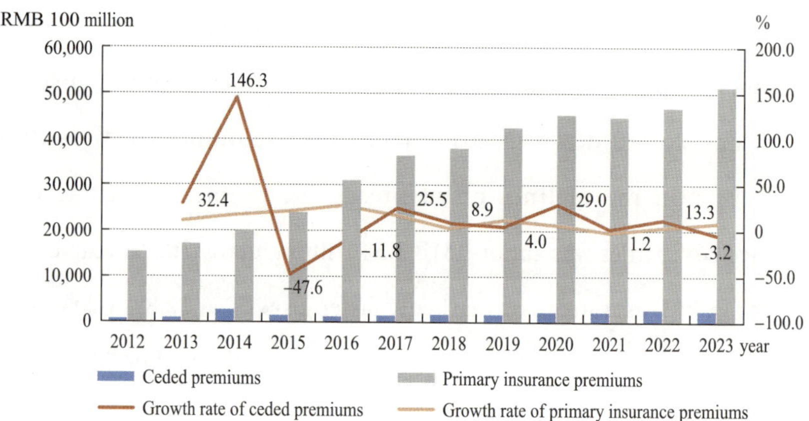

Figure 1 Primary Insurance Premiums, Ceded Premiums and Growth Rates (2012-2023)

(Source: Yearbook of China's Insurance and National Financial Regulatory Administration)

Table 1 Ceded Premiums, Primary Insurance Premiums and Cession Rates (2012-2023)

Unit: RMB 100 million, %

	Ceded premiums	Growth rate	Primary insurance premiums	Growth rate	Cession rate
2012	879.4		15,487.8		5.7
2013	1,164.0	32.4	17,222.1	11.2	6.8
2014	2,867.2	146.3	20,234.7	17.5	14.2
2015	1,501.6	-47.6	24,282.4	20.0	6.2
2016	1,323.8	-11.8	30,959.0	27.5	4.3
2017	1,661.2	25.5	36,580.9	18.2	4.5
2018	1,808.5	8.9	38,016.6	3.9	4.8
2019	1,881.6	4.0	42,644.8	12.2	4.4
2020	2,427.1	29.0	44,257.3	6.1	5.4
2021	2,456.8	1.2	44,900.2	-0.8	5.5
2022	2,782.8	13.3	46,958.0	4.6	5.9
2023	2,694.2	-3.2	51,247.0	9.1	5.3

Source: Yearbook of China's Insurance and National Financial Regulatory Administration.

In 2023, the premiums ceded by property insurers in the Chinese market were RMB 163.75 billion, an increase of 0.5% year-on-year, accounting for 60.8% of the total ceded premiums. Personal insurance companies ceded

RMB 105.67 billion of premiums to reinsurers, down by 8.4% year-on-year, accounting for 39.2% of total ceded premiums (see Figure 2).

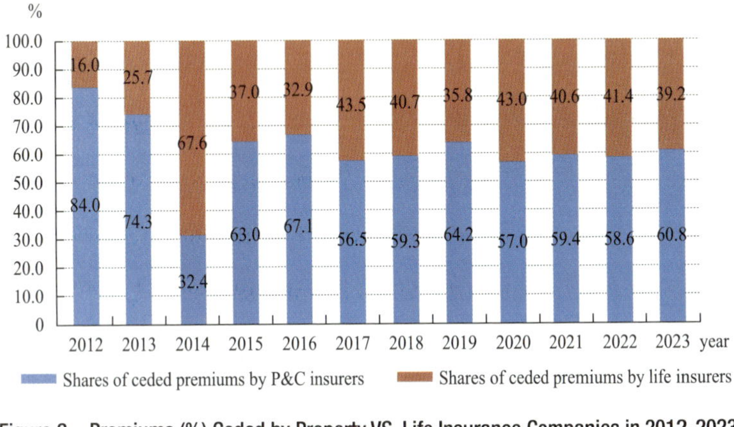

Figure 2 Premiums (%) Ceded by Property VS. Life Insurance Companies in 2012-2023

(Source: Yearbook of China's Insurance and National Financial Regulatory Administration)

From 2012 to 2023, reinsurance demand kept growing alongside China's insurance market expansion. Ceded premiums rose from RMB 87.94 billion to RMB 269.42 billion in 2023, representing an average annual growth rate of 10.7%. Over the same period, the premium income of primary insurers increased from RMB 1,548.78 billion to RMB 5,124.7 billion, an average annual growth rate of about 11.5% (see Figure 1 and Table 1). In general, ceded premiums and primary premiums have shown similar annual growth rates, yet with significant disparities in growth from year to year. Ceded premiums were obviously more volatile than primary premiums, which is a notable feature of the reinsurance business that spreads risks and smoothen fluctuations in primary insurance.

(2) Cession rates of primary insurers

The cession rate in China's insurance market was around 5.3% in 2023

(see Figure 3). By segment, the cession rate was about 10.3% for property insurers and about 3.0% for personal insurance companies. Property insurers cover a broader range of risks, including catastrophe risks in particular when compared with life insurers. Thus, property insurers have a greater demand for reinsurance and a higher cession rate.

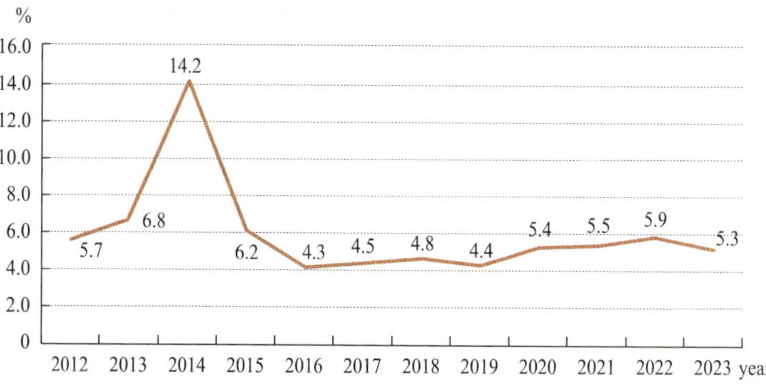

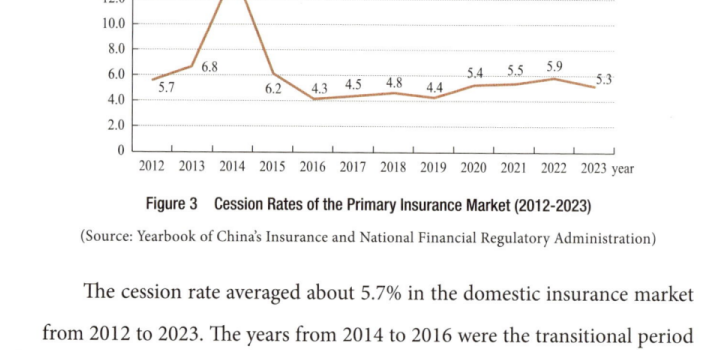

Figure 3 Cession Rates of the Primary Insurance Market (2012-2023)

(Source: Yearbook of China's Insurance and National Financial Regulatory Administration)

The cession rate averaged about 5.7% in the domestic insurance market from 2012 to 2023. The years from 2014 to 2016 were the transitional period for C-ROSS Phase II regulatory policies, the cession rate experienced drastic fluctuations. The cession rate was as high as 14.2% in 2014 due to surge in demand and then gradually went down. Excluding impact of the fluctuations from 2014 to 2016, the average cession rate was 5.2%. The overall cession rate has been increasing since 2016, with a slight decrease in 2023, indicating a gradual increase in demand to spread risks to reinsurers.

China's insurance market has a lower cession rate and a higher premium retention rate than the global market. According to estimates of the International Association of Insurance Supervisors (IAIS), the cession rate

was about 8% for the global insurance market, and close to 12% for North America.

2. Premium income in the reinsurance market

In 2023, the premium income of the domestic reinsurance market stood at RMB 229.61 billion, an increase of 2.0% year-on-year but a softer growth when compared with 2022. Specifically, the six Chinese reinsurers recorded RMB 166.01 billion in ceded premium income, up by 2.1% year-on-year, accounting for about 72.3%. The eight foreign reinsurers registered ceded premium income of RMB 63.61 billion, up by 1.8% year-on-year, accounting for around 22.7%.

From 2012 to 2023, the ceded premium income of reinsurers in China increased from RMB 69.12 billion to RMB 229.61 billion, an average annual growth rate of 11.5% (see Figure 4). Overall, the ceded premium income of reinsurers showed similar average growth to primary premium income and premiums ceded by primary insurers, but the ceded premium income of reinsurers indicated significant differences and fluctuations in growth from year to year. In particular, the ceded premium income of reinsurers fluctuated significantly from 2014 to 2016 as the C-ROSS Phase II regulatory policies were in the transitional period. After C-ROSS Phase II was fully implemented in 2016, ceded premium income grew steadily year by year

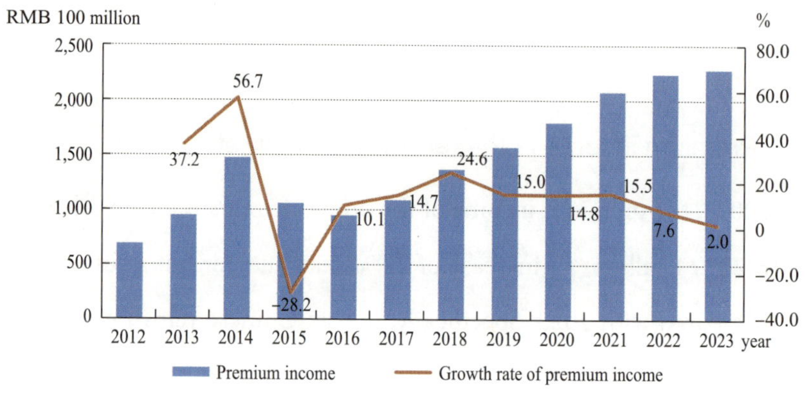

Figure 4 Premium Income of Reinsurers and Growth Rates (2012-2023)

(Source: Yearbook of China's Insurance and National Financial Regulatory Administration)

The premium income of Chinese reinsurers remained positive growth in 2012-2023 but slowed down significantly in 2023. The premium income of foreign reinsurers operating in China was more volatile over the period (see Table 2 and Figure 5), illustrating the different business strategies between Chinese and foreign reinsurers.

Table 2 Premium Income of Chinese VS. Foreign Reinsurers and Growth Rates (2012-2023)

Unit: RMB 100 million, %

	Premium income	Premium income of Chinese reinsurers	Growth rate	% of total	Premium income of foreign reinsurers	Growth rate	% of total
2012	691.2	400.3		57.9	290.9		42.1
2013	948.6	466.8	16.6	49.2	481.8	65.6	50.8
2014	1,486.0	502.5	7.6	33.8	983.5	104.1	66.2
2015	1,066.3	543.4	8.1	51.0	522.9	-46.8	49.0
2016	958.6	552.0	1.6	57.6	406.6	-22.2	42.4
2017	1,099.6	778.7	41.1	70.8	320.9	-21.1	29.2
2018	1,370.1	949.8	22.0	69.3	420.2	31.0	30.7
2019	1,576.1	1,044.9	10.0	66.2	533.0	26.8	33.8
2020	1,809.2	1,180.1	13.1	65.2	629.1	18.0	34.8

continued

	Premium income	Premium income of Chinese reinsurers	Growth rate	% of total	Premium income of foreign reinsurers	Growth rate	% of total
2021	2,090.2	1,422.9	20.6	68.1	667.3	6.1	31.9
2022	2,250.2	1,625.5	14.2	72.2	624.6	-6.4	27.8
2023	2,296.1	1,660.1	2.1	72.3	636.1	1.8	27.7

Source: Yearbook of China's Insurance and National Financial Regulatory Administration.

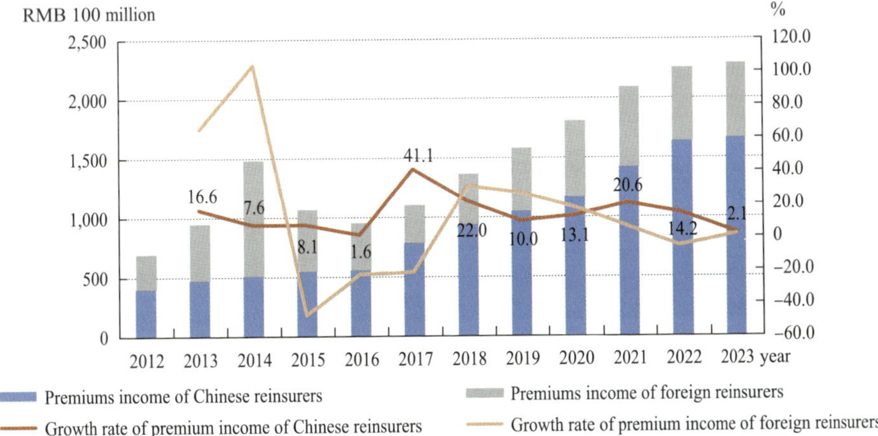

Figure 5　Premium Income of Chinese VS. Foreign Reinsurers and Growth Rates (2012-2023)

(Source: Yearbook of China's Insurance and National Financial Regulatory Administration)

3. Reinsurance claim payouts

The claim payouts of China's reinsurance industry totaled RMB 124.76 billion in 2023, up by 8.1% year-on-year, accounting for about 54.2% of the premium income for the year (see Figure 6). Specifically, the six Chinese reinsurers recorded RMB 90.68 billion in claim payouts, up by 9.0% year-on-year. The eight foreign reinsurers registered RMB 34.07 billion in claim payouts, down by 5.6% year-on-year (see Table 3 and Figure 7).

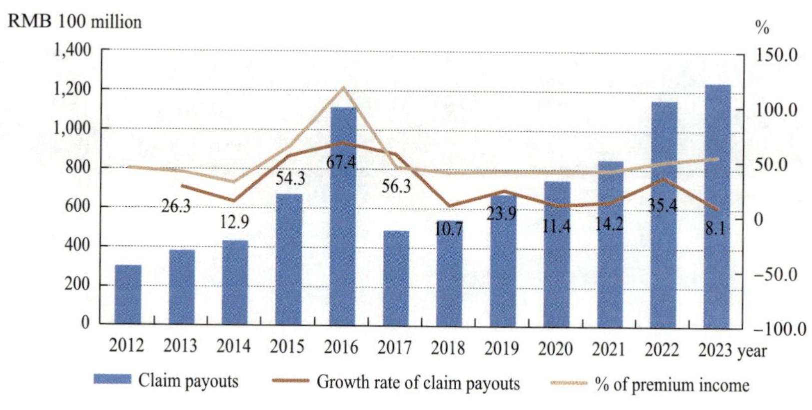

Figure 6 Reinsurance Claim Payouts (2012-2023)

(Source: Yearbook of China's Insurance and National Financial Regulatory Administration)

Table 3 Reinsurance Claim Payouts (2012-2023)

Unit: RMB 100 million, %

	Claim payouts	Chinese reinsurers' claim payouts	Growth rate	% of total	Foreign reinsurers' claim payouts	Growth rate	% of total
2012	303.8	151.8		50.0	151.9		50.0
2013	383.7	180.6	18.9	47.1	203.1	33.7	52.9
2014	433.2	210.5	16.6	48.6	222.6	9.6	51.4
2015	668.5	263.3	25.1	39.4	405.2	82.0	60.6
2016	1,119.4	301.2	14.4	26.9	818.1	101.9	73.1
2017	489.0	254.4	−15.6	52.0	234.6	−71.3	48.0
2018	541.2	278.3	9.4	51.4	262.9	12.1	48.6
2019	670.3	350.4	25.9	52.3	320.0	21.7	47.7
2020	746.5	432.7	23.5	58.0	313.8	−1.9	42.0
2021	852.6	491.0	13.5	57.6	361.6	15.2	42.4
2022	1,154.6	831.9	69.4	72.1	322.7	−10.8	27.9
2023	1,247.6	906.84	9.0	72.7	340.7	5.6	27.3

Source: Yearbook of China's Insurance and National Financial Regulatory Administration.

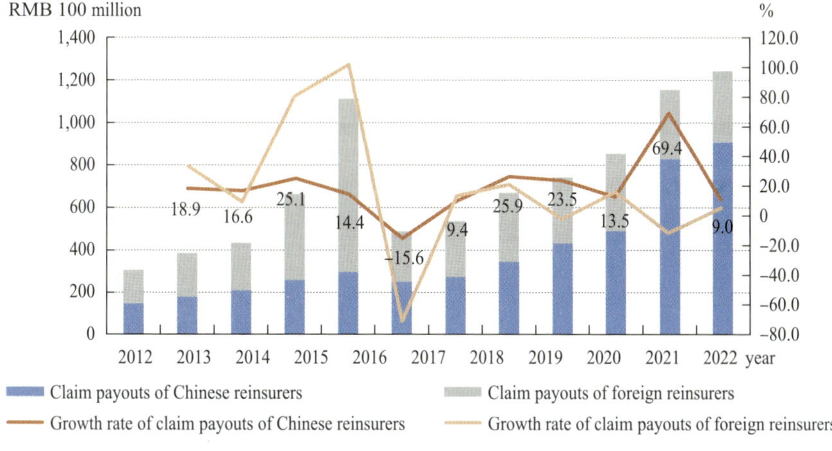

Figure 7 Claim Payouts of Chinese VS. Foreign Reinsurers and Growth Rates (2012-2023)

(Source: Yearbook of China's Insurance and National Financial Regulatory Administration)

From 2012 to 2023, the claim payouts of China's reinsurance industry rose from RMB 30.38 billion in 2012 to RMB 124.76 billion in 2023, representing an average annual growth rate of 13.7% (see Figure 6). Overall, reinsurance payouts surged in 2016 when C-ROSS Phase II was initially implemented. Personal reinsurers' claim payouts grew substantially in 2016 before a marked decline in 2017, showing great fluctuations during the policy shift.

4. Total reinsurance assets

At the end of 2023, the total assets in China's reinsurance industry were about RMB 747.15 billion, an increase of 11.2% from the beginning of the year, and 9.2 percentage points higher than the growth rate of premium income. From 2012 to 2023, the total assets in China's reinsurance industry increased from RMB 143.72 billion to RMB 747.15 billion, an average annual growth rate of about 16.2%, outpacing the ceded premium income

of reinsurers. Total assets were also volatile from 2014 to 2016 due to the impact of C-ROSS Phase II. Since 2016, total reinsurance assets in China have continued to expand steadily, in line with the development of ceded premium income.

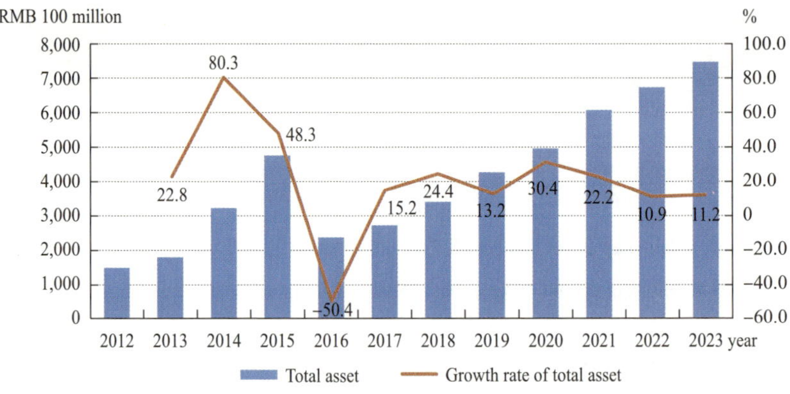

Figure 8 Total Assets of China's Reinsurance Industry and Growth Rates (2012-2023)

(Source: Yearbook of China's Insurance and National Financial Regulatory Administration)

From 2012 to 2023, the share of total reinsurance assets in the total assets of the insurance industry is relatively stable, standing at around 2.5% at the end of 2023. This shows that the reinsurance industry has gradually expanded along with the insurance market, maintaining steady growth under the evolving regulatory policies and market environment. Meanwhile, the share of total insurance assets in total assets of the financial sector increased steadily from 5.6% in 2018 to 6.5% in 2023, indicating a stronger role and position of insurance in the financial sector.

Table 4 Total Assets and Proportions of Reinsurance, Insurance and Financial Sectors (2012-2023)

Unit: RMB 100 million, %

	Total reinsurance assets	Total insurance assets	Total reinsurance assets as % of total insurance assets	Total financial assets	Total insurance assets as % of total financial assets
2012	1,437.2	68,425.6	2.1		
2013	1,765.4	77,576.7	2.3		
2014	3,183.2	96,177.8	3.3		
2015	4,722.0	119,295.7	4.0		
2016	2,343.9	142,659.0	1.6		
2017	2,699.3	146,816.7	1.8		
2018	3,358.3	163,641.0	2.1	2,940,000	5.6
2019	4,261.3	187,495.6	2.3	3.186,900	5.9
2020	4,956.3	216,156.5	2.3	3,531,900	6.1
2021	6,057.5	248,874.0	2.4	3,819,500	6.5
2022	6,719.5	271,500.0	2.5	4,196,400	6.5
2023	7,471.5	299,573.0	2.5	4,610,900	6.5

Source: Yearbook of China's Insurance, websites of the National Financial Regulatory Administration and the People's Bank of China.

(II) Market Landscape

1. Higher diversity of market players

After years of development, China's reinsurance market has gradually formed a diversified landscape with domestic professional reinsurers, offshore reinsurers and direct insurers playing in the same market.

In terms of professional market players, by the end of 2023, there were 15 professional players in China's reinsurance market, including seven Chinese reinsurers (including one conglomerate, namely China Re Group) and eight foreign reinsurers (see Table 5). Spanish reinsurer MAPFRE was

approved to establish a branch in Beijing in 2022 with working capital of RMB 500 million. Its branch opened for business in July 2024.

As for offshore market players, in recent years, offshore reinsurers have expanded their participation in the Chinese market by underwriting insurance ceded by domestic insurers through offshore transactions. In 2023, the domestic insurers conducted transactions with over 500 offshore reinsurers around the world and ceded about RMB 50 billion of premiums to overseas reinsurers.

In addition, more than 100 domestic direct insurers in the property and personal lines competed in the reinsurance market to various degrees. Some direct insurers conducted reinsurance transactions with overseas market players through business swap.

Table 5 Overview of Professional Reinsurance Companies in China

Company name	Date of establishment	Place of registration	Nature of registration	Chinese/ foreign
China Reinsurance (Group) Corporation	1996	Beijing	Group	Chinese
China Property and Casualty Reinsurance Company Limited	2003	Beijing	Stand-alone Company	Chinese
China Life Reinsurance Company Limited	2003	Beijing	Stand-alone Company	Chinese
Munich Reinsurance Group Beijing Branch	2003	Beijing	Branch	Foreign
Swiss Reinsurance Company Limited Beijing Branch	2003	Beijing	Branch	Foreign
General Reinsurance Corporation Shanghai Branch	2004	Shanghai	Branch	Foreign
SCOR SE Beijing Branch	2008	Beijing	Branch	Foreign
Hannover Re Shanghai Branch	2008	Shanghai	Branch	Foreign

continued

Company name	Date of establishment	Place of registration	Nature of registration	Chinese/ foreign
AXA Global Reinsurance (Shanghai)	2011	Shanghai	Stand-alone Company	Foreign
Reinsurance Group of America, Incorporated Shanghai Branch	2014	Shanghai	Branch	Foreign
Taiping Reinsurance (China) Company Limited	2015	Beijing	Stand-alone Company	Chinese
Qianhai Reinsurance Company Limited	2016	Shenzhen	Stand-alone Company	Chinese
PICC Reinsurance Company Limited	2017	Beijing	Stand-alone Company	Chinese
Korean Reinsurance Company Shanghai Branch	2020	Shanghai	Branch	Foreign
China Agriculture Reinsurance Corporation	2020	Beijing	Stand-alone Company	Chinese

Note: 1. The name of each reinsurance entity is abbreviated as follows: China Re Group or China Re, China Re P&C or China Re, China Re Life or China Re, Munich Re or Munich Re Beijing Branch, Swiss Re or Swiss Re Beijing Branch, General Re or General Re Shanghai Branch, SCOR SE or SCOR SE Beijing Branch, Hannover Re or Hannover Re Shanghai Branch, AXA Global Reinsurance (Shanghai), RGA or RGA Shanghai Branch, Taiping Re (China), Qianhai Re, PICC Re, Korean Re or Korean Re Shanghai Branch, and China Agriculture Re.

2. XL Insurance (China) Company Limited was established in 2011 and changed its name to XL Reinsurance (China) Company Limited in 2020 and AXA Global Reinsurance (Shanghai) in 2024.

Source: Yearbook of China's Insurance and annual reports of the reinsurance companies.

2. A pattern of two-way opening-up began to take shape

In terms of "bringing in", the reinsurance market has become one of China's financial service sectors that have opened up earliest and most widely to the outside world since China's accession to the World Trade Organization (WTO) in 2001. All the world's major reinsurers have set up branch offices and carried out business in China, providing talent, technology and capital

urgently needed by China's reinsurance market. In recent years, China's reinsurance industry has furthered its high-level opening-up, kept improving the national policies and standards in line with international standards and practices, activated the internal impetus for industry development and achieved fresh results in high-quality development.

Since the 18th CPC National Congress, China has stepped up the development of Shanghai as an international reinsurance hub. In June 2023, the National Financial Regulatory Administration (NFRA) and Shanghai Municipal People's Government jointly released the *Implementation Rules on Accelerating the Building of Shanghai International Reinsurance Center*, officially kicking off Shanghai's endeavors to create an "international board" for reinsurance. Now the "international board" for reinsurance has become home to dozens of Chinese and foreign insurance companies and brokerage firms. According to the plan, the Shanghai International Reinsurance Center will focus on building an "international board" serving as the global trading venue for ceded reinsurance business. Its purpose is to pool global factors of production to gather in Shanghai, enhance the ability to allocate global resources and build a global reinsurance trading center combining onshore and offshore operations and able to compete globally, thereby creating a hub for the domestic reinsurance market while providing a strategic link between domestic and international markets.

In terms of "going out", China's insurance market underwrites ceded reinsurance business from overseas primary insurers by means of offshore trading. The ceded premiums from overseas markets stood at about RMB

28.3 billion in 2022. Meanwhile, Chinese reinsurers are actively exploring overseas markets, which markedly improve their operation and management capabilities and enhance their international competitiveness. China Re has become the eighth largest global reinsurer and one of the Chinese financial corporations and insurance companies with the highest degree of internationalization. China Re has extended its business to 11 countries and regions outside China.

(III) Business structure

1. Ceded premium income by type of business

In 2023, the premium income of China's reinsurance market stood at RMB 229.61 billion. Specifically, the premium income of treaty business was RMB 225.24 billion, up by 0.5% year-on-year, accounting for about 98.1% of the total premium income. The premium income of facultative business was RMB 4.37 billion, down by 9.0% year-on-year, accounting for about 1.9% of the total (see Figure 9). The treaty business showed softer growth, while the facultative business saw a decline in both growth and share.

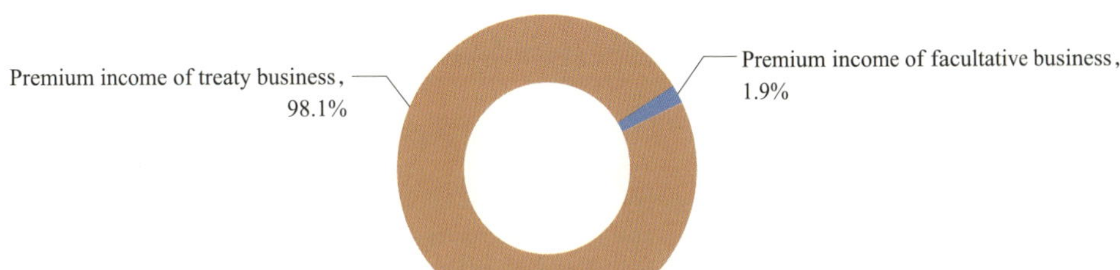

Figure 9 Proportions of Premium Income of Treaty VS. Facultative Business in 2023

(Source: National Financial Regulatory Administration)

From 2012 to 2023, the premium income of treaty business increased from RMB 68.19 billion to RMB 225.24 billion, an average annual growth rate of about 11.5%. The premium income of facultative business increased from RMB 930 million to RMB 4.37 billion, an average annual growth rate of about 15.1% (see Table 6 and Figure 10). In general, the treaty business is the dominant type of reinsurance business, accounting for more than 95%. Facultative business represents a small share with the volume of business declining in the last two years.

Table 6 Premium Incomes, Growth Rates and Proportions of Treaty VS. Facultative Business (2012-2023)

Unit: RMB 100 million, %

	Treaty business premium income	Growth rate	% of total	Facultative business premium income	Growth rate	% of total
2012	681.9		98.7	9.3		1.3
2013	940.3	37.9	99.1	8.3	-10.7	0.9
2014	1,476.7	57.1	99.4	9.23	11.6	0.6
2015	1,055.2	-28.5	99.0	11.0	19.2	1.0
2016	917.9	-13.0	95.8	37.9	243.7	4.0
2017	1,080.2	17.7	98.2	19.4	-48.9	1.8
2018	1,339.4	24.0	97.8	30.7	58.5	2.2
2019	1,539.8	15.0	97.7	36.3	18.1	2.3
2020	1,774.3	15.2	97.5	45.8	26.2	2.5
2021	2,070.7	16.7	97.7	49.5	8.1	2.3
2022	2,240.6	8.2	97.9	48.0	-3.1	2.1
2023	2,252.4	0.5	98.1	43.7	-9.0	1.9

Source: Yearbook of China's Insurance and National Financial Regulatory Administration.

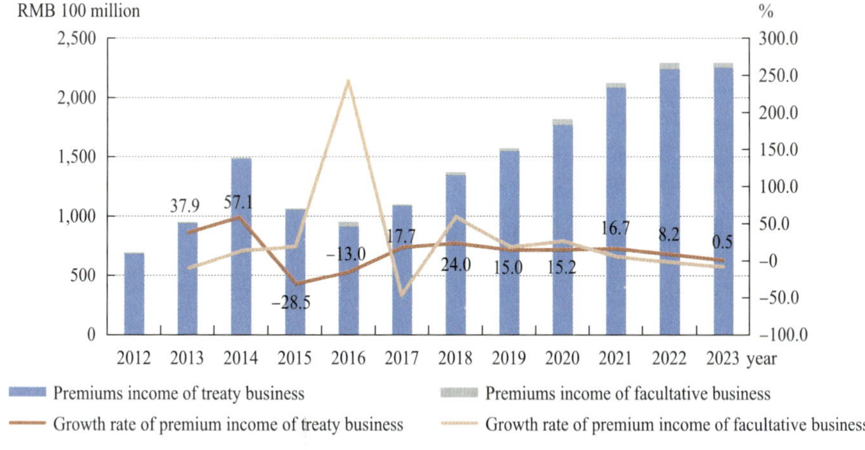

Figure 10 Premium Income of Treaty VS. Facultative Business and Growth Rates (2012-2023)

(Source: Yearbook of China's Insurance and National Financial Regulatory Administration)

2. Ceded premium income by lines of business

In 2023, property reinsurance premium income of China's reinsurance market was RMB 136.30 billion, up by 11.7% year-on-year and accounting for about 62.7% of the total. Life reinsurance premium income was about RMB 31.80 billion, down by 26.6% year-on-year and making up about 14.6% of the total. Health reinsurance premium income was RMB 44.50 billion, down by 16.4% year-on-year and accounting for about 20.5% of the total. Casualty reinsurance premium income was RMB 4.70 billion, down by 26.7% year-on-year and accounting for about 2.2% of the total (see Figure 11).

Overall, firstly, the lines of business showed divergent growth trends in premium income. Property reinsurance grew rapidly, while the life, health and casualty segments shrank in size compared with 2022. Secondly, the share of property reinsurance premium income was significantly higher

than in 2022, while the share of premium income from the life, health and casualty segments was declining. Thirdly, the life reinsurance market was under pressure on the demand, distribution and asset sides, which affected direct insurers' demand for reinsurance and led to a decline in life, health and accident reinsurance premium income.

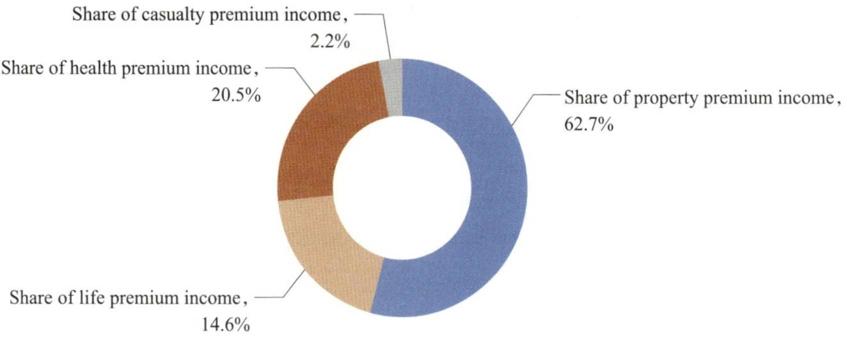

Figure 11 Proportions of Premium Income by Lines of Reinsurance in 2023

(Source: National Financial Regulatory Administration)

From 2012 to 2023, the property reinsurance premium income in China's reinsurance market increased from RMB 46.26 billion to RMB 136.30 billion, an average annual growth rate of about 10.3%. Life reinsurance premium income grew from RMB 15.30 billion to RMB 31.80 billion, an average annual growth rate of about 6.9%. Health reinsurance premium income increased from RMB 5.06 billion to RMB 44.50 billion, an average annual growth rate of about 21.9%. Casualty reinsurance premium income expanded from RMB 2.5 billion to RMB 4.7 billion, an average annual growth rate of about 5.9% (see Table 7 and Figure 12). Health reinsurance recorded the fastest growth over the period, yet showing weaker growth and a shrinking share in recent years (see Figure 13).

Table 7　Premium Income and Growth Rates by Lines (2012-2023)

Unit: RMB 100 million, %

	Property	Growth rate	Life	Growth rate	Health	Growth rate	Casualty	Growth rate
2012	462.6		153.0		50.6		25.0	
2013	562.8	21.7	297.3	94.3	63.5	25.6	24.8	−0.6
2014	588.0	4.5	799.6	168.9	65.7	3.4	32.7	31.7
2015	598.1	1.7	320.9	−59.9	112.1	70.7	35.1	7.4
2016	480.7	−19.6	285.9	−10.9	100.1	−10.8	43.5	23.9
2017	484.9	0.9	430.2	50.5	136.1	36.0	48.4	11.3
2018	600.4	23.8	484.4	12.6	218.2	60.4	67.1	38.5
2019	729.9	21.6	421.3	−13.0	353.1	61.8	73.6	9.7
2020	840.1	15.1	441.6	4.8	454.5	28.7	73.1	−0.7
2021	1,075.6	28.0	445.0	0.8	496.5	9.2	73.1	0.0
2022	1,220.5	13.5	433.4	−2.6	532.2	7.2	64.1	12.3
2023	1,363.0	11.7	318.0	−26.6	445.0	−16.4	47.0	−26.7

Source: Yearbook of China's Insurance and National Financial Regulatory Administration.

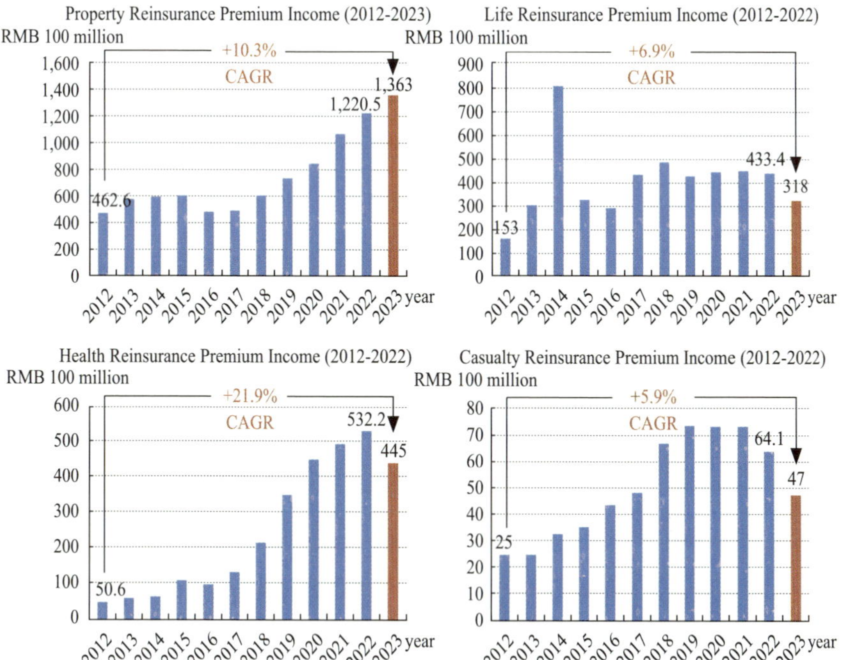

Figure 12　Property, Life, Health, Casualty Reinsurance Premium Income and Annual Growth Rate (2012-2023)

(Source: Yearbook of China's Insurance and National Financial Regulatory Administration)

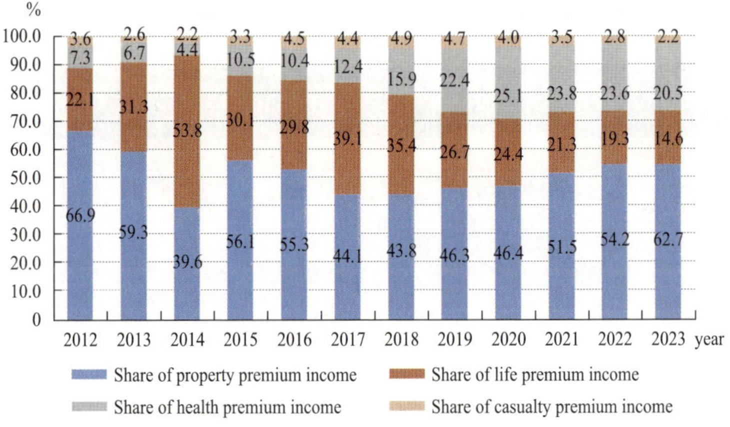

Figure 13 Proportions of Reinsurance Premium Income by Lines (2012-2023)

(Source: Yearbook of China's Insurance and National Financial Regulatory Administration)

(IV) Risk management

1. Solvency capital requirement

The core solvency ratio is the ratio of an insurance company's core capital to its minimum capital requirement (MCR). It measures the adequacy of an insurer's high-quality capital, subject to a minimum regulatory requirement of 50%. The comprehensive solvency ratio is the ratio of the available capital to MCR, which measures the overall adequacy of an insurer's capital, subject to a minimum regulatory requirement of 100%.

From the first quarter to the fourth quarter of 2023, the average core solvency ratios of reinsurance companies were 240.9%, 239.3%, 242.3% and 245.6%, respectively, all exceeding the regulatory floor of 50% and the quarterly averages of P&C insurers and personal insurance companies in the quarters.

From the first quarter to the fourth quarter of 2023, the average

comprehensive solvency ratios of reinsurance companies were 277.7%, 275.2%, 278.3% and 285.3% respectively, all exceeding the regulatory floor of 50% and the quarterly averages of P&C insurers and personal insurance companies in the quarters.

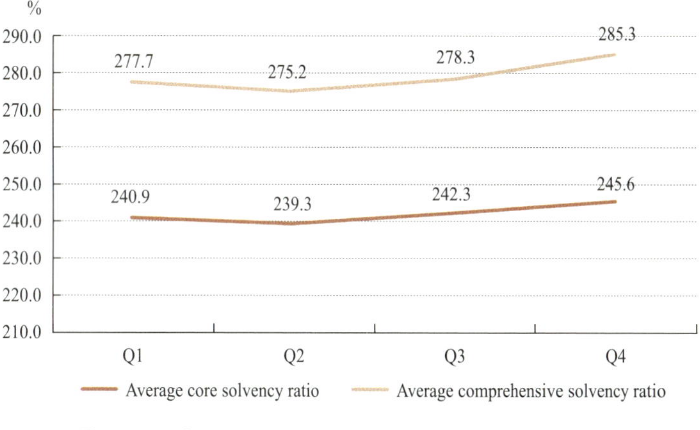

Figure 14 Solvency Ratios of Reinsurance Companies in 2023

(Source: National Financial Regulatory Administration)

2023 saw in a decline in both average core solvency ratio and average comprehensive solvency ratio of reinsurers when compared with 2022. In September 2023, NFRA published the *Notice on Improving the Regulatory Standards for Solvency of Insurance Companies* and recalibrated the regulatory standards for solvency specified in the *Rules on the Regulation of the Solvency of Insurance Companies (II)*. Since the third quarter of 2023, the solvency ratio of reinsurance companies has picked up.

2. Integrated risk rating (IRR)

IRR represents an evaluation of the integrated risk regarding an insurance company's solvency. It measures the overall solvency risk of an insurer with 4 classes: A, B, C and D, and the required regulatory rating is B.

In 2023, a total of 14 reinsurers received and disclosed their quarterly IRRs, all of which were rated Class B or higher.

3. Solvency-Aligned Risk Management Requirements and Assessment (SARMRA)

SARMRA is an important part of the functional supervision of the insurance industry. It reflects the risk management level of an insurance company by assessing the soundness of the system and the effectiveness of compliance. SARMRA is of great significance for improving the risk management level of insurers and enhancing the industry's ability to forestall and defuse risks. A SARMRA score of 80 or higher improves solvency adequacy.

In 2023, regulators conducted onsite SARMRA on 36 insurance companies, including three reinsurers, of which China Agriculture Re received the assessment for the first time. The average score of reinsurers was 78.81[①], down by 0.92 from 2022. As shown by the SARMRA results in 2023, insurance companies generally enhanced their awareness of risk management and strengthened the risk management roles and duties, making progress in risk management. They have established a comprehensive risk management framework, developed a wide range of risk management policies and procedures, established appropriate risk management working mechanisms and established a risk appetite system appropriate to their own particular circumstances.

---

① Source: The annual SARMRA results of insurance companies for 2023 published by NFRA on the website of NFRA.

(V) Development of the reinsurance brokerage market

A reinsurance broker is an insurance brokerage organization that acts on behalf of and in the interests of an insurance company or ceding company and purchases reinsurance protection or service solutions from the assuming insurer (usually a reinsurance company). With the business environment changing and risk management needs diversifying over recent years, the business model of reinsurance brokers has gradually evolved from reinsurance arrangements in the early stage to providing comprehensive services including risk advisory service and risk management techniques.

Players in China's reinsurance brokerage market are mainly international reinsurance brokers, domestic reinsurance brokers and domestic direct insurance brokers who are concurrently engaged in reinsurance business. The China Reinsurance Registration System data show that there were 232 reinsurance brokers as at the end of 2023, of which 120 were overseas brokers, accounting for 51.7%, and 122 were domestic brokers, accounting for 48.3% of the total.

At present, China's reinsurance broker market is dominated by three top-ranked foreign professional reinsurance brokers in the world, namely, Guy Carpenter, Aon and Gallagher, while Chinese reinsurance brokers are growing fast. Foreign reinsurance brokers, with professional teams and sufficient resources in place to provide a full spectrum of services and are able to make complex reinsurance arrangements across the world. Chinese reinsurance brokers and direct insurance brokers have smaller market shares, but are very market-oriented and have a good understanding of clients'

needs, with professional teams for specific lines of business offering a full range of services (see Table 8).

Table 8 Chinese VS. Foreign Reinsurance Brokers

Unit: RMB100 million

Name	Time of registration	Place of registration	Capital	Domestic reinsurance brokerage revenue in 2023
		Foreign		
Guy Carpenter	November 2003	Shanghai	0.5	2
Aon	October 1993	Beijing	0.5	1.3
Gallagher	August 2004	Shanghai	0.5	0.5
		Chinese		
Taiping Reinsurance Brokers	July 1996	Hong Kong	—	1.1
Continental Insurance Broker	August 2003	Beijing	0.5	0.7
Jiang Tai Reinsurance Brokers	July 2015	Shanghai	0.5	0.4
China Zenith Insurance Brokers	November 2004	Beijing	0.1	0.2
Mingrui Insurance Brokerage	May 2009	Shanghai	—	0.1
Huatai Insurance Brokerage	March 1993	Beijing	0.5	0.1

Note: "Domestic reinsurance borkerage revenue in 2023" Data represents the reinsurance brokerage income from customers in the Chinese mainland, excluding brokerage companies' brokerage fee income from direct insurance. Publicly disclosed data is unavailable, and the data is estimation based on market information.

Source: Information disclosed by companies to the public.

III. Reinsurance Services for Economic and Social Development

In 2023, China's reinsurance industry focused on major national strategies, economic and social development and securing living standards,

especially the five priorities of technology finance, green finance, inclusive finance, pension finance and digital finance, contributing its professional value to building China into a financial powerhouse.

(I) Vigorously developing technology insurance to help achieve greater self-reliance and self-strengthening in science and technology

With a focus on the frontier areas and key links of technological innovation, reinsurance has provided stronger support for tech firms and strategic industries, helping build a modern industrial system led by technological innovation. In 2023, the total amount insured by China Re for technological innovation exceeded RMB 430 billion, representing a year-on-year increase of 16.4%. China Re provided reinsurance service for major equipment and facilities, such as the inaugural flight of the domestically-manufactured large passenger jet C919, the launch of national key satellites and the world's first megawatt-scale floating wave energy generation device independently developed by China. Risk protection was provided for the research and development of the first set of major technical equipment, the first batch of new materials and the first release of software. It launched the first "special contract on comprehensive cover for small and medium-sized specialized and sophisticated enterprises that produce new and unique products" in China, developed auto chip insurance products and rolled out the self-driving car insurance. China Re also extended the new cyber-security insurance model of "insurance + risk management + service" to Beijing and Shanghai. PICC Re developed the underwriting and pricing platform

"Cybersecurity E Insurance" for small and medium-sized enterprises. The platform fully scans and assesses the cybersecurity of small and medium-sized enterprises, issues detailed assessment reports and gives security advice, empowering the research and development of cybersecurity products, risk underwriting and plan implementation. Qianhai Re participated in contracts on the first set of major equipment and new materials and exerted every effort to support "Made in China 2025", playing its part in the transformation and upgrading of China's major equipment manufacturing industry.

(II) Vigorously developing green insurance to help achieve peak carbon emissions and carbon neutrality

Reinsurance focuses on transformation toward low-carbon development and ecological conservation, expands the coverage of green insurance and offers innovative green insurance products, giving an impetus to the green upgrading of modern industries. In 2023, the total amount insured by China Re for green development exceeded RMB 3 trillion, representing a year-on-year increase of 26.8%. China Re, as chairman of the China Nuclear Insurance Pool, has supported commercial operation of the world's first fourth-generation nuclear power plant by providing the insurance for front-end facilities of the nuclear fuel cycle and the liability insurance for the use of nuclear technology, thus contributing to China's nuclear power development. It provided comprehensive lifecycle insurance for wind energy, solar photovoltaics and other green energy projects from construction to operation. China Re and Swiss Re were deeply engaged in the compilation of the green insurance classification guidelines of the Insurance Association

of China (IAC), contributing their expertise to the release of the *Green Insurance Classification Guidelines (2023 Edition).* Eyeing the emerging field of the transition toward green development of marine economy, Swiss Re Institute released the *Insurance for the Blue Economy*, exploring the connotation and business scope of blue insurance for the first time and driving the development of emerging business fields. Since last year, PICC Re's underwriting capacity for offshore wind energy investment has increased by 100% year-on-year, enhancing its ability to serve national strategies across the board. Qianhai Re took part in the liability insurance excess-of-loss contracts of direct property insurers to support the development of front-end environmental pollution liability insurance. It also supported the property insurance for clean energy projects including photovoltaic power stations and wind farms, such as the property and engineering insurance contracts of the insurance subsidiaries of power groups.

(III) Vigorously developing inclusive insurance to help realize a better life

First, the reinsurance industry helped forestall and defuse the business risks of micro and small businesses and keep the private sector on track. In 2023, China Re served 3.72 million micro, small and medium-sized enterprises, representing a year-on-year increase of 150.8%. It continued to focus on protecting businesses from risks, supporting the expansion of domestic demand and stabilising employment. In Shanxi Province, China Re helped launch the first ever provincial "Hui Shang Bao" product. To meet special needs regarding catering, lodging, cultural tourism and community

care, China Re developed over 540 products with industrial and local characteristics thus boosting business confidence.

Second, the reinsurance industry supported the building of a multi-tiered social security system, focusing on vulnerable groups and improving people's well-being through inclusive security. In 2023, China Re helped the Healthy China initiative by serving 210 million people, an increase of 78.5% year-on-year. In support of the governmental endeavors to benefit the people, Chine Re added special medicines, one-stop claim settlement and other quality services for "Huimin Insurance" in regions like Beijing and Suzhou. The youth series of insurance products were developed to help the young grow up healthy and safe. Qianhai Re launched nine "Huimin Insurance" projects covering Beijing, Shenzhen, Hainan Province, Guizhou Province, Anhui Province, Guangxi (Nanning City), Xiamen City, Suzhou City and Hubei Province (Yunmeng County), benefiting more than eight million people. Qianhai Re continued to promote non-standard population systems and innovative products to serve vulnerable groups. By the end of 2023, the company had cooperated with more than 10 domestic life insurance companies in launching a number of non-standard population products on five Internet insurance platforms, providing health protection for people with more than 100 diseases. In addition, on the basis of non-standard population projects, Qianhai Re has developed exclusive health insurance products for some of the common chronic diseases, such as lung nodules, breast nodules, thyroid nodules, life after thyroid cancer surgery, life after breast cancer surgery, hypertension, Trio H's (hyperglycemia, hypertension and hyperlipidemia), kidney disease, liver disease, etc. in cooperation

with a number of insurance companies. Swiss Re, with a focus on product innovation for the elderly, accelerated its shift to electronic underwriting and claims handling and participated in the compilation of the *Fourth Set of China Life Insurance Industry Life Tables*, contributing to the high-quality development of China's life insurance market.

Third, the reinsurance industry helped boost China's strength in agriculture, ensuring food security with agricultural insurance. China Re actively plays the role of agricultural risk protection, further promotes high-standard farmland insurance, explores the development of forestry and grassland carbon sink index insurance. The sum insured of serving the rural revitalisation was RMB705.15 billion in 2023, representing a year-on-year increase of 12.9%. Swiss Re, together with relevant enterprises, launched the *Operation Guidelines on Technical Inspection Service (TIS) for Inherent Defects Insurance (IDI) of High-standard Farmland Infrastructure Projects*. Based on the TIS practices in IDI insurance at home and abroad, Swiss Re helped the insurance industry deepen its understanding of new risks, learn the risk management methods, establish a risk evaluation system, develop rational and healthy underwriting and business development strategies, and improve the quality of farmland infrastructure through systematic and lifecycle risk management. Swiss Re issued the *Research on Innovation in the Agricultural Product Quality and Safety Insurance*. This report, with an eye on all the quality and safety risks through the value chain of agricultural products, pointed out that risk management has become the core of enhancing the quality and safety of agricultural products. As an effective risk transfer tool, insurance helps further enhance the quality

and safety of agricultural products in the new era by providing protections from loss prevention to risk management and economic compensation. Qianhai Re actively participated in China's first reinsurance contract for rural revitalization, focusing on opening up new lines of business regarding the "agriculture, rural areas and farmers", including the development of high-standard farmland, the improvement of agricultural mechanization rate and the beautiful countryside drive, so as to provide diversified, customized and integrated risk protection for the agriculture and rural areas, and promote the new ecosystem development serving the rural revitalization strategy. Qianhai Re also supported the reinsurance contracts of the newly established China Fishery Mutual Insurance Corporation, further enhancing the fishery risk protection in China and promoting high-quality development of the fishery industry.

Fourth, efforts were stepped up to help build a catastrophe insurance system to serve the modernization of social governance system. China Re served the country's disaster prevention, reduction and relief initiative, and undertook insurance responsibility for domestic earthquake, flood and typhoon risks amounting to RMB25.8 trillion, up 11% year-on-year. China Re participated in the catastrophe insurance pilot projects in all 19 provinces and municipalities, served as the lead reinsurer for 80% of our projects, and provided compensation payments of RMB650 million for disaster-stricken events such as the heavy rains in the Beijing-Tianjin-Hebei region and the earthquake in Jishishan county. China Re also iterated and upgraded a series of catastrophe models with independent intellectual property rights for earthquakes, typhoons, floods and other catastrophes and leading the industry in technological capabilities. Actively responding to climate

change, China Re worked with the PBC to develop a physical risk stress testing model for climate change, took the lead in the national key research and development program of the Ministry of Science and Technology on "Prevention and Control of Major Natural Disasters and Public Security", and provided advice to the State on the establishment of catastrophe insurance systems and other major issues to help enhance the country's ability to prevent and control disasters. The visualized catastrophe risk management platform "Catastrophe Altazimuth" developed by PICC Re uses the regional catastrophe risk theory and geographic information system (GIS) technology to enable insurance companies' multi-dimension, multi-scenario and multi-factor management of catastrophe risks as well as industry-wide risk reduction and sophisticated management. A total of 40 insurance companies have become registered users of the platform.

(IV) Vigorously developing pension insurance in light of the aging population trend

Reinsurance helps improve the risk protection and service level for the elderly and refine the multi-tier pension insurance system. China Re actively promote the innovation of insurance products and services for the elderly. It provided "chronic disease + critical illness + care" protection, and roposed the innovative critical illness nursing insurance in conjunction with chronic disease management services and health care services, and then promoted the implementation of these products; innovatively launched the first disability insurance in the market to move the disability care payment forward, enhancing the people's sense of gain; innovated medical

insurance for the elderly by providing medical expense protection for the elderly; promoted the "insurance + diagnosis and treatment + rehabilitation services" model, created a model of long-term care insurance in the industry, and sold more than 500,000 insurance policies of the new long-term care and disability products in 2023. Swiss Re has deepened its cooperation with the Insurance Association of China (IAC) to complete the *Study on the Risk Protection of Middle-aged and Elderly People in China*. For the first time, this report systematically reviews and analyzes the insurance protection status of the middle-aged and elderly people in China and the consumers' insurance demand preferences, laying a foundation for industry players to develop new insurance products for the middle-aged and older people. Qianhai Re pays great attention to the risk protection needs of senior people. As of the end of 2023, Qianhai Re had developed a series of health insurance products tailored for the people with chronic diseases and the silver-haired population in cooperation with more than 10 insurance companies, such as medical products with benefits up to RMB1 million for the people with chronic conditions, medical insurance for online follow-up service and reimbursement of medication for chronic diseases and the dementia protection insurance for the elderly at risk of dementia.

(V) Vigorously developing digital insurance and enhancing the capability of risk reduction services

Empowered by digital technology, reinsurance services have become more efficient with higher quality. China Re has iteratively upgraded the "Digital China Re" strategy, established China Re Digital Technology

Co., Ltd. ("China Re DT"), released the topology and roadmap for digital transition and built a new strategic framework with China Re CRM and China Re DT as the two technological wings empowering innovative development of the mainstay business of reinsurance. China Re developed and launched the "Re · Yun" agricultural insurance technology platform. Swiss Re launched the Swiss Re Agriculture Insurance Risk Management Platform (SRAIRMP). The platform, through its real-time disaster analysis function, tracked, monitored and assessed the entire process of heavy rainfall disasters in the provinces affected by Typhoon Doksuri. It has promoted agricultural risk reduction services by using big data, artificial intelligence and agricultural risk management models, and helped government agencies, insurance companies and agricultural enterprises carry out disaster prevention, mitigation and relief work more proactively and in a targeted manner. Qianhai Re selected the neural network model as the core algorithm for the intelligent pricing engine of heavy truck insurance, and developed the API interface to help insurance companies effectively solve the long-standing problem of heavy trucks' difficult access to insurance. In terms of life insurance, Qianhai Re has obtained the software copyrights in the "non-standard automatic underwriting system" and the "life insurance estimation system", and developed innovative products, such as the universal medical insurance and chronic illness insurance, together with its partners.

IV. Reinsurance Trends and Outlook

(I) Opportunities and challenges

1. Opportunities

First, China's economic growth provides a solid foundation for the reinsurance industry. The Central Financial Work Conference held in October 2023 called for efforts to create a sound monetary and financial environment. The Central Economic Work Conference held in December stressed the need to maintain the proactive fiscal policy and prudent monetary policy in 2024. Despite uncertainties in the world economy, China's economy maintained relatively steady growth with great resilience and potential as macro policies came into play. Amid the ongoing push for industry and consumption upgrading, transition toward green and low-carbon development as well as business and investment expansion of enterprises, the property reinsurance market demand has expanded, and the personal insurance products such as health insurance and pension insurance are growing rapidly to broaden the market space for personal reinsurance.

Second, China's insurance industry still has vast space for development. Since the reform and opening-up began, China's insurance industry has developed rapidly into an important sector of the modern economy and a basic instrument of risk management. However, it is still in its early stage of development, showing much room for improvement in insurance penetration and density when compared with that in developed economies. The 20th National Congress of the Communist Party of China (CPC) has

drawn up a grand blueprint of advancing the rejuvenation of the Chinese nation on all fronts through Chinese modernization. As a fundamental institutional arrangement for the modern market economy, insurance is ushering in a crucial opportunity for high-quality development. It will play a pivotal role in strengthening social resilience and safeguarding development in terms of healthcare, old-age security, environmental governance, social management, workplace safety, public security and disaster prevention and relief.

Third, there are opportunities for development in the global market. Against the backdrop of China getting increasingly integrated into the world economy, the global market has continued to show diversified development potential, offering an important strategic opportunity for China's reinsurance industry to go global faster, fully integrate itself into the international insurance market, enhance its global competitiveness and influence, and speed up the transition and upgrading of the domestic insurance industry. The cyclical recovery of the European and US markets after the COVID-19 pandemic has strengthened the growth prospects of developed insurance markets. The development of emerging insurance markets, especially in Asia and Africa, has added to the fuel for the reinsurance market growth. Meanwhile, as the Belt and Road Initiative of China goes deeper, there are prominent special risks in overseas energy, infrastructure, manufacturing and high-tech industries that are not covered. The demand for insurance coverage has become increasingly strong, providing Chinese reinsurers with overseas opportunities. In addition, the challenges from global climate change, political uncertainty and economic volatility have been

strengthening the demand for international cooperation and risk sharing, bringing opportunities for Chinese reinsurers to expand their overseas presence and expand their global influence.

2. Challenges

First, the macro environment is complex and volatile, with global fluctuations coupled by domestic transformation. Internationally, the rise of trade protectionism, geopolitical tensions, rebalancing of global supply chains and tightening of monetary policies in many countries have a direct impact on the stability of insurance demand, return on asset allocations and assessment of payout risk. At present, China is in a crucial period of shifting its development model, improving its economic structure and changing its growth drivers. This transition period is characterised by insufficient domestic demand, overcapacity in some industries, low social expectations and persisting risks in many areas, which may affect the insurance purchasing power of companies and individuals and thus indirectly put pressure on the reinsurance market. Frequent natural disasters and potential threats from global public health incidents not only test the insurance industry's ability to pay, but also pose new challenges to the actuarial models and risk assessment mechanism of reinsurance companies. As the interest rate spread with overseas markets is in a narrowing trend amid China's low interest rates that will continue, the insurance and reinsurance companies will find it more difficult to manage their assets and liabilities.

Second, the intensifying market competition adds to the pressure on business innovation and differentiated competition. In the property insurance market, the frequency of natural catastrophes has led to higher claims costs

and increased competition. In particular, in the area of catastrophe risk transfer, insurance companies are seeking more efficient solutions for risk cession, which is driving reinsurance companies to continue to innovate their products and services. In personal lines, competition for market share is fierce, placing greater demands on the ability to meet individual needs with differentiated and innovative products. For example, protection against longevity risks and critical illnesses requires life insurers to be more responsive to the market and better able to provide customised services. In health insurance, the demand for health insurance continues to grow as the population ages and medical costs rise, attracting an influx of technology companies and specialist health reinsurers. Technological capabilities in health management, telemedicine and big data analytics have become a new competitive advantage. Reinsurance companies have to be capable of processing massive personal health data and ensuring privacy and data security, significantly adding to the complexity of operations.

(II) Trends and outlook

First, reinsurance will focus on serving the development of the real economy. China's reinsurance industry will actively adapt itself to new developments in the economic restructuring and industrial upgrading across the country. Through ongoing innovation in the risk protection service model, reinsurance will provide high-quality service for the major national strategies and new demands of the real economy. In the fields of infrastructure, high-tech, modern agriculture and green energy, reinsurance will play a more important role in risk protection. For example,

stable reinsurance support over the long term will boost the funding and construction of infrastructure projects, reduce potential losses caused by natural disasters, technological risks and other factors and ensure the smooth implementation of projects. With a focus on key areas including green insurance, health insurance and micro and small business insurance, a package of customized reinsurance solutions will be provided to meet diverse needs.

Second, the reinsurance business model will continue to innovate and iterate. The insurance technology has developed rapidly in recent years. In particular, the generative artificial intelligence that gains steam is reshaping the business model and service mode in the insurance industry. Driven by digital transition, China's reinsurance industry will further advance upgrading of the reinsurance model and step up high-quality development. Efforts will continue to deepen the insurance-reinsurance integration, government-business integration and integration of industries, so as to extend the service chains and extend risk management expertise and capabilities to the larger community. The upstream and downstream resources will be integrated to lead product and service innovation, improve infrastructure development and enrich the supply of public goods. A new business model of "re-insurance + technology + service" will be developed to build a platform-based ecosystem that serves the national strategies, social governance and public wellbeing, and broaden the access to services. The operation management and business processes will be reengineered faster to become digital and intelligent, so as to enhance the ability to quantify, identify and manage risks with the digital technology, promote the intelligent

upgrading of operation management.

Third, the reinsurance market will accelerate two-way opening-up. China's reinsurance market will open up wider to shape a new pattern of two-way opening-up where domestic and overseas participants are equally important, thus making the industry more competitive worldwide. On the one hand, large international reinsurers continue to increase their presence in China and introduce advanced management practices and technologies into the Chinese reinsurance market, helping enhance the overall service level and innovation capability of the market. On the other hand, as Shanghai gains pace to build itself into an international reinsurance hub, Chinese reinsurers are "going global" faster by setting up overseas branches, participating in international reinsurance and creating a global cooperation network. They take an active part in global competition with a stronger capacity of global services.

Fourth, the reinsurance policy system will continue to improve. In October 2023, the Central Financial Work Conference called for focusing on the five priorities of technology finance, green finance, inclusive finance, pension finance and digital finance. Subsequently a series of policy guidelines were issued to chart the course of development and provide systematic planning, guiding the reinsurance industry to further improve the quality and effectiveness of services for the real economy and public wellbeing. In September 2024, the *Opinions of the State Council on Strengthening Supervision and Preventing Risks to Promote High-quality Development of the Insurance Industry* (Guo Fa [2024] No. 21) was issued, requiring that the insurance industry should fully function as an economic shock absorber

and a social stabilizer with a stronger insurance capacity and higher service level. With such a clear policy direction, the insurance industry will enhance compliance of operations, strengthen risk management and create a better competitive environment and market order. Also, reinsurance companies will enhance their professional capabilities in risk management, product and service innovation and risk reduction toward high-quality and sustainable development.

Chapter II

Review and Outlook on China's P&C Reinsurance Market in 2023

I. Market Size

(I) Size of ceded premiums

In 2023, the total ceded premiums of China's P&C insurance companies stood at RMB 163.75 billion, up by 0.5% year-on-year. During the same period, the total primary insurance premiums of P&C insurers amounted to RMB 1.58678 trillion, up by 5.6% year-on-year, and the growth rate of ceded premiums was about 5.1 percentage points lower than that of primary insurance premiums over the same period (see Figure 1 and Table 1).

Between 2013 and 2023, the ceded premiums of P&C insurance companies in China increased from RMB 86.52 billion to RMB 163.75 billion, with an average annual growth rate of about 6.6%. During the same period, the primary insurance premiums of P&C insurers increased from RMB 648.09 billion to RMB 1.58678 trillion, with an average annual growth rate of about 9.4%. The average annual growth rate of ceded premiums was about 2.8 percentage points lower than that of primary insurance premiums over the same period (see Figure 1 and Table 1).

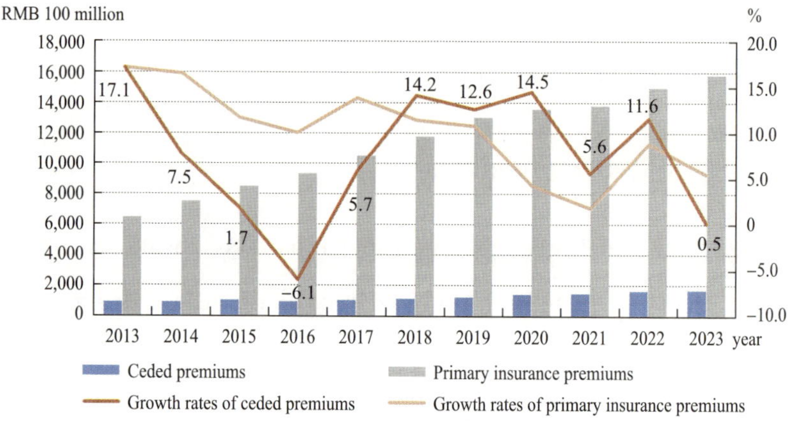

Figure 1 Primary Insurance Premiums, Ceded Premiums and Growth Rates of P&C Insurance Companies (2013-2023)

(Source: Yearbook of China's Insurance and National Financial Regulatory Administration)

Table 1 Ceded Premiums, Primary Insurance Premiums and Cession Rates of P&C Insurance Companies (2013-2023)

Unit: RMB 100 million, %

Years	Ceded premiums	Growth rates	Primary premiums	Growth rates	Cession rates
2013	865.2	17.1	6,481.2	17.2	13.3
2014	929.8	7.5	7,544.4	16.4	12.3
2015	946.0	1.7	8,423.3	11.6	11.2
2016	887.9	-6.1	9,266.2	10.0	9.6
2017	938.8	5.7	10,541.4	13.8	8.9
2018	1,072.3	14.2	11,755.7	11.5	9.1
2019	1,207.7	12.6	13,016.3	10.7	9.3
2020	1,383.4	14.5	13,583.7	4.4	10.2
2021	1,460.5	5.6	13,816.2	1.7	10.6
2022	1,629.5	11.6	15,019.4	8.7	10.8
2023	1,637.5	0.5	15,867.8	5.6	10.3

Source: Yearbook of China's Insurance and National Financial Regulatory Administration.

(II) Cession rates

In 2023, the cession rate of China's P&C insurance companies was about 10.3%, exceeding 10% for the fourth year in a row, down by 0.5 percentage points year-on-year (see Figure 2).

The P&C cession rates saw a year-on-year decline from 2013 to 2015, yet remaining above 10%, and showed a falling trend followed by a rising one from 2016 to 2022. In 2023, the rate dropped by 0.5 percentage points to 10.3%. The P&C cession rate declined sharply to below 10% in 2016, mainly due to the implementation of C-ROSS II, and further dropped to less than 9% in 2017 amid the continued impact of C-ROSS II. Since 2018, the P&C cession rates have increased over time due to growing non-motor insurance business. The rates remained above 10% from 2020 through 2023.

Figure 2 Cession Rates of P&C Insurance Companies (2013-2023)

(Source: Yearbook of China's Insurance and National Financial Regulatory Administration)

II. Demand-side Analysis

(I) Distribution of ceded premiums

In 2023, four P&C insurance companies had P&C ceded premiums over RMB 10 billion, totaling RMB 101.49 billion and accounting for 61.8% of the industry's total ceded premiums. A total of 18 P&C insurers had P&C ceded premiums ranging from RMB 1 billion to RMB 10 billion, totaling RMB 42.96 billion and accounting for 26.2% of industry-wide ceded premiums. A total of 49 P&C insurers had P&C ceded premiums ranging from RMB 0.1 billion to RMB 1 billion, totaling RMB 19.27 billion and accounting for 11.7%. A total of 18 P&C insurers had P&C ceded premiums of less than RMB 0.1 billion, totaling RMB 0.56 billion and accounting for 0.3% of the total (see Table 2).

Table 2 Distribution of Ceded Premiums from P&C Insurance Companies in 2023

Unit: company, RMB 100 million, %

Size	Number	Total ceded premiums	% of total
Ceded premiums of more than RMB 10 billion	4	1,014.9	61.8
Ceded premiums of RMB 1 billion to RMB 10 billion	18	429.6	26.2
Ceded premiums of RMB 100 million to RMB 1 billion	49	192.7	11.7
Ceded premiums of less than RMB 100 million	18	5.6	0.3

Source: National Financial Regulatory Administration.

(II) Changes in ceded premiums

In 2023, 55 P&C insurance companies saw a year-on-year increase in P&C ceded premiums, accounting for 61.8% of the total. Specifically, 14 P&C insurers had a year-on-year increase of less than 10%, accounting for 15.7% of the total; 13 had a year-on-year increase from 10% to 20%, accounting for 14.6% of the total; and 28 had a year-on-year increase of over 20%, accounting for 31.5% of the total (see Table 3).

Table 3 Distribution of Ceded Premiums Growth Rates of P&C Insurance Companies in 2023

Unit: company, %

	Number	% of total
P&C insurance companies with a YoY increase in ceded premiums	55	61.8
Of which: Companies with a YoY increase less than 10%	14	15.7
Companies with a YoY increase of 10% to 20%	13	14.6
Companies with a YoY increase over 20%	28	31.5

Source: National Financial Regulatory Administration, excluding the business of Lloyd's China.

(III) Distribution of cession rates

In 2023, 40 P&C insurance companies had a P&C cession rate of over 20%, accounting for 44.9% of the total, a decrease of one company year-on-year; 7 had a P&C cession rate from 15% to 20%, accounting for 7.9% of the total, and an increase of one company year-on-year; nine had a P&C cession rate from 10% to 15%, accounting for 10.1% of the total, an decrease of one company year-on-year; 15 had a P&C cession rate from 5% to 10%, accounting for 16.9% of the total, a decrease of one company year-on-year;

18 had a P&C cession rate of less than 5%, accounting for 20.2% of the total, an increase of four companies year-on-year (see Table 4).

Table 4 Distribution of Reinsurance Cession Rates of P&C Insurance Companies (2016-2023)

Unit: company

Cession rates	2016	2017	2018	2019	2020	2021	2022	2023
>20%	26	26	28	34	32	38	41	40
15% to 20%	4	5	8	2	10	5	6	7
10% to 15%	12	12	11	15	7	8	10	9
5% to 10%	14	17	15	11	12	18	16	15
<5%	24	24	25	25	26	17	14	18
Total	80	84	87	87	87	86	87	89

Source: National Financial Regulatory Administration.

III. Supply-side Analysis

In 2023, there were 12 professional reinsurance companies registered and/or engaging in P&C reinsurance business in China. Five of these companies were Chinese reinsurers and seven were foreign reinsurers. China Re P&C played its role as the main market channel of reinsurance in China, ranking first in terms of market share.

(I) Motor line of business

In 2022, the P&C reinsurance market recorded RMB 19.94 billion in professional reinsurers' premium income from the motor line of business, down by 2.5% year-on-year. From 2012 to 2022, the average annual growth rate was about -3.3%, showing an overall downtrend in business size. The annual premium income from the motor line showed the fastest growth in 2013, at around 27.7%, and the sharpest decline in 2016, at about 42.6%.

The business size shrank to around RMB 20 billion from more than RMB 30 billion in 2016, and fell below RMB 20 billion for the first time in 2022 (see Table 5).

Table 5 Premium Income of Professional Reinsurers from the Motor Line (2012-2022)

Unit: RMB 100 million

	2012	2013	2014	2015	2016	2017	2018	2019	2020	2021	2022
China Re P&C	147.0	170.0	174.9	181.5	94.3	91.2	88.4	83.5	98.1	81.0	84.6
Munich Re Beijing Branch	39.3	65.6	46.6	45.5	43.3	30.3	41.6	28.3	28.7	25.7	22.6
Swiss Re Beijing Branch	78.2	103.1	106.3	83.1	38.3	38.5	33.8	42.9	44.7	42.9	32.7
SCOR SE Beijing Branch	3.7	9.1	14.1	16.4	14.6	12.5	12.1	10.6	4.5	4.3	4.5
General Re Shanghai Branch		0.1	0.1	0.2	0.2	0.2	0.2	0.2	0.2	0.2	0.1
Hannover Re Shanghai Branch	10.3	3.7	3.4	20.7	6.2	4.6	8.2	12.0	14.4	14.6	13.5
Taiping Re (China)		4.0	4.6	6.4	6.3	7.6	11.5	11.8	11.9	11.6	15.7
Qianhai Re						1.4	2.5	5.2	3.9	3.8	3.3
PICC Re						15.6	10.1	10.6	21.6	20.4	22.2
Korean Re										0.1	0.2
Total	278.4	355.5	350.0	353.8	203.2	201.8	208.4	205.1	228.1	204.5	199.4

Source: Yearbook of China's Insurance.

Among market players, China Re P&C ranked first industry-wide by premium income from the motor line, which stood at RMB 8.46 billion in 2022 for China Re P&C, versus less than RMB 4 billion for all other players.

(II) Non-motor lines of business

In 2022, the P&C reinsurance market recorded RMB 95.65 billion in professional reinsurers' premium income from the non-motor lines of

business, up by 16.2% year-on-year. From 2012 to 2022, the average annual growth rate was about 17.9%, showing rapid overall growth in business size. The annual premium income from non-motor lines remained the positive growth, except in 2015 and 2017. The non-motor lines showed strong growth, with the premium income passing the marks of RMB 40 billion, RMB 50 billion and RMB 90 billion in 2018, 2019 and 2022, respectively (see Table 6).

Table 6 Premium Income of Professional Reinsurers from Non-motor Lines (2012-2022)

Unit: RMB 100 million

	2012	2013	2014	2015	2016	2017	2018	2019	2020	2021	2022
China Re P&C	93.5	114.2	118.1	114.8	123.6	128.9	162.9	203.7	235.4	269.3	336.4
Munich Re Beijing Branch	25.4	23.1	26.3	27.6	41.2	16.5	41.5	46.6	38.9	50.3	53.7
Swiss Re Beijing Branch	46.2	53.2	52.6	60.3	59.3	37.0	58.8	76.7	81.0	95.9	89.9
SCOR SE Beijing Branch	12.6	15.2	18.3	19.2	23.1	22.8	21.3	22.1	23.0	29.7	28.7
General Re Shanghai Branch	0.2	0.3	0.5	0.4	0.3	0.7	1.5	1.9	3.2	2.2	2.9
Hannover Re Shanghai Branch	6.3	5.5	30.7	10.5	16.2	20.7	33.4	54.5	81.4	68.4	77.3
AXA Global Reinsurance (Shanghai)										4.8	3.1
Taiping Re (China)		9.4	11.0	12.0	14.2	22.8	32.5	38.9	39.0	39.8	47.5
Qianhai Re						4.7	19.1	18.2	21.3	25.5	25.5
PICC Re						19.1	38.8	47.0	29.9	40.6	45.0
Korean Re									0.7	5.0	5.7
China Agriculture Re										191.7	240.8
Total	184.2	220.8	257.4	244.8	278.1	273.2	409.8	509.6	553.8	823.1	956.5

Source: Yearbook of China's Insurance.

Among market players, China Re P&C ranked first industry-wide by premium income from the non-motor lines, which stood at RMB 33.64 billion in 2022 for China Re P&C, versus less than RMB 25 billion for all other players.

IV. Opportunities and Challenges in the P&C Reinsurance Market

(I) Opportunities for development of the P&C insurance market

1. Focusing on the "five priorities" of finance, the P&C insurance industry has ample room for development in such fields as fostering strategic emerging industries, promoting green and low-carbon development and improving public wellbeing.

At the Central Financial Work Conference held in October 2023, the central leadership called for focusing efforts on the five priorities of technology finance, green finance, inclusive finance, pension finance and digital finance. The P&C insurance industry will focus its development on the five priorities. The following types of insurance will have great growth potential.

First, customized urban home P&C insurance. The home property version of the "Huimin Insurance" provides integrated "insurance + services" protection, available to buyers in several provinces and cities. Second, drone liability insurance. According to the *Interim Regulations for Managing Unmanned Aerial Vehicle (UAV) Flight*. The drone liability insurance will become compulsory in 2024, requiring that insurance should

be procured for commercial flights of UAVs and non-commercial flights of UAVs other than micro and light UAVs. Third, private commercial space insurance. At present, private commercial space enterprises have developed many models and types of rockets. The insurance industry has explored a "stepwise insurance" model. Fourth, fishery insurance. The 2023 No. 1 Central Document "encourages the development of fishery insurance". The China Fishery Mutual Insurance Corporation was approved to open, adding to the segments of commercial insurance market. Fifth, catastrophe insurance. The catastrophe insurance pilot project was introduced in Henan Province in the second year of the extreme rainstorm disaster in Zhengzhou. The "Beijing-Tianjin-Hebei" rainstorm and flood disaster in 2023 has again shed light on the inadequate catastrophe risk protection at present, implying growth room for catastrophe insurance. Sixth, cybersecurity insurance. The Ministry of Industry and Information Technology (MIIT) and National Financial Regulatory Administration jointly issued a document to ensure well-regulated and sound development of cybersecurity insurance. The global cybersecurity insurance market has reached a premium size of 10 billion US dollars. By contrast, the domestic enterprises have insufficient protection against cybersecurity risks, suggesting huge space for development.

2. Policies are shifting P&C insurance to risk reduction services over the medium and long terms.

In January 2023, the former CBIRC issued the *Opinions on Promoting Risk Reduction Services in the P&C Insurance Industry*, requiring efforts to step up the development of risk reduction services in the P&C insurance

industry. P&C insurers have made a variety of explorations. For example, in commercial truck insurance, insured trucks are equipped with video monitoring devices to reduce the risks associated with blind spots and drowsy driving. Workplace safety liability insurance provides risk education and training, as well as screening for potential hazards. For construction projects, inherent defect insurance (IDI) engages third party organizations to review construction quality risks throughout the project. In the construction project insurance, engineers conduct an onsite survey and give advice on disaster and loss prevention. In the elevator insurance, the maintenance and repair services are integrated to ensure timely and adequate maintenance of the equipment.

In addition, P&C insurance companies innovate their services, tap deep into particular market segments, create new service models, enhance customer convenience, and speed up the integration of technological innovation and risk reduction services. For example, by integrating cross-sector information such as underwriting and claim data, geographic data as well as weather and meteorological data, risk maps are drawn with a focus on risk scenarios, so that the big data technology provides data inputs for decision making on risk reduction service in more scenarios. The satellite-based remote sensing is used for risk survey of the surrounding environment of projects, give early warnings and detect risks of forest fires, and give alerts to agricultural meteorological disasters. The unmanned aerial vehicles are used to conduct power grid line inspection, project risk survey and pesticide spraying to prevent and control agricultural diseases. The Internet of Things (IoT) technology is applied to build an intelligent firefighting platform,

conduct electrical fire monitoring and implement smart monitoring of flooding.

(II) Opportunities for development of the P&C reinsurance market

First, reinsurance helps serve national strategies with a focus on the five priorities of finance. Focusing on the five priorities of finance, P&C insurance companies have expanded insurance coverage and introduced new insurance types in technology insurance, green insurance and inclusive insurance, among others. Reinsurance helps serve national strategies by providing reinsurance services for agricultural, catastrophe and other insurance. Also, reinsurers cooperate with direct insurers in risk research and product innovation centering on the five priorities of finance.

Second, reinsurance helps innovate products and services with a focus on the development of new quality productive forces. Accelerating the development of new quality productive forces has become a new requirement posed by high-quality development. With a focus on low-altitude economy, new energy and other emerging fields, P&C insurers need step up their innovation in products and services. Reinsurance is naturally based on platform. Capitalizing on its strengths in data accumulation, technological capacity and cooperation network, reinsurance supports direct insurers in innovative product design, product pricing, terms and conditions design and risk management.

Third, reinsurance helps provide risk reduction services with a focus on risk reduction. Reinsurance has a unique role in driving risk reduction

services in the P&C insurance industry. Reinsurers can join P&C insurers in providing risk reduction services in the fields of natural disaster risks, agricultural risks, building quality risks and emerging risks.

(III) Risks and challenges facing the P&C insurance and reinsurance markets

First, as medium- and long-term climate risks are escalating, natural disasters are expected to result in heavier losses. Asia remains the world's most disaster-hit region as the impact of climate change is intensifying[①]. According to the *Blue Book on Climate Change of China 2024* published by the Climate Change Center of the China Meteorological Administration (CMA), China's temperatures are rising faster than the global average, and China's Climate Risk Index has shown an upward trend, as evidenced by higher frequency and intensity of extreme heat events, more extreme precipitation events and increased fluctuations in the average typhoon intensity. Also, the World Meteorological Organization announced that El Niño conditions began to develop, which will further complicate the climate in China. The meteorological authority has predicted a number of scenarios, including heavy rainfall in most parts of the country in some years, floods in the Huaihe River basin in some years, floods in the Yangtze River basin in some years and heavy rainfall in areas south of the Yangtze River in some years.

Natural disasters hit China frequently in 2023, resulting in heavier losses. In late May, a run of wet weather during the wheat harvest season in

① State of the Climate in Asia 2022, World Meteorological Organization.

southern Henan led to a reduction in summer grain production by more than 2.5 billion kilograms, pushing the insurance payouts beyond RMB 2 billion. In late July and early August, Typhoon Doksuri and torrential rains and floods in the Beijing-Tianjin-Hebei region hit more than 10 provinces and cities, with insured losses estimated to be more than RMB 10 billion. Given the rising losses caused by disastrous extreme weather, the P&C insurance industry has seen its liability for natural disasters building up rapidly, with the compound annual growth rate of typhoon and flood risk exposures exceeding 10%, faster than the premium growth of relevant insurance products over the same period. The premium adequacy ratio for disaster risks remains under pressure.

Column: Natural Disasters[①] and Insurance Payouts[②] in China in 2023

In 2023, natural disasters in China were mainly floods, typhoons, earthquakes and geological disasters. Droughts, hailstorms, low temperatures and snow disasters, sandstorms and forest and grassland fires also hit China to varying degrees. In early summer, a long run of wet weather hit Henan and other places, adversely affecting the summer harvest. In the major flood season, major disasters such as super Typhoon Doksuri, catastrophic flood in the Haihe River basin, and heavy rainstorms and floods in the Song-Liao River basin occurred one after another. In mid-December, the disastrous winter storms in Shanxi and other places had a great impact on the work and life of local people. On December 18, a Magnitude 6.2 earthquake hit Jishishan County, Gansu Province, resulting in heavy casualties in Gansu and Qinghai provinces.

① Source: The basic data on natural disasters that occurred in China in 2023, published by the Ministry of Emergency Management on its website.

② Source: "IAC Organizes Industry-wide Work on the National Disaster Prevention and Reduction Day 2024", published on the website of the Insurance Association of China (IAC).

In the year, 95.444 million people were affected by natural disasters in varying degrees, with 691 deaths and missing persons on record and 3.344 million people relocated or moved in emergency. There were 209,000 houses collapsed, 623,000 severely damaged and 1,441,000 moderately damaged. The affected area of crops is 10,539,300 hectares; direct economic losses amounted to RMB 345.45 billion. Compared with the average for the past five years, the number of people affected by disasters, the number of deaths and missing persons due to disasters and the crop area affected by disasters decreased by 24.4%, 2.8% and 37.2% respectively, while the number of collapsed houses and direct economic losses increased by 96.9% and 12.6% respectively.

In terms of insurance payout, the insurance industry paid out about RMB 25.259 billion in losses caused by major natural disasters in 2023, invested about RMB 661 million in disaster prevention and mitigation, used manpower of about 113,100 people in disaster prevention and mitigation, gave early warning messages to about 130 million people and screened risks of corporate customers for about 171,400 times, expected to reduce disaster-caused losses by about RMB 3.709 billion.

Second, the workplace safety risks deserve attention. According to the data disclosed by the emergency management authority, the total number of workplace accidents and the death toll in the past five years decreased by 80% and 50% respectively as compared with that in the previous five-year period. Since 2023, however, the number of major accidents has picked up. In particular, the safety risks in mines, fire safety and hazardous chemicals deserve extra attention.

Third, the increasing number of new types of insured assets poses new challenges. Many new types of insured assets have emerged in recent years, such as offshore pastures, domestically built large cruise ships, offshore photovoltaic farms, electric ships and offshore floating wind farms. Some of them have started large-scale application. However, the limited insurance

data and latency of related risks have posed new challenges to underwriting of such emerging assets.

Fourth, the new-energy vehicles (NEVs) shipping risk has emerged. The surging export of Chinese NEVs has brought about new risk variables. In 2022, there were more than ten fires on new energy vehicle carriers. Once a fire occurs on a car carrier ship, the rescue is a big difficulty. Thus, the shipping insurance is subject to a large risk exposure. Marine shipping of motor vehicles, including NEVs, has become a focus of the shipping industry, bringing new challenges to shipping insurance.

Fifth, there are large exposures to the safety risks in buildings. As for the risk in building materials, the safety accidents caused by hollowing and peeling-off of the external wall insulation layer made of inorganic mortar will result in huge payouts from the inherent defect insurance (IDI) of buildings, with a risk exposure of RMB 1 billion. In May 2023, a residential community in Tianjin experienced sudden land subsidence, resulting in loss of residential properties. In July, a high-school indoor stadium in Heilongjiang Province collapsed, causing injuries/deaths and property losses. The building safety hazards have aroused public concerns. The insurance risk reduction service should play a greater role in ensuring building safety.

Sixth, due attention should be paid to the risks ceded by overseas insurers. On the one hand, the natural catastrophe risks ceded from overseas insurers pose a huge exposure that will trigger massive payouts once a covered business disruption occurs. Take the global insurance policies in the automobile and chemical industries as an example, there are many cases of payouts exceeding USD 100 million, much higher than the expected loss

level of similar target assets in the domestic market. On the other hand, the price information is not transparent from direct insurance to reinsurance, coupled by large price gap between domestic and overseas markets. The related business risks deserve due attention.

V. Outlook on the P&C Reinsurance Market

(I) Outlook on the changes in demand for ceding to reinsurance

In the conventional lines of insurance, P&C insurance companies maintain stable demand for reinsurance in general. The impact of traditional risk factors has continued. Extreme weather brought about by climate change has aggravated disaster-related losses. Catastrophe risks such as earthquakes, floods and typhoons build up rapidly at insurance companies, becoming the major threat to stable operation of the industry. Against such a backdrop, P&C insurance companies are expected to have stronger demand for transferring risks to the reinsurance market.

Second, in the emerging risk areas, P&C insurers have still-strong demand for reinsurance service. Emerging risks such as cyber risks, new energy vehicle risks, new liability risks and overseas risks are prominent. The risk mix of insurance business is becoming increasingly complex. Reinsurance demand keeps growing. Reinsurance companies will, in cooperation with direct insurers, develop more targeted insurance products for emerging risks and provide a broader range of risk protection. Also, reinsurance will give full play to its platform and professional strengths, endeavor to build an industry-wide platform by integrating industry and

third-party resources, accelerate the development of risk management model tools and continuously improve the comprehensive risk reduction service capabilities across the industry.

Third, P&C insurance companies will attach greater importance to cooperation with professional reinsurers with sound financial strength. In selecting and rebalancing reinsurers, the P&C insurers will further shift their cooperation toward domestic professional reinsurers that are financially sound.

(II) Outlook on changes in the underwriting strategy of professional reinsurers

In the overall "hard market" environment of international reinsurance market, reinsurers will be more cautious about the chief quotation due to constraints from the external market attention and internal pricing floor.

From a price and risk perspective, in a "hard market" environment of international reinsurance market, reinsurers feel pressure on their own business operations, with the retrocession cost rising. Due to the impacts of extreme weather, payouts under the reinsurance contracts for historical years have swelled, and the non-model losses related to rainstorm and waterlogging have become worse. However, the additional pricing of extreme weather risks is inadequate in the domestic reinsurance market at present, putting reinsurers under increasing business risk pressure.

From the perspective of market landscape, on the one hand, as the new risks and challenges affecting the insurance business are on the rise, it takes time for reinsurers to improve their response and management capabilities.

On the other hand, the external environment affecting reinsurance supply has become more challenging and complex. Reinsurance supply shows a trend of strengthening local reinsurance support and shrinking external reinsurance supply.

Overall, extreme weather will aggravate disaster-inflicted losses, adding to the difficulties in reinsurance business management and pricing profitability. Meanwhile, the impact of climate change has made reinsurance companies more cautious about their risk appetite. Reinsurance companies are subject to more internal "hard constraints" and the supply-demand relationship in the reinsurance market is in a "tight balance". The reinsurance market is expected to further improve the price level to reflect changes in risk trends.

Chapter III

Review and Outlook on China's Life Reinsurance Market in 2023

I. Market Size

(I) Overview

In 2023, China's life insurance market continued to move forward in transformation. The long-term savings lines grew fast while the protections lines showed a short-run decline. Life insurers are under pressure in operation and have increased demand for capital, which brought both opportunities and challenges to the development of the life reinsurance market.

In terms of business size, the premium income of China's life insurance companies totaled RMB 3.5379 trillion in 2022, up by 10.2% year-on-year on a comparable basis.

In terms of business mix, in 2023, the life insurance premium income was RMB 2.7646 trillion, up by 12.8% year-on-year. The health insurance premium income was RMB 728.3 billion, up by 3.0% year-on-year, slowing a mild recovery from 2022 but still in the territory of low growth. The casualty insurance premium income was RMB 45 billion, down by 9.8% year-on-year, a moderate slowdown when compared with 2022.

(II) Size of ceded premiums

In 2023, the total ceded premiums of life insurance companies in China stood at RMB 105.67 billion, down by 8.4% year-on-year. During the same period, the total primary insurance premium income of life insurance companies was RMB 3.5379 trillion, up by 10.2% year-on-year on

a comparable basis (see Figure 1 and Table 1). Overall, the amount of ceded life premiums fluctuated from year to year. At present, China shows strong resilience in its macroeconomy, seeing the basic trend of steady long-term growth remaining unchanged. However, the Chinese economy still faces a number of challenges, including insufficient effective demand, weak social expectations and many risks and hidden dangers. Due to the US interest rate hikes and other factors, the capital market became more volatile and the direct insurance market was under the pressure of transition, posing certain shocks and challenges to growth of the life reinsurance market.

The ceded premiums of China's life insurance companies increased from RMB 29.88 billion in 2013 to RMB 105.67 billion in 2023, with an average annual growth rate of about 13.5%, securing a steady increase. The ceded premiums increased rapidly from 2013 to 2014, followed by a significant decline from 2015 to 2016 before a volatile pick-up from 2017 to 2020. After 2020, the life reinsurance market remained above RMB100 billion in size.

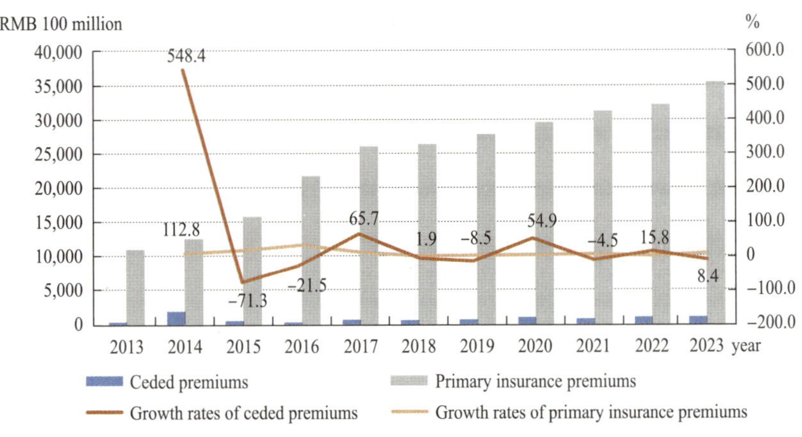

Figure 1 Primary Insurance Premiums, Ceded Premiums and Growth Rates of Life Insurance Companies (2013-2023)

(Source: Yearbook of China's Insurance and National Financial Regulatory Administration)

Table 1 Ceded Premiums, Primary Insurance Premiums and Cession Rates of Life Insurance Companies (2013-2023)

Unit: RMB100 million, %

(RMB100 million)	Ceded premiums	Growth rate	Primary premiums	Growth rate	Cession rates
2013	298.8		11,010.0		2.7
2014	1,937.4	548.4	12,592.3	14.4	15.4
2015	555.6	-71.3	15,724.0	24.9	3.5
2016	435.9	-21.5	21,662.8	37.8	2.0
2017	722.4	65.7	25,972.7	19.9	2.8
2018	736.2	1.9	26,232.5	1.0	2.8
2019	673.9	-8.5	27,792.6	5.9	2.4
2020	1,043.7	54.9	29,500.7	6.1	3.5
2021	996.3	-4.5	31,224.0	14.0	3.0
2022	1,153.3	15.8	32,091.0	2.8	3.6
2023	1,056.7	-8.4	35,379.0	10.2	3.0

Source: Yearbook of China's Insurance and National Financial Regulatory Administration.

(II) Cession rates

In 2023, the cession rate of China's life insurance companies was around 3.0%, down by 0.6 percentage points year-on-year (see Figure 2). At present, China's life reinsurance cession rate is below the global average. Traditional protection-oriented reinsurance business accounted for a relatively large cession share, while savings-oriented life insurance business has a lower share. Meanwhile, affected by such bulk transactions as international mergers and acquisitions, annuities, among others, the overseas existing market is stable with limited growth at present.

From 2013 to 2023, the cession rates of life insurance companies as a whole recorded a steady increase (see Figure 2). The cession rates increase to

a peak from 2013 to 2014, a significant decline in 2015 and a steady pick-up from 2016 to 2020. After 2020, the cession rate remained at around 3%.

Figure 2 Cession Rates of Life Insurance Companies (2013-2023)

(Source: Yearbook of China's Insurance and National Financial Regulatory Administration)

II. Demand-side Analysis

(I) Distribution of ceded premiums[①]

In 2023, 11 life insurance companies had ceded premiums over RMB 5 billion, totaling RMB 71.08 billion, accounting for 66.4% of the industry's total ceded premiums. 15 had ceded premiums between RMB 1 billion and RMB 5 billion, totaling RMB 27.16 billion, accounting for 25.4% of the total. 61 had ceded premiums of less than RMB 1 billion, totaling RMB 8.73 billion, accounting for 8.2% of the total (see Table 2).

① The values of ceded premiums by some life insurance companies in 2023 are negative.

Table 2 Distribution of Ceded Premiums from Life Insurance Companies in 2023

Unit: company, RMB 100 million, %

Size	Number	Total ceded premiums	% of total
Ceded premiums of more than RMB 5 billion	11	710.8	66.4
Ceded premiums of RMB 1 billion to RMB 5 billion	15	271.6	25.4
Ceded premiums of less than RMB 1 billion	61	87.3	8.2

Source: National Financial Regulatory Administration.

(II) Changes in ceded premiums

In 2023, 42 life insurance companies saw a year-on-year increase in life ceded premiums, accounting for 48.8% of the total. Specifically, 16 life insurers had a year-on-year increase of over 50%, accounting for 18.6% of the total; three had a year-on-year increase from 20% to 50%, accounting for 3.5% of the total; and 23 had a year-on-year increase of less than 20%, accounting for 26.7% of the total (see Table 3).

Table 3 Distribution of Ceded Premiums Growth Rates of Life Insurance Companies in 2023

Unit: company, %

Size	Number	% of total
Life insurance companies with a YoY increase in ceded premiums	42	48.8
Of which: With a YoY increase over 50%	16	18.6
With a YoY increase of 20% to 50%	3	3.5
With a YoY increase less than 20%	23	26.7

Source: National Financial Regulatory Administration.

III. Supply-side Analysis

In 2023, there were 10 professional reinsurance companies registered/engaging in life reinsurance business in China. Specifically, one company had a market share of over 50%. One company had a share from 10% to 15%, three with a share from 5% to 10%, and five with a share of less than 5%. China Re Life plays its role as the main channel of reinsurance in China, ranking first in terms of market share. Other major participants include the largest global reinsurers and Chinese reinsurers, such as Qianhai Re, Taiping Re (China) and PICC Re.

(I) Life line of business

In 2022, the life reinsurance market recorded RMB 51.97 billion in professional reinsurers' premium income from the life line of business, down by 11.5% year-on-year. From 2012 to 2022, the average annual growth rate was about 13.0%, showing a volatile uptrend (see Table 4). The annual premium income from the life line increased significantly from 2013 to 2014, decreased notably from 2015 to 2016 and began to pick up steadily in 2017. Except for in 2019 and 2022, the sector maintained positive growth from 2017 to 2022.

Table 4 Premium Income of Professional Reinsurers from the Life Line (2012-2022)

Unit: RMB 100 million

	2012	2013	2014	2015	2016	2017	2018	2019	2020	2021	2022
China Re Life	125.7	142.2	166.0	178.1	252.9	368.5	404.6	390.0	464.8	443.7	379.4
Munich Re Beijing Branch	4.0	20.4	23.1	30.3	9.3	6.2	4.2	5.0	7.9	6.1	6.6

continued

	2012	2013	2014	2015	2016	2017	2018	2019	2020	2021	2022
Swiss Re Beijing Branch	1.0	0.8	1.3	1.6	0.8	1.9	2.4	1.1	3.4	3.4	4.5
SCOR SE Beijing Branch	0.3	10.6	19.0	10.8	2.1	3.8	10.1	7.3	8.0	40.0	27.3
General Re Shanghai Branch	2.3	2.6	3.1	3.8	4.0	5.1	5.6	7.1	8.0	9.8	12.1
Hannover Re Shanghai Branch	19.7	120.7	586.9	96.3	16.7	9.3	12.5	17.6	18.8	16.4	10.2
RGA Shanghai Branch				0.1		2.1	2.9	2.0	2.4	2.5	2.7
Taiping Re (China)										0.1	0.2
Qianhai Re						33.3	42.2	29.0	49.1	62.5	71.1
PICC Re										2.4	5.5
Total	153.0	297.3	799.6	320.9	285.8	430.2	484.4	459.0	562.5	587.1	519.7

Source: Yearbook of China's Insurance.

Among market players, China Re Life ranked first industry-wide by premium income from the life line of business, which stood at RMB 37.94 billion in 2022 with a market share of about 73.0%, followed by Qianhai Re and SCOR SE with the market shares of 13.7% and 5.3% in 2022, respectively. The remaining market players each recorded less than RMB 2 billion in premium income from the life line.

(II) Health line of business

In 2022, the life reinsurance market recorded RMB 47.74 billion in professional reinsurers' premium income from the health line of business, down by 0.6% year-on-year. From 2012 to 2022, the average annual growth

rate was about 25.2% (see Table 5). The premium income from the health line has grown rapidly in recent years, with its value in 2022 being 9.4 times that of 2012. But the premium income from the health line generally shrank, showing a marked moderation in growth across the industry.

Table 5 Premium Income of Professional Reinsurers from the Health Line (2012-2022)

Unit: RMB 100 million

	2012	2013	2014	2015	2016	2017	2018	2019	2020	2021	2022
China Re Life	16.2	26.8	25.1	32.5	37.3	50.6	97.6	139.3	175.6	212.3	261.3
Munich Re Beijing Branch	10.6	10.8	10.8	17.3	24.5	28.5	26.3	36.4	44.3	37.5	23.8
Swiss Re Beijing Branch	18.9	18.7	21.1	20.3	21.5	20.1	17.3	38.1	46.6	48.6	48.5
SCOR SE Beijing Branch	1.5	2.0	2.5	1.4	1.2	5.0	13.7	21.8	30.7	26.3	23.8
General Re Shanghai Branch	0.5	0.4	1.2	2.1	2.9	7.8	23.4	37.0	40.9	41.7	26.0
Hannover Re Shanghai Branch	2.9	4.8	4.7	38.2	12.7	19.7	28.8	41.6	51.9	58.4	47.0
RGA Shanghai Branch				0.4		3.9	7.8	8.5	8.2	8.9	11.4
Taiping Re (China)								0.6	1.4	2.4	3.0
Qianhai Re						0.4	2.1	12.2	27.8	39.8	26.0
PICC Re									0.4	4.6	6.6
Total	50.6	63.5	65.4	112.2	100.0	135.9	216.9	335.6	427.8	480.5	477.4

Source: Yearbook of China's Insurance.

Among market players, China Re Life ranked first industry-wide by premium income from the health line of business, which stood at RMB 26.13 billion in 2022 with a market share of about 54.7%. Swiss Re, Hannover Re,

General Re, Qianhai Re, Munich Re and SCOR SE each recorded from RMB 2.0 billion to RMB 5.0 billion in premium income from the health line in 2022. Other companies each recorded less than RMB 1.5 billion in premium income from the health line.

(III) Casualty line of business

In 2022, the life reinsurance market recorded RMB 5.01 billion in professional reinsurers' ceded premium income from the casualty line of business, down by 23.9% year-on-year. From 2012 to 2022, the average annual growth rate was about 7.6%, showing an uptrend but significantly decrease in 2022 (see Table 6).

Table 6 Premium Income of Professional Reinsurers from the Casualty Line (2012-2022)

Unit: RMB 100 million

	2012	2013	2014	2015	2016	2017	2018	2019	2020	2021	2022
China Re Life	17.1	13.6	18.3	18.1	22.2	23.0	21.5	25.1	24.6	37.0	21.2
Munich Re Beijing Branch	2.8	1.3	6.2	3.8	5.5	8.3	11.5	12.6	13.0	11.6	11.3
Swiss Re Beijing Branch	1.9	0.9	0.6	1.1	–0.6	0.5	0.9	1.5	1.7	1.4	1.5
SCOR SE Beijing Branch	0.6	0.9	2.2	3.8	4.8	3.9	2.2	2.1	2.3	2.6	2.0
General Re Shanghai Branch	0.2	0.3	1.3	3.6	5.3	5.2	6.8	7.7	6.3	4.9	5.1
Hannover Re Shanghai Branch	1.4	7.0	3.1	4.1	5.5	6.0	12.3	13.1	14.1	6.8	8.2
Taiping Re (China)								0.3	0.5	1.0	0.2
Qianhai Re						0.1	0.6	0.5	0.6	0.4	0.3
PICC Re										0.1	0.3
Total	24.1	24.0	31.7	34.6	42.8	46.8	55.7	62.9	63.0	65.8	50.1

Source: Yearbook of China's Insurance.

Among market players, China Re Life ranked first industry-wide by premium income from the casualty line of business, which stood at RMB 2.12 billion in 2022 with a market share of about 42.3%, followed by Munich Re, Hannover Re and General Re with a market share of 22.6%, 16.4% and 10.2%, respectively. The remaining market players each recorded less than RMB 500 million in premium income from the casualty line.

(IV) Global market landscape for life reinsurance

In the global market, according to AM.Best data, life reinsurance generated at least 30% of the total premium income of global reinsurance groups, showing a fairly stable pattern of business. In the ranking of global life reinsurance companies for 2022, all reinsurance groups saw a decline in the size of life reinsurance and remained stable in rankings. Canada Life Re stayed in the first place, while China Re Life took the seventh spot (see Table 7).

Table 7 Top Ten Global Life Reinsurance Groups in 2022

Unit: USD 100 million

Rank	Company name	Gross reinsurance premiums
1	Canada Life Re	234.1
2	Swiss Re	159.9
3	Munich Re	146.0
4	RGA	138.2
5	SCOR SE	103.7
6	Hannover Re	96.4
7	China Re	91.8
8	Berkshire Hathaway	51.9
9	Transatlantic Re	30.0
10	Assicurazioni Generali SPA	24.5

Source: AM. Best.

IV. Opportunities and Challenges in the Life Reinsurance Market

In 2023, China's economy made fresh breakthroughs in transformation of development model, adjustment of structure and enhancement of growth drivers in a world with a weak recovery and more divergencies among economies. China continued to outperform major economies in terms of growth, recording 5.2% year-on-year GDP growth and 6.3% year-on-year growth in per capita disposable income. China's life insurance industry also got back to the double-digit territory of growth in premiums in 2023. At present, the Chinese life insurance industry is still in an in-depth transition with many challenges. The industry should grasp the important historic opportunity in the new stage of high-quality development, break through the development bottlenecks and realize long-term value growth.

(I) Opportunities for development of the life insurance market

First, a string of favorable government policies have come out. The Chinese government's top-level design defines a clearer role and attaches greater importance to life insurance. The Central Financial Work Conference has called on the insurance industry to work as an economic shock absorber and a social stabilizer. Among the "five priorities" of finance, the inclusive finance and pension finance have received great attention. China's life insurance industry will have great growth potential in elderly care and medical services, becoming an important part of the multi-tier social security system. The tax preference and deferral policies are been gradually refined

and implemented. Since 2023, the individual income tax (IIT)-preferential health insurance and tax-deferred pension policies have been introduced successively, with supporting rules implemented effectively. These policy moves have opened up broad space for growth, becoming a major driver for sustainable development of commercial health and pension insurance services.

Second, the macroeconomy is in a recovery and poised for long-term growth. The growth pace of the life insurance market is highly correlated with the macroeconomy. China's GDP grew by 5.2% in 2023 in a continuing recovery. New achievements were made in high-quality development, laying a solid support for high-quality development of the insurance industry. According to the experience of mature markets, insurance will enter a relative saturation period when the GDP per capita reaches about USD 30,000. At present, China's GDP per capita is about USD 12,600, suggesting huge growth space for the insurance industry.

Third, the aging pollution brings new opportunities. Data from the National Bureau of Statistics shows that at the end of 2023, China had 217 million people aged 65 and above, accounting for 15.4% of the total population of the country. As the Chinese population has been further aging, there will be huge demand for health and pension insurance and services in the future. In the long run, the life insurance market will diversify into life, pension and health insurance and gradually scale up.

Fourth, the digital technology drives innovative development. The accelerated application of new technologies is profoundly changing every sector, including life insurance. The big data has greatly expanded the

boundaries of underwriting. Artificial intelligence-assisted claims settlement and underwriting have significantly improved the operating efficiency. By applying new technologies to innovate business models, insurance and reinsurance companies will enhance their operating results and service capabilities, giving a strong impetus to high-quality development of the industry over the long term.

(II) Risks and challenges facing the life insurance market

First, there are some supply-demand mismatches in the market. On the demand side, customers have limited awareness of insurance products and have yet to gain a deeper and more detailed understanding of the personal risk protection demand and the products and services they purchased. The commercial insurance payouts as a share in total medical expenses is still not high. On the supply side, there is still much room for improvements in the functions of insurance, and in the liabilities of medical insurance products. The integration with services of hospitals, doctors and other stakeholders is not adequate. Insurance companies operate commercial medical insurance in the way they operate life insurance. The coverage of the elderly, patients with chronic conditions and other groups in urgent need of insurance is still limited. The pension product design is tilted toward financial attributes and limited in service features. It lacks features such as long-term security and related health care services, substantially the same as other financial and wealth management products.

Second, the traditional traffic-driven model gradually fails. With the population increasingly aging and the demographic dividend fading,

alongside the emergence of new business models such as livestreaming and delivery services, the traditional agency income has lost its comparative advantage, and the huge-crowd strategy for personal insurance has become outdated. Since 2023, the regulatory policy has strictly required "as-is reporting" of channel fees, bringing additional discipline to the bancassurance channel. On the Internet platform, the cost of Internet traffic has seen a multi-fold increase. It is increasingly difficult to launch blockbuster products through Internet channels. On the whole, the extensive growth model driven by traffic has become uncompetitive, and the channel is under pressure of transformation.

Third, the traditional profit model is to be reconstructed. The domestic bond market sees interest rates on a downward trend over the medium to long terms, and faces risk challenges such as credit risk. The traditional profit model of life insurers mainly relies on the interest rate spread, which has significantly narrowed nowadays. The profit model is facing challenges and reconstruction. In a low interest rate environment over the long term, life insurance companies should strengthen asset-liability matching management to better guard against risks. It is even more necessary to strengthen fine management, enhance business quality and efficiency and seek potential income out of expense gain and mortality gap.

(III) Risks and challenges facing the life reinsurance market

Development opportunities: First, amid the growing demand for health insurance and the keen supply-side expectations for the health insurance market in China, the regulatory authorities have issued a series of policies to

boost the market demand for product innovation in key areas, such as long-term care insurance, disability insurance, IIT-preferential health insurance, inclusive health insurance and short-term health insurance. Reinsurance, with a professional edge in product innovation and risk management, can provide crucial support and play a leading role in innovation. Second, as the direct insurance channels are undergoing transformation and upgrading, with the products and services experiencing supply-side structural reform, insurance companies have significantly stronger demand for reinsurance services in terms of data, products, services and sales support. Reinsurance will further manifest its professional value in risk definition, product upgrading and risk pricing and management. Third, in the innovative integration of insurance and health industries, reinsurance acts as a bridge under the new model of "insurance + service", better playing its role as a platform and professional value by coordinating resources and linking all stakeholders together. Fourth, reinsurance will continue to leverage its strengths in data technology to play its part in building the life insurance infrastructures, such as life tables, critical illness tables and accident tables. Fifth, the new policies such as C-ROSS Phase II and IFRS 17 put insurance companies generally under solvency pressure, giving rise to the demand for reinsurance.

Development challenges: First, China is still facing multi-faceted pressure, and on a fragile footing of recovery. This macro environment has certain impact on the development of the life insurance and reinsurance industries. Second, the life insurance market is under great pressure on the demand, sale and asset sides. The demand for insurance has not been

effectively unleashed in the short term, the willingness to save money in the long run continues to rise and direct insurers have weak demand from risk ceding, which will impede development of the life reinsurance industry. Third, the experience in critical illness continues to deteriorate amid mounting medical expenses. The long-term medical insurance management mechanism remains to be improved. The health insurance is facing such problems as increased risk exposure and increasing difficulty in business management. Fourth, overseas reinsurers have stepped up their participation in the Chinese market by way of offshoring. The life reinsurance market has become increasingly fierce.

V. Outlook on the Life Reinsurance Market

At the Central Financial Work Conference, the central leadership of China called for focusing efforts on the five priorities of technology finance, green finance, inclusive finance, pension finance and digital finance. The Third Plenary Session of the 20th CPC Central Committee has charted the course for the insurance and reinsurance industries in further deepening the reform and innovation and speeding up high-quality development. From the perspective of products and services, life insurance products are still the main products in the life insurance industry in the short term. The people still have strong demand for products that create stable income and preserve asset value. Compared with other financial products such as funds, savings and banking wealth management, the life insurance products have their advantage in longer terms and stable performance. Meanwhile, with the predetermined interest rate of life insurance products adjusted, the life

insurance products with the savings feature alone become less appealing. The life insurance products with both savings and protection features can better meet the people's ever-increasing demand for health protection. Health insurance may make fresh breakthroughs in long-term care insurance. From the perspective of business channels, the regulatory authorities continue to implement the "as-is reporting" policy to strengthen the fine and scientific management of products in different channels, which will bring additional discipline to sales activity and enhance well-ordered competition in the market. In the future, the development of business channels will be company-specific to highlight the strengths and characteristics of insurers. The transformation will focus on in-depth understanding of customer needs, optimization of product mix and improvement of customer experience and service quality, so as to achieve more targeted and effective market penetration, thus driving sales growth. From the perspective of assets, as the medium- and long-term interest rates are moving lower, preventing the risk of interest rate spread loss will become a key task of the industry for some time to come. The industry will gradually reduce the cost of liabilities. To cope with uncertainties in the investment environment, the industry will emphasize the prudence and safety of the asset allocation strategies to ensure sufficient liquidity of assets.

Reinsurance will also unleash its professional strengths in product innovation, ecosystem-wide collaboration and data technology, continue to deepen the insurer-reinsurer partnership and effectively transform the industrial development. First, reinsurance will lead the innovation in products. The industry will drive the supply-side structural reform of life

insurance, accelerate the development and promotion of long-term care insurance, disability insurance and other types of insurance, and enhance the supplementary role of commercial health insurance. Second, ecosystem-wide collaboration will be enhanced. Cooperation will strengthen with medical and health service organizations to further promote the integration of medical and insurance industries and explore and make breakthroughs in chronic disease management, health management and other areas. Reinsurance will assist direct insurers in upgrading the product mix to drive the professional development of channels and empower the innovation and transformation of sales channels. Third, artificial intelligence and other cutting-edge technologies will be employed to develop and utilize data resources in depth, so as to help direct insurers reduce costs and increase efficiency and enhance the capabilities of risk prevention, risk control and fine management, and help the industry transform and upgrade to diverse value creation and achieve high-quality development.

Chapter IV

Review and Outlook on Two-way Opening-up of China's Reinsurance Industry in 2023

China's insurance industry has been opening wider and deeper to the outside world as China advances its institutional opening-up of the financial sector. A pattern of two-way opening has also begun to take shape in China's reinsurance market. On the one hand, China's reinsurance market is increasingly opening up, with the world's major reinsurers setting up offices and doing business there, becoming new drivers of the market. In addition, the drive to build Shanghai into an international reinsurance center has been gaining momentum, with the aim of developing the Chinese city into a global reinsurance center with both onshore and offshore operations. On the other hand, Chinese reinsurers steadily advance international development, strengthen their global network, enhance their ability to manage internationalized operation and take active part in global risk governance, manifesting increasing competitiveness and influence in the international markets.

I. Development of Foreign Reinsurance Companies in China

(I) Overview

China's accession into WTO in 2001 was a milestone in the opening-up history of the Chinese financial sector. Reinsurance became China's first financial market to open up after it became a WTO member. From 2002 to the end of 2005, cross-border business restrictions on reinsurance and reinsurance brokerage services were gradually lifted, allowing foreign reinsurers to establish a physical presence and conduct business in the Chinese market. The percentage of statutory reinsurance has been gradually

reduced over the years and was eliminated in 2006, with a complete shift to commercial reinsurance. Reinsurance has become one of the most open and internationalized financial markets in China.

By the end of 2023, there were 15 professional players in China's reinsurance market, including seven Chinese reinsurers (including one conglomerate, namely China Re Group) and eight foreign reinsurers (see Table 1). Top international reinsurers actively participate in China's market by setting up branches in China.

Table 1 Ranking of Foreign Reinsurers by Premium Incomes in China in 2023

Unit: RMB 100 million

Rank	Foreign reinsurers in China	Reinsurance premiums in 2023
1	Swiss Re Beijing Branch	195.5
2	SCOR SE Beijing Branch	134.9
3	Hannover Re Shanghai Branch	128.7
4	Munich Re Beijing Branch	113.6
5	General Re Shanghai Branch	43.9
6	RGA Shanghai Branch	13.8
7	Korean Re Shanghai Branch	5.8
8	AXA Global Reinsurance (Shanghai)	0.1

Source: Annual disclosure reports of the companies for 2023.

Foreign reinsurers adopted differentiated development strategies for the Chinese market according to their own operating characteristics. For example, some foreign reinsurers focused their business in China on the governmental and sci-tech sectors. On the one hand, they cooperate with the Chinese government by providing coverage for health, agricultural and liability risks in priority areas identified by the government, including healthcare, agriculture, rural areas and farmers, environmental pollution and food safety. On the other hand, they have advanced sci-tech innovation to

cooperate with direct insurers in Internet of Vehicles, Internet of Things, data mining and other technology-intensive areas. For another example, some foreign insurers pay more attention to quality of business and emphasize sustainable and profitable growth in business, thus placing a particular emphasis on technology upgrading, market research and early investment. Some other foreign reinsurers emphasize business performance. They attach more importance to business profits and are good at reducing costs through fine management to remain more profitable than competitors.

(II) Operations of foreign reinsurers in China in 2023

In 2023, foreign reinsurers maintained steady business development in China with growing profitability and competitiveness, becoming an integral part of China's reinsurance market.

1. Business size

From 2018 to 2023, foreign reinsurers kept their business scale stable in China. Foreign reinsurers experienced a slight increase in premium income in 2023 compared to the previous year Swiss Re Beijing Branch and SCOR SE Beijing Branch recorded a rise in premium income over 2022, while Hannover Re Shanghai Branch and Munich Re Beijing Branch saw a decline in premium income from 2022. By business size, Swiss Re Beijing Branch remained the top foreign reinsurer operating in China with a premium income of RMB 19.55 billion in 2023. SCOR SE Beijing Branch recorded RMB 13.49 billion in premium income in 2023, surpassing Hannover Re Shanghai Branch and Munich Re Beijing Branch to rank second (see Figure 1).

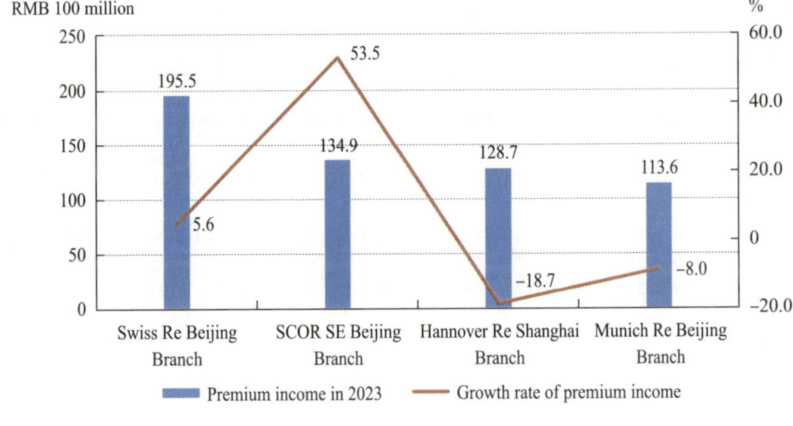

Figure 1 Foreign Reinsurers' Premium Income and Growth Rates in 2023

(Source: Annual disclosure reports of the above companies for 2023)

(1) Swiss Re Beijing Branch

By premium income, Swiss Re Beijing Branch, as the top foreign reinsurer operating in China, had a premium income of RMB 19.55 billion in 2023, up by 5.6% year-on-year. Swiss Re Beijing Branch has achieved solid growth in the property segment over recent years, which contributed about 70% of its total premium income, far more than that from life and health segments.

By business mix (see Table 2), the property segment contributed 69.1% of the premium income of Swiss Re Beijing Branch in 2023, with property and liability insurance (41.9%) and motor insurance (19.5%) taking bigger shares. Premium income from personal insurance accounted for 30.9%. In the past two years, premium income from the personal line of business has continued to grow, driven by the positive outlook of China's life and health insurance markets.

Table 2 Business Mix of Swiss Re Beijing Branch

Unit: RMB 100 million, %

Business line	Premium income in 2023	% of total
Personal insurance	**60.4**	**30.9**
Life insurance	11.0	5.6
Health insurance	49.4	25.3
Property insurance	**135.1**	**69.1**
Motor insurance	38.2	19.5
Property and liability insurance	81.8	41.9
Marine insurance	13.2	6.7
Others	1.9	1.0
Total	195.5	100

Source: Annual disclosure report of Swiss Re Beijing Branch for 2023.

(2) SCOR SE Beijing Branch

The premium income of SCOR SE Beijing Branch was RMB 13.49 billion in 2023, up by 53.5% year-on-year, surpassing Hannover Re Shanghai Branch and Munich Re Beijing Branch to become the second-largest foreign reinsurer in China. Specifically, the life segment recorded RMB 10.68 billion in ceded premium income, up by 101.1% year-on-year, while the non-life segment registered ceded premium income of RMB 2.81 billion, down by 19.3% year-on-year.

By business mix (see Table 3), SCOR SE Beijing Branch has seen its life segment taking up a share of over 60% in recent years, which even further expanded significantly to 79.2% in 2023 versus 20.8% of non-life segment.

Table 3 Business Mix of Scor SE Beijing Branch

Unit: RMB 100 million, %

Business line	Premium income in 2023	% of total
Life insurance	106.8	79.2
Non-life insurance	28.1	20.8
Total	134.9	100

Source: Annual disclosure report of Swiss Re Beijing Branch for 2023.

(3) Hannover Re Shanghai Branch

Hannover Re Shanghai Branch recorded RMB 12.87 billion in ceded premium income in 2023, down by 18.7% year-on-year.

By business mix (see Table 4), Hannover Re Shanghai Branch reported a 45.5/54.5 split between life and non-life segments. Of the life segment, health insurance took the largest share of 31.2%. Of the non-life segment, credit insurance accounted for 12.9%, liability insurance 12.7%, property insurance 9.5% and motor insurance 8.8%.

Table 4 Business Mix of Hannover Re Beijing Branch

Unit: RMB 100 million, %

Business line	Premium income in 2023	% of total
Life insurance	58.6	45.5
Health insurance	40.2	31.2
Life insurance	11.4	8.8
Casualty insurance	7.1	5.5
Non-life insurance	70.1	54.5
Liability insurance	16.3	12.7
Property insurance	12.2	9.5
Credit insurance	16.7	12.9
Motor vehicle and third-party liability insurance	11.3	8.8
Agricultural insurance	4.0	3.1
Engineering insurance	4.7	3.7
Cargo transportation insurance	2.3	1.8
Health insurance	–0.2	–0.1
Hull insurance	1.8	1.4
Casualty insurance	0.5	0.3
Others	0.6	0.5
Total	128.7	100

Source: Annual disclosure report of Swiss Re Beijing Branch for 2023.

(4) Munich Re Beijing Branch

The ceded premium income of Munich Re Beijing Branch was RMB 11.36 billion in 2023, decrease of 8.0% compared to the previous year. Specifically, the non-life segment recorded RMB 8.44 billion in ceded premium income, up by 3.4% year-on-year, while the life segment registered ceded premium income of RMB 2.92 billion, down by 30.1% year-on-year.

By business mix (see Table 5), Munich Re Beijing Branch reported a 25.7/74.3 split between life and non-life segments in 2023. Life premium income showed a downward trend.

Table 5 Business Mix of Munich Re Beijing Branch

Unit: RMB 100 million, %

Business line	Premium income in 2023	% of total
Non-life insurance	84.4	74.3
Life insurance	29.2	25.7
Total	113.6	100

Source: Annual disclosure report of Swiss Re Beijing Branch for 2023.

2. Profitability

In 2023, foreign reinsurers operating in China showed steady profitability (see Table 6). It should be noted that given the high retrocession rate of foreign reinsurers, their profitability will be impacted by retrocession arrangements, so the net profit indicators do not necessarily provide an objective and full picture of their operations and business quality.

Table 6 Net Profits of Foreign Reinsurers in China

Unit: RMB 10,000, %

Company	Net profit in 2022	Net profit in 2023	Growth rate
Swiss Re Beijing Branch	27,617	22,104	-20
SCOR SE Beijing Branch	24,129	19,726	-18

continued

Company	Net profit in 2022	Net profit in 2023	Growth rate
Hannover Re Shanghai Branch	-84,973	9,466	111
Munich Re Beijing Branch	39,374	19,730	-50

Source: Annual disclosure reports of the above companies for 2023.

3. Solvency

The four foreign reinsurers mentioned above had high solvency ratios in 2023, of which Swiss Re Beijing Branch boasted the highest solvency ratio of 343% (see Table 7). Foreign reinsurance companies generally maintain strong capital reserves to lay a solid foundation for their further expansion in China's reinsurance market.

Table 7 Solvency Ratios of Foreign Reinsurers in China

Unit: %, RMB 100 million

Company	End-2023 comprehensive solvency ratio	End-2023 working capital	End-2023 net assets
Swiss Re Beijing Branch	343	43.5	87.2
SCOR SE Beijing Branch	247	20.6	29.5
Hannover Re Shanghai Branch	241	72.5	71.5
Munich Re Beijing Branch	266	16.5	48.1

Source: Annual disclosure reports of the above companies for 2023.

II. International Development of Chinese Reinsurance Companies

In the two-way opening-up of China's financial sector, Chinese reinsurers including China Re and Taiping Re are going global to compete in the global reinsurance market and integrate into the global insurance

value chain at a faster pace. Meanwhile, as Shanghai's drive to become an international reinsurance hub gains pace, Chinese reinsurers will further integrate into the global reinsurance market and make the Chinese reinsurance market more competitive and influential worldwide.

(I) International development of China Re

As the forerunner of Chinese reinsurers going global, China Re Group has been steadfast in implementing its international strategy over the years, with its international business landscape taking shape. China Re received its initial rating in 2010, entered the Lloyd's market in 2011, went public in Hong Kong in 2015 and acquired the British insurer Chaucer in 2018. It has set up China Re Asset Management (Hong Kong), Singapore Branch and China Re Life (Hong Kong) successively. At present, China Re operates overseas institutions in 11 countries and regions and has over 1,000 partners across the world, with its international business covering more than 200 countries and regions. China Re is one of the most internationalized Chinese insurance companies.

(II) International development of Taiping Re

Taiping Reinsurance Co., Ltd. ("Taiping Re"), the parent of Taiping Re (China), was incorporated in Hong Kong in September 1980. As a specialized reinsurance subsidiary of China Taiping Insurance Group, Taiping Re underwrites property and life reinsurance worldwide. Headquartered in Hong Kong, Taiping Re operates wholly-owned subsidiaries in Beijing and London, a branch office in Labuan, Malaysia and representative offices in

Tokyo and Macao.

Relying on the strong support of its listed parent company, China Taiping Insurance Holdings Co., Ltd., and its strategic shareholder, Belgium-based Ageas Insurance International N.V., Taiping Re maintains prudent, efficient and flexible underwriting policies and management methods. In recognition of its sound financial strength and good performance, Taiping Re has received a Financial Strength Rating of A from international rating agencies like Standard & Poor's, A.M. Best, and Fitch for consecutive years.

Taiping Re is a well-known professional reinsurer in Asia and the No. 1 player in Hong Kong's property reinsurance market, with its own scope of business covering more than 100 countries and regions across five continents and serving more than 1,000 customers. In 2023, Taiping Re realized HKD 9.42 billion in revenue from insurance services. It recorded HKD 48.18 billion in total assets .

(III) Chinese reinsurers' service for the BRI cooperation

China Re actively serves the real economy with its principal duties and activities, providing high-quality services for the Belt and Road Initiative (BRI) cooperation by advancing the supply-side structural reform in the insurance industry and enhancing the capacity of overseas risk protection. First, China Re helped improve the top-level design of the BRI insurance mechanism. In 2020, China Re led the insurance industry in establishing the China Belt and Road Reinsurance Pool (CBRRP), the only industry platform in China to specialize in the BRI risk management, serving as the chairman and manager of the organization. It also led the establishment

of reinsurance industry organizations for BRI insurance in Singapore and the UK, providing risk protection for China's overseas interests in the BRI. Second, a comprehensive risk protection service network was created for the BRI. China Re has endeavored to build a comprehensive service system for the BRI leveraging its global network. With the three reinsurance industry platforms established for BRI insurance in Beijing, Singapore and the UK, China Re has shaped a "circle of friends" for strategic cooperation in 136 countries and regions, serving projects along the Belt and Road where China has overseas interests. In the past three years, China Re provided over RMB 900 billion of comprehensive risk protection for BRI projects. Third, China Re kept leading the innovation in BRI insurance products and services. China Re has connected the domestic and international markets by successfully introducing special risk protection projects, including political violence and terrorism insurance into the Chinese market, creating the first ever terrorism risk assessment system of foreign countries from a Chinese perspective. In stronger collaboration with the largest companies, China Re has provided reinsurance service for landmark projects with global influence, including the China-Laos Railway and Gwadar Port. In strengthening technological empowerment, China Re took the lead in using the satellite-based remote sensing technology to conduct risk survey and risk reduction management, supporting the major BRI projects in accessing comprehensive risk protection. In driving green transformation, China Re introduced green factors for the first time into the insurance pricing for the Karot Hydropower Project in the China-Pakistan Economic Corridor, which is an innovative green finance solution.

(IV) Development of the Shanghai International Reinsurance Center

In June 2023, the National Financial Regulatory Administration (NFRA) and Shanghai Municipal People's Government jointly issued the *Implementation Rules on Accelerating the Building of Shanghai International Reinsurance Center*, officially initiating Shanghai's efforts to create an "international board" for reinsurance. The move is to, focused on building an international reinsurance exchange that is globally competitive, upgrade China's reinsurance market from "one-way opening-up" to "two-way opening-up" by setting Chinese standards and rules, take an in-depth part in the global cooperation in reinsurance, provide Chinese solutions to the global risk protection and financial governance system and help maintain a diversified and stable international landscape and financial cooperation relationship for risk protection.

In August 2024, the NFRA issued the *Implementation Opinion on Accelerating the Building of Shanghai International Reinsurance Center* in conjunction with Shanghai Municipal People's Government, planning to develop Shanghai into a global reinsurance hub by setting up the Shanghai International Reinsurance Exchange in the Lingang Special Area of China (Shanghai) Pilot Free Trade Zone. The exchange is designed to be a platform with clustering elements and centralized transactions, active in trading under a complete set of rules. China endeavors to develop the new space of reinsurance development, strengthen the capacity of reinsurance supply, improve the risk management policies and mechanisms and effectively

unleash the role of reinsurance in ceding insurance risks, in a bid to build a modern reinsurance market system.

Since Shanghai started its push for the "international board" of reinsurance, all the relevant work has accelerated and yielded a series of breakthroughs in strategic positioning, development path, rules framework and trading system. In terms of rules-making, the first four sets of rules were officially released for registration, trading, premium calculation and differentiated supervision of the "international board" of reinsurance. In the second round, another four sets of rules for exchange-traded reinsurance, trading desks and information were formulated. In addition to regulatory policies being put in place, the "international board" of reinsurance has become home to a growing number of insurance organizations in its first year. As for business activity, the "international board" of reinsurance has launched an international reinsurance platform with such functions as trade confirmation, contract filing, bill confirmation and clearing. Based on this business platform, the first overseas reinsurance contract was officially signed at the Shanghai International Reinsurance Exchange. As insurance organizations made their first deals on the platform one after another, the "international board" of reinsurance can provide unimpeded services of registration, trading, clearing and settlement, aiming to make ongoing improvements and expand the platform size going forward. In the future, Chinese reinsurers are expected to further expand their overseas underwriting capacity, assume risks from overseas insurers on a solid footing, keep improving their risk management capability and continue to boost the global competitiveness and influence of China's reinsurance market.

III. Outlook on International Development of China's Reinsurance Industry

(I) Foreign reinsurers' outlook on the Chinese market

In terms of market potential, China's insurance market is huge in size with the potential for sustained development. The Chinese economy is resilient with higher quality of growth. Swiss Re Institute estimated China's growth in 2024 to be about 4.5%. A solid economic recovery will add luster to the overall performance of the insurance industry. The Chinese market will remain a major growth engine for the global insurance industry, accounting for an increasing share of the global insurance market. In the next decade, the Chinese insurance market is expected to double in size and become the largest insurance market and the second largest reinsurance market of the world. The main growth drivers are steady economic growth, expansion of the middle-income bracket and growing public awareness of risk.

In terms of regulatory policies, the Chinese insurance market remains two-way opening up with a favorable and predictable regulatory environment. In recent years, the National Financial Regulatory Administration (NFRA) has introduced more than ten measures for opening-up of the insurance industry. Foreign reinsurers are rushing to expand their strategic distribution in China. Swiss Re, for example, initially positioned China as an emerging market but now has repositioned China as a high-growth market. SCOR SE has recently announced to invest more in the Chinese market to capitalize on

the long-term growth opportunities of China..

(II) Outlook on international development of Chinese reinsurers

Thanks to the post-pandemic economic recovery, the sharp increase in commercial insurance rates and the growth of emerging markets, the global insurance market has gradually regained growth momentum. Chinese reinsurers will seize opportunities to further devise their international development strategies and improve their capability of internationalized operation management. They will gain insights into the cyclicality of the international market and the global macro-finance, actively study and steadily advance their overseas presence, keep refining the overseas institution management models and management mechanisms, enhance their capability of global asset investment research and allocation and sharpen their global competitive edge. In addition, Chinese reinsurers will take the opportunity of building the Shanghai International Reinsurance Center to strengthen coordination of domestic and overseas operations, improve the cross-border service capacity, take better part in international competition and make positive contributions to the new development pattern featuring dual circulation, which takes the domestic circulation as the mainstay and the domestic and overseas circulations reinforcing each other.

At present, the high-quality development of the BRI cooperation focuses on creating a multi-dimensional BRI connectivity network, promoting green development, carrying out pragmatic cooperation and improving international cooperation mechanisms. Chinese reinsurers will give full play

to their strengths in global, platform-based and professional operations to strengthen the risk protection mechanism, improve the service network, enhance the risk protection level and comprehensive service capacity and make more contributions to the high-quality development of the BRI cooperation.

Meanwhile, Chinese reinsurers will balance development and security to pursue robust and steady international development. They will be proactive in coping with geopolitical risks, climate change and capital market volatility in the course of going global, strengthen risk assessment, improve the risk management system and response mechanism, keep improving the risk management capability and effectively forestall cross-border risks.

Chapter V

Review and Outlook on China's Reinsurance Regulation in 2023

In 2023, China's reinsurance regulation maintained the political and people-oriented nature of financial work, integrated all efforts to prevent risks, strengthened supervision and promote development, guided the insurance and reinsurance industries to continuously enhance protection capability and service level. In the year, the National Financial Regulatory Administration (NFRA) was inaugurated, marking a crucial step forward in China's organizational reform in financial regulation, and providing strong support for forestalling and defusing financial risks and advancing high-quality development.

I. Overall Regulatory Framework of the Reinsurance Industry

(I) A three-pillar reinsurance regulatory framework

After decades of development, China's insurance and reinsurance industries have formed a three-pillar regulatory framework, with solvency regulation as the core, corporate governance regulation as the foundation and market practice regulation as the emphasis.

Specifically, solvency regulation lies at the core of regulating the modern insurance industry. It is intended to ensure that insurers are solvent enough to meet underwriting requirements and keep the insurance market stable through comprehensive evaluation, supervision, and inspection of insurance companies' solvency adequacy ratios, comprehensive risk profile and risk management ability. In 2021, the former China Banking and Insurance Regulatory Commission (CBIRC) successfully completed the C-ROSS Phase II and issued the *Regulations on the Administration of Solvency of Insurance*

Companies (CBIRC Order No. 1 of 2021) and the *Rules on the Regulation of the Solvency of Insurance Companies (II)* (Y.B.J.F. 〔2021〕 No. 51). These regulatory policies have clearly established a three-pillar framework for solvency regulation, consisting of quantitative capital requirements (Pillar I), qualitative regulatory requirements (Pillar II) and market discipline mechanism (Pillar III) and introduced three closely connected indicators of solvency regulation, namely core solvency adequacy ratio, comprehensive solvency adequacy ratio and integrated risk rating. These policies have further tightened and refined the solvency regulatory requirements for direct insurers and reinsurers, making the insurer solvency supervision more scientific, effective and comprehensive, and guiding China's insurance market down the road for robust and healthy development. In 2023, the NFRA published the *Notice on Improving the Regulatory Standards for Solvency of Insurance Companies* (J.G. 〔2023〕 No. 5) and further improve the regulatory standards for solvency of insurers. These regulatory standards guide insurance companies back to their principal duty of insurance, better serve the real economy and the general public.

Corporate governance is the cornerstone of the modern enterprise system. Its purpose is to improve the governance of an enterprise and maintain sound and steady operations of an insurance institution through the establishment of a corporate governance framework that includes governing bodies like the (general) meeting of shareholders, board of directors, board of supervisors and senior management, defining the scope of roles and requirements of performing duties for these bodies, and improving mechanisms like risk control, checks and balances, and

incentives and restraints. In January 2006, the former China Insurance Regulatory Commission ("CIRC") issued the *Guiding Opinions on Regulating the Governance Structure of Insurance Companies (Trial)* (B.J.F.〔2006〕No. 2), formally introducing corporate governance supervision into the regulatory system of China's insurance industry. Since then, China has gradually enriched and improved corporate governance regulation in both practical and theoretical terms. Regulatory authorities have issued a series of regulatory policies on corporate governance, including the *Code of Corporate Governance of Banking and Insurance Institutions* (Y.B.J.F.〔2021〕No. 14) and the *Measures for Regulating the Conduct of Majority Shareholders of Banking and Insurance Institutions (Trial)* (Y.B.J.F.〔2021〕No. 43), detailing and clarifying the composition, division of duties and working mechanisms of insurers' governing bodies, namely the general meeting of shareholders, the board of directors, the board of supervisors and the management. As a Chinese characteristic, the Party leadership has been integrated into every aspect of the corporate governance of insurance institutions. The corporate governance requirements for insurance institutions have been comprehensively and systematically standardized to keep refining the regulatory system for corporate governance in the insurance industry.

Regulation of market practices, as an important guarantee to ensure orderly operation of the insurance market, covers the formulation of insurance terms and premium rates, and the regulation of insurance practices concerning sales, intermediaries, services and anti-frauds. Putting protecting the rights and interests of insurance consumers at the core, it aims to maintain order of the insurance market by bringing discipline to market

practices of insurance institutions. The regulatory policies and measures are closely related to the particular market practices of regulated entities. Considering the differences between P&C insurance, personal insurance and reinsurance in terms of trading entities, management model, business nature, and risk characteristics, regulators usually adopt a category-specific approach to regulating various insurance institutions and business. As for reinsurance, the former CBIRC revised and issued the *Provisions on the Administration of Reinsurance Business* in July 2021 (CBIRC Order No. 8 of 2021), strengthening the supervision of insurance institutions in respect of top-level reinsurance strategy formulation, reinsurance security management and reinsurance management standards. It emphasized that insurance companies should use reinsurance tools properly and stay committed to the core role of reinsurance as "insurance for insurers"

(II) Regulatory policy system for the reinsurance industry

At the legislative level, both insurance and reinsurance in China are governed by the *Insurance Law of the People's Republic of China.*

At the level of regulatory policy, NAFR has introduced the following two categories of regulatory policies on reinsurance. (1) Regulatory policies applicable to the insurance industry as a whole, such as regulatory policies on solvency, corporate governance and the use of insurance funds. Such regulatory policies are based on the common characteristics of reinsurance and direct insurance, usually applicable to both reinsurers and direct insurers, or applicable to direct insurers and applicable mutatis mutandis to reinsurers. (2) Special regulatory policies applicable to the reinsurance

industry, which cover the regulation of reinsurance market practices and the special regulation targeting the international nature of reinsurance. These special regulatory policies include standardizing the establishment of reinsurance companies, clarifying the norms for reinsurance business management and strengthening the safeguards for reinsurance by establishing an information disclosure mechanism for connected reinsurance transactions, creating a reinsurance registration mechanism and requiring offshore reinsurers to provide qualifying guarantees. To ensure effective implementation of the above regulatory policies, NAFR combines on-site supervision with off-site supervision and adopts such regulatory methods as formulating management standards, carrying out capacity assessment and imposing administrative penalties on illegalities or irregularities of insurance institutions, thereby urging insurers to maintain reasonable solvency, improve corporate governance and bring discipline to market activities.

In light of policies issued by other relevant regulatory authorities, in addition to the three-pillar regulatory framework of the National Financial Regulatory Administration, China's insurance and reinsurance industries are subject to supervision by the People's Bank of China, the Ministry of Finance and the Cyberspace Administration of China in terms of anti-money laundering, counter-terrorist financing, finance and accounting, state-owned assets management as well as cybersecurity and personal information protection. In addition, the guidelines and plans issued by the CPC Central Committee, the State Council and relevant regulatory agencies with respect to the national economic and financial work also have a far-reaching effect on the regulatory policies for China's insurance and reinsurance industries.

II. Important Reinsurance Regulatory Policies Issued in 2023

In 2023, National Financial Regulatory Administration (NFRA) was established based on the former China Banking and Insurance Regulatory Commission. The important reinsurance regulatory policies issued by the NFRA and the former CBIRC in 2023 mainly address the operational risk management of insurance institutions, prevention and control of criminal cases, identification and assessment of systemically important insurance companies and refinement of the solvency regulatory criteria, giving a boost to high-quality development of the reinsurance industry.

(I) Organizational reform of financial supervision: the establishment of the NFRA

The *Reform Plan for Party and State Organizations* was issued in March 2023, planning to set up the National Financial Regulatory Administration (NFRA) based on the former CBIRC to take charge of financial supervision excluding the securities business. In May 2023, the NFRA was inaugurated. In November 2023, the *Provisions on Functions, Organizational Structure and Staffing of the National Financial Regulatory Administration* was published. This document has defined the main duties, organizational structure and staffing of the NFRA.

In terms of main duties, the NFRA expands its duties from the former CBIRC's functions to the larger financial industry (excluding securities). Incorporating the PBOC's day-to-day supervision of financial conglomerates,

such as financial holding companies, the financial consumer protection duties of the PBOC and the investor protection duties of the China Securities Regulatory Commission (CSRC).

As for organizational structure, the NFRA retained, cancelled or merged some internal bodies of the former CBIRC and created new bodies required to perform its functions. First, 17 internal bodies and their basic functions, including the General Office (Party Committee Office), were retained, and some of them were renamed. Second, the former Major Risk Event and Case Resolution Bureau (Banking & Insurance Safety & Security Bureau) was cancelled. Third, the former Policy Bank Supervision Department and some other internal bodies were merged and new internal bodies were created to take over their functions. Specifically, the former Policy Bank Supervision Department and State-controlled Large Commercial Bank Supervision Department were replaced by the Large Bank Supervision Department. The former National Joint-Stock Commercial Bank Supervision Department and City Commercial Bank Supervision Department were replaced by the Joint-Stock and City Commercial Bank Supervision Department. The Insurance Intermediary Supervision Department was merged into the Property and Casualty Insurance Supervision Department (Reinsurance Supervision Department). The Financial Innovation Supervision Department, Insurance Fund Investment Supervision Department and Trust Institution Supervision Department were replaced by the Asset and Wealth Management Institution Supervision Department. Fourth, some new bodies were created to take over functions shed by former internal bodies and new functions of the NFRA. These new bodies include the Financial Institution Authorization

Department, the Technology Supervision Department, the Institution Recovery and Resolution Department, the Investigation Bureau, the Administrative Penalty Bureau, the Internal Audit Department (Office of the Party Committee's Inspection Leadership Team), the Party-related Affairs Bureau (Party Committee's Publicity Department) and the Investigation Task Force.

In terms of insurance supervision, the Corporate Governance Supervision Department, the Property and Casualty Insurance Supervision Department (Reinsurance Supervision Department), the Personal Insurance Supervision Department and the Asset and Wealth Management Institution Supervision Department of the NFRA take charge of the offsite monitoring, onsite investigation, risk analysis, supervisory evaluation, regulatory enforcement and risk case handling for insurance conglomerates, P&C insurers/reinsurers/insurance intermediaries, life insurers and insurance asset management organizations, respectively. The Corporate Governance Supervision Department has a new function of serving as the principal supervisory body for insurance conglomerates. The Property and Casualty Insurance Supervision Department (Reinsurance Supervision Department), the Personal Insurance Supervision Department and the Asset and Wealth Management Institution Supervision Department shed their functions of insurer authorization and exit management to the newly established Institution Authorization Department and the Financial Institution Recovery and Resolution Department, respectively. In addition, the Insurance and Non-bank Institution Examination Bureau retains its function of onsite examination over insurance institutions, while the new Investigation Bureau,

Investigation Task Force and Administrative Penalty Bureau take charge of the investigation and evidence collection for financial non-compliance incidents and hearing of administrative penalty cases of financial institutions, including insurance institutions.

(II) Improving the operational risk management requirements for banking and insurance institutions.

Operational risk is one of the main risks in the business management of banking and insurance institutions. Previously, the operation risk management of insurance institutions was mainly governed by the *Insurer Solvency Regulation (II)* (Y.B.J.F. 〔2021〕 No. 51) issued in October 2021, while the operation risk management of banking institutions were mainly governed by the *Guidelines for Operational Risk Management of Commercial Banks* (Y.J.F. 〔2007〕 No. 42) issued by the former China Banking Regulatory Commission in May 2007. Given the increasing complexities in operational risk prevention and control, however, these regulatory rules no longer met the operational risk management needs of banking and insurance institutions as they did not reflect the latest developments or were not detailed and refined enough. In December 2023, therefore, the NFRA revised and issued the *Administrative Measures for Operational Risks of Banking and Insurance Institutions* (NFRA Order No. 5 of 2023)[①] to improve and unify

① The *Guidelines for Operational Risk Management of Commercial Banks* (Y.J.F. 〔2007〕 No. 42) and the Notice of the China Banking Regulatory Commission on Strengthening the Guard Against Operational Risks (Y.J.F. 〔2005〕 No. 17) were superseded by the *Administrative Measures for Operational Risks of Banking and Insurance Institutions* on its effective date.

the requirements for operational risk management of banking and insurance institutions.

The new policy defines the basic principles, responsibility assignment, basic requirements and procedures/methodologies of operational risk management in banking and insurance institutions. As for responsibility assignment, the new policy emphasizes the three lines of defense mechanism for operational risk management. At banking and insurance institutions, the business and management departments, the lead departments for operational risk management and measurement and the internal audit departments perform the functions of direct management, guidance and supervision as well as supervisory evaluation of operational risks, respectively. In terms of basic requirements, the new policy requires that banking and insurance institutions should develop the basic policies for operational risk management, the operational risk management evaluation mechanism and operational risk appetite that be commensurate to their own characteristics, monitor and warn operational risks on an ongoing basis, and establish an information system with operational risk management functions. In terms of procedures and methodologies, the new policy requires banking and insurance institutions to carry out operational risk identification, assessment, control and mitigation according to their operational risk appetite, develop and effectively implement the business continuity plans and other management processes, establish working mechanisms such as the internal regular reporting mechanism for operational risks, and advise banking and insurance institutions to properly use management tools such as operational risk loss databases. Meanwhile, considering the different

types of institutions, the new policy adopts differentiated supervision distinguishing between banking institutions and insurance institutions, larger institutions and smaller institutions. For example, although the new policy is applicable to insurance companies, it applies mutatis mutandis to insurance conglomerates (holding companies), reinsurance companies and insurance asset management companies. The new policy requirements on risk measurement and provision for capital are not applicable to insurance companies. A transitional period of one year and two years is allowed for larger and smaller banking/insurance institutions, respectively.

(III) Strengthening case risk prevention and control of banking and insurance institutions

To regulate case management of banking and insurance organizations, the former CBIRC issued the *Administrative Measures for Criminal Cases of Banking and Insurance Institutions (Trial)* (Y.B.J.F. 〔2020〕 No. 20) in June 2020 setting forth the basic working principles, responsibility assignment and case handling mechanism for banking and insurance institutions. For banking and insurance institutions to move forward the case risk prevention and control to earlier stages, the NFRA issued the *Administrative Measures for Prevention and Control of Criminal Case Risks of Banking and Insurance Institutions* (J.G. 〔2023〕 No. 10)① in November 2023 to further enhance the soundness, reasonableness and effectiveness of the case risk prevention and control work of banking and insurance institutions.

---

① The *Notice of CBRC General Office on Issuing the Measures for Case Risk Prevention of Banking Institutions* (Y.J.B.F. 〔2013〕 No. 257) was superseded.

This policy emphasizes that the case risk prevention and control work of banking and insurance institutions should abide by the following principles: "prevention first; earlier start; full coverage; well-focused; tiered responsibility system in which the legal person assumes the primary responsibility; responsibility assignment and collaboration; territorial supervision and integration into day-to-day work". The policy is intended to establish a pattern of case risk prevention and control featuring broad-based collaboration and joint efforts. Banking and insurance institutions are required to establish sound mechanisms for case risk prevention and control, supervision and inspection of case risk prevention and control, internal accountability, case risk clues discovery and detection, case risk prevention and control performance review and case risk prevention and control assessment as well as other working mechanisms. They shall formulate policies on case risk investigation and resolution and the professional code of conduct. The training on case risk prevention and control and case-based warning education shall be carried out, and relevant IT system development shall be stepped up, thereby building a comprehensive governance mechanism for case risk prevention and control.

(IV) Establishing an assessment and identification mechanism for systemically important insurance companies

The stable operation of systemically important financial institutions plays a crucial role in ensuring sound development of China's financial system and real economy. In November 2018, the PBOC, the former CBIRC and CSRC jointly issued the *Guidelines for Improving Supervision*

of Systemically Important Financial Institutions (Y.F.〔2018〕No. 301)[①] to create a mechanism for identification, supervision and resolution of systemically important financial institutions. In order to implement this opinion and lay a solid foundation for differentiated supervision of systemically important insurance companies, the NFRA issued the *Measures for Assessment of Systemically Important Insurance Companies* (Y.F.〔2023〕No. 208) in October 2023, further clarifying the assessment and identification mechanism of systemically important insurance companies. The policy sets forth the assessment procedures and methodologies for systemically important insurance companies. Quantitative assessment indicators are adopted to calculate the systemic importance score of insurance companies, and give a regulatory opinion based on other quantitative and qualitative information to comprehensively assess the systemic importance of participating insurance companies. This policy further refines the quantitative sub-indicators and their weights based on the assessment indicators defined by the *Guidelines for Improving Supervision of Systemically Important Financial Institutions,* such as size, interconnectedness, complexity, substitutability and asset liquidity (see Table 1).

Table 1　Assessment Indicators for Systemically Important Insurance Companies

Unit: %

Assessment indicators	Quantitative sub-indicators	Weight
Size (20%)	Total assets	10
	Total income	10

① *Guidelines for Improving Supervision of Systemically Important Financial Institutions* (Y.F.〔2018〕No. 301) became effective on the date of issuance.

continued

Assessment indicators	Quantitative sub-indicators	Weight
Interconnectedness (30%)	Inter-financial institution assets	7
	Inter-financial institution liabilities	7
	Assets under management	7
	Assets of non-insurance affiliates	7
	Derivative financial assets	2
Asset liquidity (30%)	Short-term financing	10
	Complexity of fund utilization	10
	Level 3 assets	10
Substitutability (20%)	Number of branch offices and number of policy holders	6.67
	Payout amount	6.67
	Premium income from specified business	6.67

Source: National Financial Regulatory Administration.

(V) Refining the regulatory standards for insurer solvency

To improve the regulatory standards for solvency of insurance companies and bring insurance companies back to their original mission on a steady course of operation, the NFRA issued the *Notice on Improving the Regulatory Standards for Solvency of Insurance Companies* (J.G. [2023] No. 5) in September 2023 On the basis of maintaining the unchanged regulatory standards of 100% comprehensive solvency adequacy ratio and 50% core solvency adequacy ratio, optimized the solvency regulatory standards for insurance companies in accordance with the actual development of the insurance industry. First, the implementation of differentiated capital regulation. Differentiated regulation for insurance companies of different sizes, with minimum capital measured at 95% for medium-sized companies and 90% for small-sized companies. Second, the capital measurement

standards are refined, guiding insurers back to their original mission of insurance by developing long-term protection products and setting aside reserves prudently, and guiding insurers to enhance their ability to manage asset-liability matching. Third, risk factors are refined, guiding insurers to serve the real economy and technological innovation. The minimum capital measurement requirements are updated for technological insurance, encouraging insurers to conduct long-term value investment (see Table 2).

Table 2 Risk Factors before versus after Refining of the Regulatory Standards for Insurer Solvency

Target assets of investment	Risk factors, before	Risk factors, after
Constituent stocks of CSI 300 Index	0.35	0.30
Ordinary stocks listed on the STAR Market	0.45	0.40
Parts of REITs not covered by see-through supervision	0.60	0.50
Equity interests in unlisted companies in the national strategic emerging industries	0.41	0.40

Source: National Financial Regulatory Administration.

III. Trends in Reinsurance Regulation

In 2024, China's reinsurance industry will maintain a sound momentum while facing challenges from the macro economy, geopolitics, climate change and aging population. Adhering to the principle of "strong and strict supervision", the reinsurance industry will continue to adjust regulatory policies in line with macroeconomic guidance and industrial development trends, pursue high-quality development and effectively serve the national economy and public wellbeing.

First, persistent efforts will be made to strengthen supervision of

the reinsurance industry and improve the risk prevention and control mechanism. General Secretary Xi Jinping pointed out that "we should strive to forestall and defuse financial risks, especially systemic risks", "financial supervision should be tough and keen-edged, and "strict law enforcement should be carried out for market access, prudential supervision and behavioral supervision, so as to ensure financial supervision is fully implemented, both vertically and horizontally". In the future, the "strong and strict supervision" will remain unchanged. Financial regulators will further enhance the foresight, accuracy, effectiveness and synergy of supervision, enhance the supervisory synergies with other regulatory agencies and continue to intensify the crackdown on non-compliances in financial risk resolution and financial crimes and intensify accountability.

Second, reinsurance will continue to serve the real economy and public wellbeing better. As an important segment of the financial sector, insurance and reinsurance play an important role in spreading risks in economic and social activities, ensuring and improving public wellbeing, preventing and reducing losses and serving the real economy. At the Central Financial Work Conference, the central leadership called on the financial sector to focus on the five priorities of technology finance, green finance, inclusive finance, pension finance and digital finance. Insurance and reinsurance regulators will continue to encourage and guide insurance market to play their roles as economic shock absorbers and social stabilizers, vigorously improve the insurance protection capability and service level, building China into a financial powerhouse and serving the Chinese modernization.

Third, reinsurance institutions will be further encouraged to pursue

innovative development. Digital transformation will be accelerated across the reinsurance industry for higher efficiency of operation and management. Reinsurers are encouraged to use artificial intelligence, big data and other technologies to improve marketing services, risk management and investment management, enhance their professional capability of risk management and provide stronger technical support for the pricing, underwriting and claim settlement for risks in high-tech fields such as electronic information, advanced manufacturing, biomedicine, modern agriculture, intelligent traffic, new energy and aerospace, in a bid to enhance the overall insurance capacity to better serve the real economy, especially the new quality productive forces. The reinsurance industry will be encouraged to play a greater role in establishing a sound national catastrophe insurance system, effectively transfer and spread catastrophe risks, develop and utilize catastrophe risk models, improve risk reduction service capabilities and support disaster prevention, mitigation and relief.